D0205627

SOVIET MAN AND HIS WORLD

SOVIET MAN
AND
HIS WORLD

KLAUS MEHNERT

Translated from the German by
MAURICE ROSENBAUM

GREENWOOD PRESS, PUBLISHERS
WESTPORT, CONNECTICUT

Library of Congress Cataloging in Publication Data

Mehnert, Klaus, 1906-
Soviet man and his world.

Translation of Der Sowjetmensch.
Reprint of the 1962 ed. published by Praeger, New
York, which was issued as no. 100 in the Praeger
publications in Russian history and world communism.
Includes index.
1. Russia--Social life and customs--1917-1970.
2. National characteristics, Russian. 3. Russia--
Social conditions--1917-   I. Title.
[DK268.3.M453 1976]   947.084   76-14778
ISBN 0-8371-8567-X

First published in Germany under the title
DER SOWJETMENSCH
and later in Great Britain under the title
THE ANATOMY OF SOVIET MAN

The present edition has been revised and
brought up to date by the author

© 1958 Deutsche Verlags-Anstalt GmbH, Stuttgart

English translation © 1961
by George Weidenfeld and Nicolson, Ltd., England

Originally published in 1962 by Frederick A. Praeger, Publisher, New York

Reprinted with the permission of Praeger Publishers, Inc.

Reprinted in 1976 by Greenwood Press
a division of Williamhouse-Regency Inc.

Library of Congress Catalog Card Number 76-14778

ISBN 0-8371-8567-X

Printed in the United States of America

To the memory of my
MOTHER
Luise Mehnert, née Heuss,
born 1882 in Moscow, died 1946 in Holstein
who, though German, taught me to talk Russian
and to love the Russians

The Author

KLAUS MEHNERT was born in Moscow of German parents in 1906. His paternal great-grandfather had moved from Dresden to Moscow in 1828 to accept a post as musician with the Bolshoi Theatre; his grandfather, an engineer, built bridges and railways in Czarist Russia; his father was a painter and co-owner of a printing plant in Moscow. Julius Heuss, his maternal grandfather, migrated to Russia from the Black Forest in 1854; eventually, he founded the Moscow chocolate factory Einem (now 'Red October'). All these men married German women and remained German citizens. The family moved to Germany in 1914, at the outbreak of World War I. The author's father was killed in action in Flanders.

Klaus Mehnert studied modern history (specialising in Russian history) in Germany and at the University of California. He received his Ph.D. degree from the University of Berlin. Between 1929 and 1933, as Editor of the Berlin monthly *Osteuropa* (*Eastern Europe*), he made annual trips to the Soviet Union. He left Germany in 1934, and initially worked as Moscow correspondent for various German newspapers. From 1936 to 1945, he taught and lived in the United States and in China, while continuing to study Russian and Soviet affairs. Since his return to Germany in 1946, he has served as Editor of *Osteuropa* (revived in 1951), *Osteuropa-Recht*, *Osteuropa-Wirtschaft*, and *Osteuropa-Naturwissenschaft*. Mr Mehnert is also a political commentator for the South German radio service in Stuttgart.

The author travelled extensively all around the periphery of the U.S.S.R., from Finland to Japan, with visits to almost all Asian countries, including China and the Mongolian People's Republic. He accompanied Chancellor Adenauer on his trip to Moscow in 1955, and went there again as correspondent for various German newspapers and all German radio stations in 1956 (for four months), 1957, and 1959. Altogether, between 1929 and 1959, he has visited the U.S.S.R. thirteen times, spending about six years there and travelling to most parts of the country, north as far as the Polar Sea and south to the Persian and Chinese borders.

Klaus Mehnert's first book, *Jugend in Sowjetrussland* (*Youth in Soviet Russia*), was published in 1932 and was later translated into eight languages, including English. His other books include: *The Russians in Hawaii, 1804–1809*, published in 1939; *Weltrevolution durch Weltgeschichte. Die Geschichtslehre des Stalinismus* (*Stalin versus Marx*, in the American and British editions), published in 1953; and *Asien, Moskau und Wir* (*Asia, Moscow and Ourselves*), published in 1956 and now in its eleventh edition.

Of *Der Sowjetmensch*, the original German edition of this book, 421,000 copies have been printed in Germany alone. In addition to the present British and American editions, translations into Dutch, Finnish, French, Japanese, Spanish, and Swedish have already been published.

CONTENTS

INTRODUCTION

PRODUCTION FIGURES for coal, steel, and atomic power in the Soviet Union, the contribution of collectivized agriculture to the Soviet economy, the number of planes in the Soviet Air Force—such data are secondary to the central problems: will all these activities be controlled in the future by Bolsheviks, or will people like ourselves be in charge?

At the moment, Russian policy, for the most part, is in the hands of men who played a role in the Revolution and have been confirmed Bolsheviks for many years. But the day will come when the sons and grandsons of the Revolution will no longer hold the reins; control will then pass to their descendants. What sort of men will these be?

Will our children have to deal with Stalins and Khrushchevs—with the fanatical upholders of a revolution that threatens the rest of the world with a vast, ant-like community of robots? Have the people of the Soviet Union been transformed by Communist upbringing and conditioning? Or will their way of life and their aims begin to bear resemblance to our own as the Revolution of 1917 recedes further and further into the past? Finally, will human factors prevail over politics? In brief, is Soviet man more 'Soviet' or more 'man'?

Some say there is no such thing as 'Soviet man', that the people of the Soviet Union are simply Russians, and that Bolshevism is merely the logical evolution of the Russian character. At the other extreme are the Soviet leaders and ideologists who contend that 'Soviet man' exists and is a type of man the world has never seen before.

The traditional Russian of the nineteenth century is familiar to all of us through Russian literature. This book now attempts to establish which of the old Russian traits have disappeared during the last four decades, what new features have emerged, and what the result of this dual process is.

Since 1929, in the course of thirteen visits spread over thirty years, I have spent a total of about six years in the U.S.S.R., travelling all over the country. As a German born and bred in

1

Moscow, my natural familiarity with the language and customs has been a great help. But an observer's conclusions depend not only on the number of journeys he makes and his linguistic skills; perhaps even more important is the attitude he brings to his task. In my own case, this attitude can be summarized as objective, but not neutral.

There are obvious limits to the degree of objectivity one can attain, but within these limits I have tried to be as objective as possible, to see things as they are, and to avoid preconceived notions. But neutral, no. I am against the Soviet attempt to force Russians, Chinese, Yugoslavs, Arabs, Germans, and others into one ideological mould. I am equally opposed to the concept of class warfare that is, in fact, being used to camouflage the rise of a new privileged group in the Soviet state. I abhor the use of human beings as material for totalitarian planning towards a utopian goal, in a spirit of utter godlessness. It did not require the flight of over three million people from the Soviet zone of Germany to the West or the struggle for freedom in Hungary and Berlin to convince me that the triumph of the Communist regime would be unbearable to nations that have tasted freedom. Hence my determined repudiation of Bolshevism as a political philosophy, and of its endeavour to inflict Communism on my own people.

It is because of this attitude that I have made an even greater effort to write with objectivity. I have deliberately eschewed extreme expressions of opinion. I do not intend either to scare the reader with Red bogeymen or to soothe him with gentle lullabies. I have written this book for an adult audience, including the younger generation, which I know to be perfectly capable of grasping the fundamentals of politics. It is particularly among the latter group that I hope to find readers. They will have to continue to coexist with the peoples of the Soviet Union, and they will have to find some *modus vivendi* with them. I like to think that this book might be of some use in that respect.

Quoting Stalin is out of fashion in the U.S.S.R., but I recall one of his comments made during Germany's worst hour: 'The Hitlers', he said toward the close of World War II, 'come and go, but the German people remain.' I return this compliment to those who allowed Stalin to rule them for such a long time.

The people of the Soviet Union remain, but the Stalins come and go. And not only the Stalins.

I owe thanks to numerous specialists on Russian and Soviet affairs throughout the world; there are too many of them to list their names, but some appear in the notes at the end of the book. There exists today a whole army of these experts, subdivided into many schools and fields of research. I should like to compare them to the highly specialized medical researchers—the ophthalmologists, cardiologists, dermatologists, neurologists, and so on—who have contributed so much to our knowledge of man by their extraordinary familiarity with minute details and their use of the most up-to-date methods. As for myself, I am more like the family doctor, who, while following avidly the results of the specialists' research, himself belongs to none of their schools, but bases his diagnosis on a lifelong and intimate knowledge of his patients and their background.

Occasionally, while reading critical remarks about this book in the official Soviet press, I have wondered what the ordinary Soviet man's judgment of it would be—if he had a chance to read it. To this question I received an unexpected answer.

Some time ago, I found a letter in my mail, written on the stationery of a German university and signed by a well-known professor. He wrote that during a recent visit to Moscow, while walking along Red Square with a German colleague, he had been approached by a young Russian. Having heard them talking German, the stranger wanted to know whether they were from the Federal Republic. When they nodded, he asked them to give his greetings to their countryman Klaus Mehnert and to tell him the following:

A Russian translation of Mehnert's *Soviet Man* had been published in Moscow in an edition of only 100 copies, meant exclusively for high Party functionaries. He himself, the Russian continued, had been able to borrow the book from a relative and had read it from cover to cover. 'I could not imagine' the professor quoted the Russian as saying, 'a better and more objective description of the Soviet Union today. The book tells the pure truth, and I could not help underlining every word of it. All people with a mind of their own who have read the book and with whom I have talked about it are of the same opinion.' The Germans asked him whether, in case of a new edition, he had any corrections to suggest. After thinking for a moment, the young Russian answered determinedly: 'I would not change a word.'

Stuttgart   *Klaus Mehnert*
1 September 1961

The notes at the back of the book, to which the numbers in the text refer, cite sources and are needed only for reference, not for an understanding of the book.

Although the Russian language has no accents, I have used them on the vowels of Russian words and names to indicate on which syllable the emphasis should be placed; if the word appears frequently the accent is used on the first occasion only. The apostrophe after consonants (indicating the so-called soft sign of the Russian alphabet) shows that the consonant it follows is pronounced soft; it has been used throughout the book.

The roubles mentioned are those prior to the currency reform of 1 January 1961.

CHAPTER 1

WHAT CAN AND CANNOT BE SEEN

THE SCEPTICAL READER might ask: what is the use, even if you know the language, of visiting a country which deliberately shuts itself off from foreign observers—a country where the foreigner is recognizable a mile away and is treated accordingly, so that he sees only 'Potemkin villages'?

This is not altogether true, however. A foreigner in the Soviet Union—at any rate, a man—is less conspicuous today than he was twenty years ago. The new privileged groups in Russia now wear suits similar to our own in style. Women's fashions lag behind those of the West, but well-dressed men look much the same in Marseilles, Hamburg, or Leningrad, except that Western cloth is of far better quality than Russian.

In the autumn of 1955 I went to a Moscow law court. A notice in the lobby listed the cases to be heard that day. 'Court 3, 10 o'clock, *Khuligánstvo*', I read. (*Khuliganstvo* is the Russian for hooliganism.) Here, I thought, I may learn something about Soviet rowdies. At 10 o'clock, when I went into the court, there were very few people present. A handful of spectators were sitting on the public benches, and a secretary was tidying the judge's desk.

When she caught sight of me, she said, 'I suppose you are the lawyer?' 'No,' I replied, 'just a spectator,' and I sat on one of the public benches, realizing that my appearance must correspond to the secretary's image of a Soviet lawyer.

A year later, in a provincial town, I was passing a school and decided to have a look inside it. On the threshold I met a pupil, a girl of about seventeen. 'Good morning, comrade director,' she said. 'The conference is on the first floor. Shall I show you the way?'

In other words, I found that a middle-aged European journalist, provided he did not make himself conspicuous, could easily pass as a member of the 'intelligentsia', a section of Soviet (and former Tsarist) society of which I shall have more to say later.

In the spring of 1956, on a flight from Moscow to Siberia, I discovered to my surprise that I had an effective means of making friends in the Soviet Union. Knowing that there would be slush and muddy roads, I had put on a strong pair of ski-boots. It was still dark when we left Vnukovo Airport in Moscow, and we touched down at Kazan for breakfast. I had just given my order when a stranger sat down at my table. '*Továrishch*,' he exclaimed, 'that's a grand pair of boots you're wearing. May I look at them?'

He examined them in detail—the grooved heel, the crossed straps, and the heavy, treaded rubber soles—and we found ourselves breakfasting together. Then he called a friend over to admire my boots, and soon a sizeable group was gathered round our table. The same thing happened again and again during my journey. One man admired my boots so much that he pulled off his shoes and overshoes and offered them in exchange, with a fountain pen and a pound of apples thrown in. Luckily, he took a much larger size, or it might have been difficult to refuse.

In Stalin's day, a Soviet citizen who found himself face to face with a foreigner became tense and reserved. He feared that a careless word, or even a phrase that had been misunderstood, might be reported to the state security agencies, with the possibility of most unpleasant consequences. I came across this attitude frequently in those days, and the following incident is typical.

In the summer of 1935, when it was almost impossible to get on the overcrowded trains at the smaller stations, I managed to board the Moscow express at Vyatka (now Kirov) on my way back from the Arctic—but only by jumping aboard when the train had already travelled a few hundred yards past the station. Some time later a doctor walked through the corridor, asking whether anyone needed his services. 'Yes, I do!' called a girl who was curled up on the luggage rack of the compartment outside which I was standing, 'I need something quickly.' And in a loud voice, with that complete lack of embarrassment typical of her country, she described what was wrong.

'Castor oil,' said the doctor, pouring out a generous dose. The girl climbed down from her perch, sniffed the medicine, and made a face. I felt sorry for her, advised her to throw the stuff away, and gave her two of my infallible pills instead. She swallowed them and was so grateful that she invited me to sit with her and her friends. 'I'll tell them that we know each other,' she said, 'and that we studied together at the university.'

The next few hours passed very pleasantly. We spread ourselves all over the three tiers of the compartment—a group of girls on their way to a student spa in the Crimea, a few young men who had joined them on the train, and myself. We sang, joked, played word games, and took turns rushing out at each station to get hot water for tea. Then Lida, one of the girls, noticed that I was wearing a ring on the little finger of my left hand. She had never seen a man wearing a ring before and was intrigued. A lively discussion started. My castor-oil friend, Irina, put an end to the argument by saying dogmatically: 'If the *tovarishch* is a professional man, it's all right, but if he works with his hands, it's just plain silly.'

This was generally regarded as reasonable, and I admitted that I was a professional man. Lida was not satisfied with this, however, and when there was a lull in the conversation she suggested that we all tell the stories of our lives and describe our work to pass the time. School, a skilled trade, college, Komsomól (the Communist youth organization), work in a factory— these were the life stories until my turn came.

'I won't tell you what I am,' I said.

'What do you mean? Of course you must tell us. Why not?'

'If I do, you'll all run away.'

'Rubbish!' said the girls, solemnly promising that they would do no such thing. And in any case, as Lida pointed out, 'We couldn't, even if we wanted to.'

'Well then,' I said, 'I'm a German journalist.'

There was dead silence except for the rumbling of the wheels. The faces of my travelling companions froze in astonishment. For a few seconds they wore looks of blank incredulity, as though they had suddenly lost their train of thought in the middle of a speech. Then they glanced furtively at each other, and one of the girls giggled. 'You're joking,' she said. To them 'German' meant 'fascist', and 'journalist' was synonymous with 'spy'. Either was bad enough; but the combination made their hair stand on end.

Irina's face was red. It was she, after all, who had introduced me to them; worse, she had spoken of our having studied together.

'Yes,' I repeated, 'I'm a German journalist.' And I took my identity card out of my pocket and passed it round.

The card itself, the seal of the Soviet Commissar for Foreign Affairs, my photograph and my signature were all meticulously examined. At that moment the train stopped at a station. Outside our carriage peasant women were selling eggs, gherkins, milk, and roast chickens, and we all ran out to buy things. When we got back to our seats, everyone was very friendly, but there was an air of reserve. My companions' curiosity had evaporated. They didn't ask a single question about Germany.

It is easy to understand this attitude. Under the notorious Article 58 of the Criminal Code of 1926, it is an indictable offence to give unpublished economic information to a foreigner, and this law has been made still tougher.[1] State secrets which it is a punishable offence to divulge include industrial production figures and information about internal and external trade, the transport system, finance, patents, and mineral resources. In the 1930's, and probably later, Russians were given long prison sentences not because they had betrayed these so-called 'secrets' to foreigners, but because they had had contact with foreigners and could not prove—how could they?—that they had *not* divulged secrets to them.

Two or three years after the war, I got a letter postmarked Frankfurt from a Russian whose name I did not know. He said he had come across my name in a German newspaper, and asked whether I had been in Moscow in the early thirties and if so, whether I had attended a rifle meeting organized by the semi-military *Osoaviakhím* organization. I replied that I had.

A few days later I was visited by a young Russian whom I remembered having met fifteen years before when, with official permission, I was studying the *Osoaviakhím* organization. I had gone one Sunday to their meeting at a rifle range near Moscow. My visitor—I will call him Petrov—had been the captain of one of the competing teams. This is what he told me:

'During those years, foreigners often came to watch our rifle meetings. One day some of them invited me to dine with them afterwards. They didn't ask me any indiscreet questions, nor did I volunteer information of any sort. But in 1937 I was arrested in the middle of the night and banished to a penal camp in the Arctic on a charge of betraying state secrets. I was given no chance to defend myself. Indeed, I felt that I was lucky to escape with my life. When war broke out, I was taken out of the camp, promised a pardon, and put into the army. In the first battle I deserted to the Germans.'

I asked Petrov whether he had been anti-Communist before his arrest. He shook his head.

'When you came to watch our rifle meeting,' he said, 'I must have been about seventeen or eighteen. I was a member of the *Komsomol* and had never been outside the Soviet Union. To me Stalin was the great leader. I would never have dreamed of giving away a state secret to a foreigner, or even of discussing a tricky political question with one. But a few years later I began to have my doubts; arrests were made here, there, and everywhere, and men of whose integrity and political loyalty I was convinced suddenly vanished without a trace. Then, when they grabbed me, I had only one thought—to get out.'

After Stalin's death, there was a considerable improvement. The feeling of panic which, during Stalin's reign of terror, gripped everyone when confronted with a foreigner, abated. The following incident will illustrate what I mean.

In the autumn of 1955 I decided to see Sofronov's play *The Heart Does Not Forgive*. It started at half past eight, but I did not get to the theatre until half past nine, during the first intermission. When I found my seat, a Russian woman of about thirty, who was sitting next to me, asked me why I had bothered to come at all, since I had already missed half the play.

'Instead of reproaching me,' I said, 'it would be kinder if you gave me a summary of what has happened up to now, so that I can understand the rest of the play.'

'The central figure,' she said, 'is Yekaterina, the zealous supervisor of a *kolkhóz*. Her husband, Stepan, is a wastrel, and she not only despises him for that but has stopped having any feeling of love for him at all. At the same time she is more and more attracted by the efficient and conscientious director of a neighbouring *sovkhóz*.'

'In other words, the eternal triangle.'

'Yes, the eternal triangle. Nevertheless, one side—Stepan—is receding rapidly. And when one of the three sides of a triangle disappears, what remains? A line, a direct connection between two points. But we'll see what happens.'

'Thank you very much,' I said. 'I feel as though I'd seen the play from the beginning.'

'But you haven't told me why you were so late,' she said.

'I have a perfect alibi,' I replied. 'I was in the Kremlin—I'm a journalist.'

'Which paper?'

'I work for a number of German papers and the German radio. I am German.'

'How very interesting! East Germany, or West?'

'The Federal Republic—West Germany.'

'Even more fascinating! Tell me more.'

Just then the house lights were dimmed, and the curtain went up. In the last act there was a violent quarrel between Yekaterina and her husband. She made it quite plain that she would have nothing more to do with him and no longer regarded him as her husband. 'The heart does not forgive!' she cried. But Stepan refused to believe that his idleness was the only cause; he guessed that he had a rival. His suspicions fell on the director of the neighbouring *sovkhoz*, and he decided to kill him. But at the crucial moment Yekaterina knocked the weapon out of his hand.

It was a lovely evening, and after the play we strolled towards the centre of town. We agreed that the play had been very poor, and my new acquaintance was particularly critical of the melodramatic ending, which had no logical connection with the rest of the plot.

Then why, I asked, had she chosen this play? She replied that she did not live in Moscow and had bought a ticket at random. She added that she wrote poetry. I asked her to recite some of it to me, and to the sound of our footsteps in the gentle Moscow night she recited a love poem, each verse of which ended with the words: '*I ya tebyá, a ty drugúyu*' (I mean you, but you mean another).

'Another triangle!' I said, and we both laughed. Then she asked me to tell her about Germany, particularly about the theatre and literary magazines. Eventually we reached the house where she was staying, and I said good-night.

Her carefree attitude would have been almost unthinkable during Stalin's lifetime; even now the memory of those days is so vivid that Soviet citizens shrink from developing close relationships with foreigners, and hesitate to visit them in their hotels or to invite them to their homes. Exceptions are to be found among diplomats, journalists, artists, and men of letters, to whom the privilege of mixing with foreigners is granted as part of their job, perhaps even as part of their duty.

Lately the atmosphere has become more hostile. Again, Russians seen with foreigners are questioned by the police. As a result diplomats and journalists in Moscow are always complaining that it is quite impossible to establish any normal social relations with individual Russians or Russian families. Under these conditions the most rewarding conversations are those with chance acquaintances. In railway compartments, diners, or hotels people talk fairly freely. They have little or no fear that a conversation which took place by chance, which did not last long, which they themselves did not initiate, and which will not be repeated, might some day be produced as evidence against them.

The Soviet citizen is keenly interested in foreigners. As a rule, the first question he asks a stranger is 'What country do you come from?' In Russian eyes the difference between, say, an Englishman and a Frenchman is less important than that between a genuine and what might be described as a semi-foreigner. A genuine foreigner is one who comes from the other side of the iron curtain; a man from Poland or Rumania is merely a semi-foreigner because he lives under a regime like that in the U.S.S.R. Visitors from iron curtain countries have nothing particularly new to say. They have to be cautious, and tend to agree with everything a Russian tells them. On the other hand, a Russian knows that from a 'real' foreigner he can learn something authentic about that almost unknown and therefore fascinating part of the world which lies beyond the Soviet bloc. This accounts for the innumerable searching questions fired at 'real' foreigners by every Russian they meet.

I use the word 'satellite' only reluctantly. But the attitude of the Soviet citizens towards an East German or, let us say, a Rumanian frequently carries just that connotation. A Soviet technician in Manchuria referred to the East European countries, in a conversation with me, as 'our satellites' (*náshi satellíty*). When, in September, 1955, a group of journalists from both East and West Germany visited Moscow, the representatives of the West German press were more in demand and asked many more questions by the Russians than were their colleagues from the Soviet zone of Germany, to whom little attention was paid. Of course, all official speeches stress the fraternal ties with the Soviet zone Germans, but in personal contacts there is little evidence of such feeling. The rising in East Germany on 17 June 1953 has contributed to this. And the confidence of the Russians in the peoples of the Communist orbit has been shaken even more by the events of 1956 in Poland and Hungary. The Russian has the vague, uneasy feeling that the German from the Soviet zone is not candid, that he assumes a loyal and fraternal manner, but that his feelings are entirely different; the Russian knows that the West German, on the other hand, is free to voice his opinion. I will never forget a German from the zone whom I once met in Moscow. In his contacts with the Russians he was an eager 'people's democrat', filled with admiration and love for the Soviet Union, but in talking to me he confessed that these protestations of loyalty caused him great pain. In the long run, this dichotomy cannot be hidden from the Russians.

Once—it was in September 1955—I took a taxi at midnight to Vnukovo to catch a plane for Tashkent. The wide highway, lightly travelled even in daytime, was empty, and we went along at a fast clip. It had rained a bit, enough to make the asphalt surface slippery. I said: 'There's no need to rush, we have lots of time; I'd rather not land in a ditch.'

The driver slowed down. 'You're right, *tovarishch*, there are too many accidents. Only yesterday a car landed in a ditch.'

'Well, well,' I said, without too much curiosity. 'Who was it?'

'It was a German,' he replied.

Now I became curious. It couldn't have been Adenauer, because I knew he had just returned safely to Bonn. But some of my colleagues had remained in Moscow, and it occurred to me that one of them might have had an accident.

'What kind of a German was he?' I asked.

And I got the classic reply: 'Thank God it was one of ours, or there would have been a world-wide scandal.' I cannot think of a better example of the Russian attitude towards 'their Germans'—or their Hungarians or Czechs for that matter.

Anyone with a normal visa for a Western country may go where he likes and see anything that interests him, with the exception of military installations and a small number of firms which have trade secrets to protect. In the Soviet Union things are different. A Soviet visa is valid initially only for Moscow. It is true that people travelling via Intourist are not restricted to the capital, but they have to keep to a pre-arranged itinerary. Once a foreigner reaches Moscow, his freedom of movement is confined to a twenty-five-mile radius of the capital; and even within those limits there are forbidden areas. For all other journeys the traveller must get permission from the Soviet Ministry for Foreign Affairs. Large tracts of the Soviet Union are completely barred to foreigners, some temporarily and some permanently.

When I was planning to tour Siberia in April 1956, I outlined my plan to the Press Department of the Foreign Ministry in Smolensk Square two months ahead of time. I was told to submit a list of the places I wanted to visit. A third of the places on my list were struck out, including Karaganda in Kazakhstan (which I had visited in 1935) and Chelyabinsk in the Urals, although that town is on the main line from Moscow to Siberia. The towns I was allowed to visit were then entered on the Russian-language identity papers which every foreigner, except tourists on short visits, must have. I then had to say when and for how long I would be in each place. All these formalities were not completed until a few days before I had planned to start, and only then was I allowed to buy tickets for the journey. When I finally left Moscow, officials in every stop on my route knew in advance that I was coming, when I would arrive, and how long I planned to stay.

It was explained officially that this was because the Soviet Government wanted to make my journey as comfortable as possible and to ensure that it would be trouble-free. In point of fact, though, the authorities were thereby able to keep watch on all my movements. This supervision, disguised as concern for one's welfare, can become tiresome. I remember one occasion when I had an hour's stopover during a flight. I was taken in charge the moment I stepped off the plane and led, with every possible courtesy, to the airport building. There, in a special room furnished in the ostentatious style of the Stalin era, I sat alone at a table laid for twenty people. A waitress was already in attendance, and the airport restaurant manager came to see that I was comfortable. I felt as though I was in a gilded cage.

During my Siberian tour in 1956 I went to the theatre whenever I could. I preferred to buy my own ticket so that if the play was uninteresting I could leave before the end. Sometimes, however, I couldn't get a seat, so I went as the guest of the management. Once when this happened the manager invited me to his office before the performance, and he didn't escort me to my seat until the curtain was about to go up. At intermission he was waiting to take me to the restaurant and offer me a drink. The restaurant filled up quickly, and very soon every seat was taken except two at our table. But whenever anyone tried to take one of the vacant seats, he was shooed away by the waitress, who watched over our table with an eagle eye. In addition a policeman had taken up his position at the doors of the restaurant. When our waitress turned her back for a moment two young girls came and sat beside us, and then one of them went to get something to eat. In a flash our waitress was by her side, talking earnestly. The girl came back to our table in some distress, whispered to her companion, and they both got up and disappeared into the crowd.

It is particularly difficult in the Soviet Union to distinguish between true and false hospitality because the Russians, in general, are naturally friendly and well-disposed towards strangers. Every hotel, particularly in the provinces, wants to show its best side to foreigners. From the manager to the chambermaids, the entire staff do their best to please foreign guests. One evening in Akmolinsk (in Kazakhstan) I returned from a tour of the neighbouring villages too late for dinner. The inn where I was staying was far from luxurious, and the maid had gone off duty. Nevertheless, on her own initiative she had left a meal ready for me in my room, complete with a packet of tea and a note telling me where I could find boiling water. The next morning, when she found that I had not returned until late at night and, having eaten well during the trip, had not needed the meal she had left, she cleared it away and refused to accept any payment for it.

Before I left the Kuzbas (the Kuznetsk Basin) for Barnaul, capital of the Altay province, I asked the local authorities to reserve a room for me. I reached Barnaul by train at three o'clock in the morning, and a driver was waiting to take me to the hotel, where everyone was waiting up for me. The manageress herself showed me to my room. The chambermaid asked if there was anything I needed, and when I said that all I wanted was to get some sleep she seemed quite disappointed. Tea and something to eat had been prepared for me, so I had to sit down to a meal at three in the morning while the maid ran a bath for me.

I learned later that all this was the doing of the good Pyotr Romanovich. I did not meet him until the next morning, when I visited the municipal authorities. He was a man of medium height with a typically Russian face. He said he was anxious to do all he could to help me in my work in Barnaul and the whole of the Altay province. He did not bother me, but left me alone when I wanted to be on my own and was ready to lend a hand when I needed help. Pyotr Romanovich obviously worked on the sound principle that more harm was done by giving a foreign visitor the feeling that his freedom of movement was being restricted than by letting him have his head, even if this enabled him to see one or two things that the authorities would rather not have shown him. At any rate, I certainly cherish happier memories of Barnaul than of any other city in Siberia.

When I am travelling I never bother much about normal mealtimes—or, in fact, about food at all. This is something the Russians just cannot understand. In Stalinsk (in the Kuzbas), when the mayor heard that I had not yet eaten breakfast, he immediately opened the big restaurant, much against my will. Normally meals were not served there before one o'clock, but for my benefit cooks and waitresses were mobilized at half past ten.

In 1956, when I was flying back from Siberia to Moscow, I learned at Sverdlovsk that until half an hour before we had landed there the airports ahead of us had been closed because of bad weather. The planes that had been held up at Sverdlovsk had just begun to resume westward flights, and it would be at least two hours, I was told, before our flight to Moscow could be continued. I asked if there was any chance of transferring to another plane that would leave earlier. The girl on duty, a most attractive blonde, made enquiries and found that the next plane was just about to take off. With a porter she hurried out into the night to get my luggage from the plane in which I had arrived and to delay the take-off of the other one until I and my belongings were safely aboard.

This sort of consideration is not shown towards Russians, but everybody is ready to make a special effort for a foreigner. I have often seen a Russian official or salesman brush aside a fellow countryman and turn, obviously eager to please, to attend to the needs of a foreigner. And it always seemed to me that this eagerness was more genuine when the Russian found he was dealing with a 'real' foreigner, rather than with a customer from one of the other iron curtain countries.

There may be several reasons for this attitude towards foreigners. First there is the Russian tradition of hospitality. Then there is the lively and largely unsatisfied interest in the outside world, about which the Russian has for decades heard only the official Soviet version, a version he accepts only with strong reservations. Then again, every 'genuine' foreigner, whether he is from the West or from India or from Egypt, is regarded as the harbinger of a return to normal international relations: 'If these people come travelling happily round our country, then surely the danger of war can't be as great as we thought.' Although Soviet films, novels, and short stories pour out a constant stream of warnings about wicked foreign agents, the individual foreign visitor is usually regarded as a symbol of the easing of political tension, rather than as a potential spy. But perhaps the strongest motive of all is the Russians' intense love of and pride in their own country. They naturally want to behave towards foreigners in such a way that the visitors will always remember with pleasure the time they spent in Russia.

When I ask myself what has impressed me most during my Russian journeys over the years, the answer is the friendliness of the people, and I am sure other foreign visitors would say the same. Whether they travel as private individuals or as VIPs, they always find the obviously genuine delight that the Russian people display at the sight of a foreigner. The enthusiasm aroused by Nehru's visit, for example—an enthusiasm predominantly genuine and only to a very minor degree officially inspired—was a factor of real significance in world affairs. It made a profound impression on the sensitive Indian and influenced his attitude towards the people themselves as well as towards the regime. Indeed, the natural, eager hospitality of the ordinary Russian is one of the most effective means the Kremlin has for making a favourable impression on the outside world.

But all this refers to the spontaneous friendliness of the people themselves. Dealings with the appropriate authorities of the central administration are not nearly so pleasant. One morning in 1956, for example, a friendly and jovial American journalist named O'Malley suddenly disappeared from Moscow. Some days before, he had been sent for by the Foreign Ministry. There he had been told that he had broken the currency regulations, but that the authorities were prepared to forgo criminal proceedings if he left the country at once. So far as he knew he had never infringed any currency regulations, but he knew the authorities regarded him with a jaundiced eye because of the reports he had been writing. It is extremely difficult to prove in court in a totalitarian state that you have invariably observed the currency regulations, so the wise man gives way gracefully.

In any event, how *can* one be absolutely sure, in a totalitarian state, that he has not in some way violated the currency regulations? Also, it is easy to fall into a trap without realizing it. I remember once going to the State Bank in Moscow to change my foreign currency into roubles. There was some delay, and I was afraid I would be late for an appointment. To be on the safe side, I went to telephone the friend I was to meet. In the waiting-room, a girl in her early twenties came up to me with a heart-warming smile and asked if I would do her a great favour. I replied that it depended on what she wanted me to do. She pulled a hundred-dollar bill from her blouse. 'Will you take this American money?' she asked. 'If I try to get it changed myself I will get into trouble. If you'll do me this favour, I'll let you have it cheap.' She then launched into an improbable story about a dress sent to her by some relations abroad. She said that while she was altering it to fit her, she had found the hundred-dollar bill in the lining. I did not believe a word of it, and I was fairly sure I was dealing with an *agent provocateur*. If I had changed the money for her, I would have committed an offence against the currency restrictions, and the authorities could have filed a suit against me any time they liked, if—as with the American journalist—they suddenly wanted to get rid of me. So I refused to play.

If you ask me whether I was usually shadowed, I can only say that I didn't pay any attention to that. On my travels I never looked back over my shoulder, and I always behaved as though no-one were watching me; after all, I had nothing to hide. I didn't want my attention to be distracted from whatever I was doing by worrying all the time whether someone was dogging my footsteps. My whole object was to meet and get to know the Soviet citizens as fellow human beings, not merely at official receptions for foreigners. Forty years of bitter experience under Bolshevism have compelled the Russians to adopt an attitude of conformity, which they wear like a protective shell. This mask has already been described often enough. I was more concerned with trying to find out what went on behind the mask, and what the ordinary Russians were really like.

In common with other foreigners, I succeeded only occasionally during my journeys in scratching the shell of Soviet reality. A German prisoner-of-war returned from the U.S.S.R., a Russian *kolkhoz* peasant, a workman from the Caucasus—each of these has experienced the Soviet way of life in different environments and contexts and would probably confirm only one aspect of what I have found to report; yet each would be right from the viewpoint of his own experience. Life in the Soviet Union is uncommonly varied, and each individual can see only a few facets of it.

CHAPTER 2

THE SOCIAL FRAMEWORK

THE RUSSIANS, like other people, live in groups and combinations of all kinds which condition their emotions, thoughts, and actions and therefore often provide clues which help us to understand them. I refer to social and economic groups and not to the many nationalities found in the Soviet Union. Throughout I shall concentrate on the Russians in the narrower sense of the term, the so-called Great Russians, because it is they who have been mainly responsible for the characteristic features of both the empire of the Czars and that of the Soviet Union. Communism, although it originated in western Marxism, began to develop long before 1917 as part of their history. Only later was it imposed on the other nationalities of the U.S.S.R.

Four decades after the Revolution, the various generations are not only physically differentiated, as trees are by their age-rings, but they are also quite different in their outlook. Those who remember life as it was before the Revolution are now nearing sixty or more. The majority of them, particularly the countryfolk, held aloof from the Revolution, feeling that they were the passive material of an experiment rather than its active participants.

The middle-aged group, those now between thirty-five and sixty, spent their most impressionable years under the Revolution, the civil war, and the First Five-Year Plan. Most of the townspeople, and an active minority in the rural areas, were moved by the emotional appeal of the Revolution and became its champions. This generation carried the major burden of those decisive years; their great achievement was the transformation of the Soviet Union from an agrarian to an industrial state, their most bitter disillusionment the reign of terror during the second half of the 1930's, with its cynical betrayal of all the principles in which they had believed.

For the younger generation, the Revolution is something they learn about in schoolbooks and occasionally in films. Their picture of the world has been shaped by other things: industrial expansion; a war fought in the name of patriotism and won at

19

the cost of heavy losses; professional advancement through school, technical studies and college; and the big gaps in status among the various social groups.

They now take for granted many of the things for which their fathers fought and suffered, and the memories to which their elders cling are to the younger generation a matter for indifference or at best romanticism, at which they smile. The Revolution has been carried through, the independence of the fatherland has been asserted in World War II, and the security of the state is safeguarded by a deep defensive belt of allied countries. When shall we be able to think of our own affairs, they ask, if not now?

Apart from the differences among the generations, to which we shall return later, there is a further differentiation worth studying—that determined by professional or social status. And here the main emphasis can be laid on the new elite.

First there are the leaders of industry—the directors, chief accountants, and managers of various departments and planning sections in the industrial enterprises, the 55,000 *kolkhozes* (collective farms) and 6,500 *sovkhozes* (state farms), in the shops, restaurants, banks, railroads, shipping and civil aviation, in the postal and telegraph services, in the communal enterprises and hotels. These probably total something like two or two and a half million people.[1]

In my travels through Russia I visited numerous industrial and agrarian enterprises, and met many executives. Like his Western counterpart, the Russian executive has a private office, guarded by one or more secretaries in an outer office, and furnished in a solidly bourgeois manner: panelled walls hung with pictures of his plant and products, carpeting, comfortable leather chairs for visitors and, most important, a huge desk for the comrade director. Resting on this imposing desk are a number of 'phones and, inevitably, a huge desk set, an inkwell, a container full of well-sharpened pencils, and a blotter—usually made of colourful semi-precious stones from the Urals. The absence of family photographs is notable.

The career of a Soviet works manager, if he belongs to the older generation, does not differ much from that of his American counterpart of a few decades ago; in many cases the Russian, too, started at the bottom. But when one of the younger Soviet directors talks about his career he sounds more like a young executive from Western Europe. He did not have to start as an ordinary factory hand, but as the son of a member of the new elite he reached his present job by way of a college education. The 'Red Directors' of the thirties, who sat at the head of industrial concerns purely as Party functionaries, are no longer typical. There are now about 3,700,000 technicians of all types (including agronomists etc.) with a college or intermediate education, and every year between 400,000 and 500,000 more enter industry and agriculture.

Next come the doctors, teachers, and lawyers (including junior personnel) who together numbered nearly 3,900,000 at the end of 1959, and who show an annual increase (not counting deaths and retirement) of about 300,000.

Technically all Soviet citizens are state employees, since the state is the sole employer. But there are also officials in the more restricted sense of the word—those who work in the administrative departments. No classified statistics are available for these. Among them are the functionaries of the trade unions, co-operatives, and similar organizations.

The number of paid full-time Party officials, which in practice means those in the more senior positions, is about three-quarters of a million, while the number of Party members (and candidates) was announced at the Twenty-first Party Congress in early 1959 as 8,200,000.[2] Transfers from a Party career to that of a state civil servant, and vice versa, are frequent; and I, for one, find it difficult to follow those who speak of the Party and state hierarchies as though they were separate entities, composed of different groups of citizens with different interests.

Among Russia's top people, we know more about the artists —writers, painters, actors, and dancers—than about any other group. They are the class most accessible to foreigners, they travel abroad, and their works or their performances are often widely known. The artists are of particular importance to everyone interested in the internal workings of the Soviet Union since they are, to some extent, the spokesmen of a people who communicate very little with the outside world. But I shall deal with this group in more detail in the chapter on freedom of thought.

The officers' corps must be regarded as a class apart, and this has been especially true since the creation during World War II of military academies for the officers of the future. The authorities lay particular stress on the standards required of officers' wives. Moreover, the officers lead lives segregated from the troops in their own barracks and clubs, and the discrepancy between their standard of living and that of the men in the ranks is enormous. In the course of a trip, my train was on a siding for fifteen minutes, alongside a troop transport. The enlisted personnel had already spent four days in freight cars; the officers were travelling in coaches.

The members of all the groups mentioned thus far are classed together in the Soviet Union as 'intelligentsia', a term far more comprehensive in its Russian usage than it is in the West. During the Revolution scant thought was given to the intelligentsia; the emphasis was on workers, peasants, and, of course, soldiers. But during the First Five-Year Plan it was realized that industrial expansion would result in the emergence of a group which obviously could not be classed as either workers or peasants. Stalin referred to this group at first as the 'cadres', but later he seemed to prefer intelligentsia, a concept which has steadily grown until the word is now virtually a synonym for that upper stratum which is not supposed to exist in a socialist state. From the available statistics, I estimate that this upper stratum of Soviet society, including families, consists of about 25 to 30 million people. Whatever the exact figure, it is certain that Russia has never had such a wide-ranging upper and middle class before.

The white-collar workers as a sociological group are not easy to describe, and aside from the top level, they represent a relatively colourless section of the population, comprising mostly those without special qualifications. They are to be found everywhere—as hotel employees, in the clerical and accounts sections of factories and offices, and in the railway and postal services—and the women far outnumber the men. They wear themselves out at their daily tasks and at the same time try to improve their qualifications, and thereby increase their incomes, by attending foreign-language courses or seeking other aids to self-improvement; but they rarely get any further and are always overshadowed by the 'workers', who have risen far above them in the social order. I estimate that there are (including families)

20 to 25 million of these employees who do not belong to the upper stratum.

The workers and peasants form the broad base of the social pyramid. They are not only less accessible to foreigners than the 'top people', but they are less frequently encountered in contemporary Russian literature, since most writers prefer to deal with the life of the intelligentsia, which they know so much better.

In 1959 the U.S.S.R. had close to 17 million people working in industry. To these must be added about 15 million in the transport services, *sovkhozes*, and non-industrial branches of the country's economy, making in all about 32 million workers, who, with their families, represent a grand total of about 60 million people.

Soviet industrial labour is predominantly peasant in origin. Industrialization and urbanization have been parallel processes. The vast increase in the number of industrial workers was made largely at the expense of the villages.

The Soviet labour force today shows signs of a split personality. On the one hand, the workers are flattered by the official myth that they are the sector on which the growth of the state is based; on the other, they are dissatisfied with their standard of living, which is still low, and by their arduous working conditions and the constant strain of piecework and output targets. Three-quarters to four-fifths of them are on piecework rates, and for these the fixing of norms and the quota laid down for a day's work are of vital concern. It is therefore over these details that day-to-day friction occurs. The wage system is so complex and so chaotic that nobody knows just where he stands, and it almost seems to invite circumvention on all levels.

It was to the villages that the Revolution brought the most radical changes. Where there used to be a more or less homogeneous mass of poor peasants, with the bigger farmers just beginning to emerge, there are now marked variations. Aside from one basic difference between the *kolkhoznik* and the industrial worker—the former's not altogether unsuccessful struggle to retain his personal property—there is in every other respect an unmistakable convergence towards urban social conditions, or at least towards those of an industrial settlement. There is, for example, no appreciable difference between the elite in a village—usually the *kolkhoz* chairman, the agronomists, and the accountants—and the corresponding group in a town. The *kolkhoznik* is becoming more and more like any worker, on a par with a fitter or a turner, and his life, like theirs, turns on the struggle to fulfil his quota. Every sign points to the fact that the peasants, as a group, are most critical of the regime. For centuries they dreamed of owning land. But no sooner had the dream come true than it was over. The compulsory collectivization of land and cattle in the early 1930's robbed the peasants once more of their hard-won gains after they had dreamed for centuries that one day they would make the land their own. When I talked with the peasants, I was constantly aware that they regarded themselves as the poorest of the poor, the lowest grade in the social scale. Including their families the Kolkhoz population numbers about 80 million.

The discrepancies in income among the various social levels are astonishing. I shall try to explain in a later chapter how this has come about, but here are the facts. In 1957, according to Soviet statistics, there were about 8 million workers and clerical employees earning between 270 and 350 roubles a month.[3] (The actual domestic purchasing power of the rouble at that time worked out to something like eight cents—about sevenpence.) On the other hand, there were then, and still are today, people with incomes of 1,000, 2,000, or 5,000 roubles a month, and even a great deal more. The highest incomes reach a million roubles a year. And apart from their high salaries, the elite enjoy many other privileges—free official residences, household help paid for by the state, rent-free country houses, official cars, theatre tickets, free treatment by the best doctors in the best hospitals, luxurious villas on the Black Sea, and generous expense allowances. If all these were reckoned in terms of cash, the monthly incomes of these privileged groups would be increased by many thousands—perhaps tens of thousands—of roubles.

Direct taxes are low, but the invisible taxes, which the consumer pays in the form of increased retail prices for his daily needs, are very high; they hit the poor much harder than the affluent. But it is largely by this means that the Soviet Government finances the state, the army, heavy industry, and foreign policy expenditure.

The Communist leaders defend themselves tooth and nail when their country is called a class state. Their argument is that one can speak of class distinction only when some people own the means of production and others are therefore economically dependent on them. That may well be one criterion of class distinction, but it is certainly not the only one, nor is it today the most important one. It is now much more a question of control rather than ownership of the means of production. Not even a Bolshevik can deny that there are people in the Soviet Union who are in charge of the means of production and others who are not and are therefore dependent on those who are.

Whether one describes the social structure of the Soviet Union as a class state, or avoids the term in deference to its wishes, the fact remains that there exists a steep social pyramid, with a vast distance between apex and base, and numerous clearly differentiated levels in between.

THE PRIVATE SPHERE

CHAPTER 3

THE RUSSIAN CHARACTER

ONE DAY, in the village near Moscow where we spent our holidays before World War I, the news got around that a hermit, a holy man, had come back from the wilds of the far north to visit his home and family, whom he had abandoned for the service of God. I hurried to the cottage he was said to be in, and on a pinewood bench in the small front garden sat a man with a grey beard who seemed to me to be as old as time, though he was probably not more than fifty. He wore a long, white, tattered shirt; his piercing eyes, deep-set in an ascetic face, completed the image of a holy man. He spoke little, and what he did say I did not understand, but the peasants listened reverently. For a few days he was the talk of the village; then things settled down again as we got used to having him around.

Only a week after he had come back, however, I was hauled out of bed early one morning by one of the village boys. Something terrible and extraordinary had happened, he said. Together we ran to the holy man's cottage. It was a smoking ruin, in the midst of which the fireplace and chimney stood forlorn. The hermit's wife and daughter were weeping noisily as they raked through the ashes, but the hermit himself had disappeared. I learned from the crowd round the cottage that the previous evening, after getting himself roaring drunk, the holy man had smashed up everything in his home, thrashed his wife, and done something dreadful (which I did not understand) to his daughter. He had then set fire to the cottage and left. Later the same day we heard that, having slept off his drunken stupor, he had given himself up to the police and had been packed off to prison in Moscow.

Those who draw more readily on literature than on life for examples of human behaviour will probably be reminded of the transformation of the loose-living Prince Nekhlyudov in Tolstoy's *Resurrection*, who suddenly gave up everything to follow a condemned woman into banishment in Siberia. Folklore contains many characters like this. The 'Volga Boat Song'—of which the whole world knows the melody, if not the words—

tells of Stenka Razin, the robber chief and friend of the people, who went sailing down the Volga with his companions and, after a night of love with his Princess, threw her into the river to drown because his men were muttering that his love affairs were beginning to make the chief a bit womanish.

In Russia there are innumerable examples, in both literature and life, of such outbursts of emotion. Their incredible intensity, suddenness, and unbridled violence offer classic examples of what is now sometimes called the 'ambivalent personality', one capable of expressing simultaneously or in rapid succession the most contradictory emotions—a personality that combines love and hate, kindness and brutality, sensual intoxication and asceticism, the sinner and the saint. The young lyric poet Yevtushénko, in the fourth volume of his works, published in 1958, writes:

> I am thus and not thus, I am industrious and lazy, determined and shiftless. I am . . . shy and impudent, wicked and good; in me is a mixture of everything from the west to the east, from enthusiasm to envy . . .[1]

A clear expression of ambivalence, after forty years of Bolshevism!

To squeeze the last drop of experience out of these extremes of temperament is a basic need of the typical expansive 'Russian soul', with its urge for unlimited, ungovernable self-expression regardless of the consequences. Time and again one sees this in everyday life—the sudden change from the joy of creation to the lust of destruction, the vast discrepancy between thought and deed, the mind soaring to sublime heights and magnificent conceptions but at the same time apparently incapable of accomplishing anything practical. These are the qualities of Goncharov's Oblomov and of Turgenev's Rudin.

The foreigner, however, was both admired for his disciplined, sustained, successful work habits, and despised as an 'eager beaver'. The fluctuation between arrogance and messianic zeal on the one hand and a feeling of inferiority on the other made Russia, even in the days of the Czars, a difficult and sometimes dangerous partner of her European neighbours.

It is outside the scope of this book to speculate on the extent to which these contradictory elements in the Russian character are the result of the boundless expanse of the land, a history rich in rapture and despair, or a long period of religious isolation. What does concern us here is that the rulers in the Kremlin consider that such characteristics impede, and even jeopardize, their plans, and that they have at times been exasperated to the point of desperation by such behaviour. Their nineteenth-century forerunners, small groups of revolutionaries and utopian idealists, insisted on complete mastery over the dull and supine masses by the revolutionary elite. They considered it as their own special mission to compel the nation, even against its will, to shape its destiny—a destiny incomprehensible to the nation itself, but clearly identified by the elite—and thus eventually to alter its very essence.

Once this minority's dictatorship had been established in the storms of revolution, Lenin, followed by the even more ruthless Stalin, used every method—terror, economic pressure and stimulation, propaganda and education—to squeeze the turbulent elements in the Russian character into the safe channel of a planned programme, to suppress undesirable urges, and to foster the qualities of industry, stability, discipline, firmness of purpose, and self-control—all necessary for the creation of a modern, industrialized power. This combination of rationalism and will-power, designed to crush and then replace the uncontrollable impulses of the past, was to produce 'new men'. And insofar as they have ruthlessly and methodically tried to eradicate all those characteristics recognized throughout the world as typically Russian, the Bolsheviks can justifiably be called 'anti-Russian'.[2]

For example, they have tried to inculcate in the Russians a sense of time, something quite foreign to the Russian mind. They have done this not only by strict rules against idleness and unpunctuality during working hours, but also by stressing the concept of time in the education of children. I remember a children's book entitled *What is the Time?*[3] With the help of many illustrations, some of them quite witty, it describes the evolution of a sense of time and the development of the means employed to measure it, from the ancient Egyptians and the Greeks through the Middle Ages to the present day, from the sundial to the chronometer—and all without a word about politics.

Another children's book, *The Precision Factory*,[4] deals with the Meteorological and Standardization Research Institute. It takes the reader through the laboratories of the Institute and explains the many instruments of all sizes by which time, distance, weights and temperature are measured, thus unobtrusively and effectively emphasizing the importance of accuracy in all things. Anecdotes and asides are skilfully interpolated in the text. The book suggests, for instance, 'Just think what would happen if all our measures and clocks suddenly became confused!' The ensuing chaos, with trains in collision and so on, is vividly presented so that the reader realizes that at this stage of human development it would be impossible to get along without calculation and precision in all our activities. This book is written in a lively style; many gifted Soviet writers have taken such an avenue of escape from the barren wastes of regimented 'socialist realism' into the oasis of non-political children's books.

The arts, too, are made to serve this branch of education. In 1956 I saw a play in Moscow which dealt with the development of an instrument to make it possible to locate the source of trouble in an electrical circuit. This objective was represented as a matter of life or death.

The Communists have come closer to their goal of making the Russians time-conscious than to any other. By various means they have conditioned the people to methodical, uninterrupted work. The word *nichevó* is rarely heard now. The Oblomovs seem to be almost extinct. The Russian of today is more moderate, more disciplined, than his forebears; his boundless energy is absorbed by exacting labour and held in check by strict laws.

This profound and apparently permanent transformation, astonishing to anyone familiar with pre-Revolutionary Russia, has not been brought about by Communism alone; it is perhaps primarily the inevitable result of industrial development, which demands a constant flow of work and makes little allowance for the extremes of human feelings. Machines—the tractor, the milking machine, the conveyor belt—were the moulders of this new image, rather than the Party official.

It may be that this education by the machine is merely superficial, that beneath the surface of this technological process the volcanic Russian temperament lies dormant, ready at any moment to break out again in all its wild unpredictability. I am not sure. But in reading some of the stories of the young author Yuri Kazakov one realizes that the 'old Russian' is by no means dead.[5]

Another point should not be overlooked. In Russia, as elsewhere, technological progress has taken its toll of human qualities. The most appealing traits of the Russians—their uninhibited naturalness and candour—have suffered most. After the collapse of Imperial Russia, the uncalculating Russian, who always acted on impulse, whether for good or ill, suddenly found himself in a new world. A calculating regime that left nothing to chance compelled him to become calculating too, to resort to dissimulation, and even to the betrayal of his fellow men—all for the sake of his own skin. During the years of the murderous purges it was not uncommon for a man facing trial on unsubstantiated charges to see people who were once close to him now bear witness against him.

In the period of comparative relaxation that followed the death of Stalin, writers were able to criticize these evils. Korneychuk's play *Wings* is an example. Years after the war a man meets the wife he had passively abandoned to the state police, although he knew the charges against her were false. It is the wife who turns out to be the real heroine; the husband is portrayed as a colourless and negative individual. This unhappy theme is treated satirically by Vladimir Polyakov in his comedy *Oh Heart!* which, though it has no literary merit, is interesting because of its subject.

The play, which I saw in Moscow in 1955, is about two middle-aged workers, Borísov and Kiparísov, inseparable friends since early childhood, who are celebrating the twenty-fifth anniversary of their employment at the same factory. A social gathering of the Party cell has been arranged to celebrate the occasion. Before the celebration begins the two friends are deeply immersed in recalling their shared experiences. The leader of the Party cell opens the proceedings by saying that there is just one rather unpleasant point to be cleared up before they can settle down to enjoy themselves. A complaint, he says, has been made against Borisov by a woman who claims that while they were at a theatre together Borisov had promised to marry her, but had broken his promise. She also suggests that during the war Borisov's behaviour was not all that it should

have been, and that he has—and this is particularly suspicious—
an aunt in America.

Borisov laughs at the accusations. The woman, he says, is a
detestable old creature whom he would not have promised to
marry even if he was blind drunk. He went to the theatre with
her, he explains, only because he couldn't get a ticket, while she
had two and had agreed to sell one to him. As far as his war
record is concerned, he will not deign to answer. Let them
ask his friend Kiparisov, who was at his side all through
the war.

Before Kiparisov rises to defend his friend, the leading Party
member whispers in his ear that there are one or two highly
placed persons who attach some importance to the complaints
against Borisov. In a split second the loyal friend turns into a
traitor.

'It is true,' he says, 'that Borisov and I were together during
the war. But I wasn't at his side all the time, of course, and
what he did when I wasn't there I wouldn't know. As a matter
of fact, it has occurred to me that I never once heard him say
anything unfriendly about America. At the time I didn't attach
any importance to it, but now I hear he has an aunt there—well,
that puts rather a different complexion on it, doesn't it?'

Borisov is horrified. The celebration peters out. When the
two 'old friends' meet later in the corridor, Borisov can hardly
restrain himself. 'If I weren't so unhappy about you,' he says,
'I'd give you a damn good sock on the jaw!' 'Go on, then . . .
Do it . . . To please me,' says another of the characters. Borisov
lets fly, Kiparisov gets what's coming to him, and the curtain
falls to thunderous applause.

The strain may well be less now than in the harshest times
under Stalin. But nobody can be certain that there never will
be a reversion to Stalin's methods, and that some candid
comment made years ago (and duly noted by someone or
other) will not be dug up again and used against him. Moreover, it is not enough just to toe the line passively, or to carry
out orders promptly. When silence is accepted as a sign of
agreement, critics of the regime need not lie, but when ex-
plicit and enthusiastic approval is expected, then a lie is the only
alternative. Nor is it enough merely to applaud and say a casual
word of praise. The tone of voice in which approval is expressed

is carefully noted. The playwright Sofronov wrote some time ago:

> One must not content oneself with merely paying attention to *what* is being said, for that may well be in complete harmony with the Party programme. One must pay attention also to the *manner*—to the sincerity, for example, with which a schoolmistress recites a poem the authorities regard as doubtful, or the pleasure revealed by a critic who goes into detail about a play he professes to condemn.[6]

One thing is certain. Bitter experience has taught the present-day Russian a lesson; he is infinitely more reserved than his forebears. This reserve is most marked among the top groups; the higher a Soviet citizen climbs the social ladder, the more cautious he becomes.

The totalitarian state does not confine its interest to the behaviour of its citizens in factories or in barracks; it wants to possess the men themselves, body and soul, and it therefore extends its inquisitive supervision to those fields of activity which are regarded in the West as more or less private.

The Soviet state conducts its campaign against drunkenness, traditionally the besetting sin of the Russians, with great zeal. Drinking hard liquor is a long-standing practice in Russia. A celebration—and the Russians love celebrations—is unthinkable without alcohol. It begins with *zakúska* (canapés) and vodka to lay a solid alcoholic foundation for the meal. As vodka is expensive—since the beginning of 1958 it has cost sixty roubles a bottle—a great deal is illicitly distilled at home.

Sheer boredom, as well as the lack of convivial company, often drives a lonely person to the bottle. It is impossible to travel in Russia without coming across alcoholics, often the result of the *ne kul'turno* (uncivilized) life of the smaller towns and vast countryside. Generally speaking, the women drink little, but drinking vodka is part of being a man. On my next-to-last journey through Siberia, in 1956, I had an illuminating and at the same time moving experience. I was living under really primitive conditions in the only hotel in an industrial town. As it did not provide food, I went to the town's one big restaurant and sat down at a table beside a man and woman.

They told me they lived in a village just outside the town. The previous day they had slaughtered a pig and had sold some of the meat in the *kolkhoz* market. Now they were celebrating. They asked me who I was and where I came from, and I told them. The man had served in the infantry during the war and had been wounded in East Prussia. He had loathed the war, and had had no stomach for shooting at Germans, who, he explained, were ordinary fellows like himself.

'Ordinary people don't want war,' the woman said, 'but what can they do about it? In Germany Hitler gave the orders; here it was Stalin, and on both sides the ordinary people had to do what they were told.' She kept repeating the phrase 'ordinary people'. 'After all,' she said, 'what does the ordinary man or woman want? A house with a bit of garden, pigs and a few chickens, enough work to keep him going, and, above all, peace and quiet. . . . I'm awfully glad that we've become such close friends with India. . . . We need all the friends we can get.'

The man then told me that while he was in the army his first wife had gone off with somebody else. He had lived alone until he met the woman who was now his second wife. 'My mother wanted me to marry him,' the woman interposed, 'even though he was older than me and had only one good leg. . . . And I'm glad I did.' Her husband worked in a factory while she looked after the house, the cabbage patch, the pigs, and the hens. From the occasional sale of garden produce she made much more than she would have earned in the factory.

When I joined them at the table they had already drunk a half-litre bottle of vodka, and now they ordered another. Nearly everyone round us was drinking vodka by the tumblerful. At most of the tables at least one of the party was drunk.

A small orchestra was playing, but the walls were plastered with notices saying 'Dancing forbidden'. 'Why can't people dance here?' I asked. 'For heaven's sake, there'd be a terrible rough-house in five minutes,' the woman replied. 'The women would constantly be bothered, and the men would start fighting.' When we got up to go, I noticed how unsteady my two companions were, and I watched them anxiously as they staggered away, arm in arm. It was pitch dark outside.

I had accepted an invitation to visit them, and the next afternoon I kept my promise. I tried to hire a taxi, but when I gave him the address, the driver, feeling sure that he would get stuck in the mud, refused me. So I started out on foot. If those two could make it home in the dark, after having drunk more than a litre of vodka, then I thought I could surely manage it sober and in broad daylight. But no sooner had I left the town than slush began to seep into my boots. It took me another half-hour to get to the cottage. The woman was alone in the house, peeling potatoes.

'How did you get home last night?' I asked. Without saying a word, the woman opened the door leading from the kitchen into the only other room in the house. On the floor lay the clothes they had been wearing the night before, completely covered with mud, indicating that they must have fallen down a number of times on their way home.

'Didn't you meet my husband on the way?' the woman asked. 'He went into town to buy half a litre. He always says half a litre is the best cure for a hangover.'

Soon afterwards the husband came back. He felt around under the bed and pulled out a bottle of home-brewed *kvas* (beer made from bread). This we finished off, along with the vodka he had brought back, and while we drank, they wanted me to regale them with stories—but not about Germany, which was something too remote for them to grasp. 'Germany,' the husband kept on telling his wife, 'is even farther away than Poland!' What interested them most and what they couldn't hear enough of were the receptions I had been to in the Kremlin. They were as fascinated as children being told a fairy tale.

When I was ready to leave, the man insisted on walking back to town with me, and we waded through the mud together. Twice a day, day after day, this man, with a disabled leg, had to make his way through this river of slush to and from work— a distance of nearly seven miles daily. The road, he said apologetically, was not very *kul'turno*, and it would be nice to have it paved. But the present plan contained no provision for it, and nobody knew whether it would ever be done. Here was a display of patient acceptance on a scale beyond our comprehension.

Alcoholism is regularly denounced as an evil, especially at Komsomol gatherings, and it is almost always mentioned as one of the sins of the younger generation. Khrushchev, who surely did not start out as a teetotaller, is one of the most vociferous opponents of alcoholism.[7] For foreigners to see long queues outside the stores or overcrowded, dilapidated houses doesn't disturb the ardent Communist nearly as much as for them to see drunks, particularly among the youth. The people themselves, especially the men, are more tolerant towards alcoholics, and are inclined to find them a fairly amusing, though at times disgusting, spectacle.

No statistics on the consumption of alcohol are available, and it is difficult to judge, simply through observation, whether it has increased or decreased during the last few decades. I am inclined to think that the per capita consumption has increased, but that total consumption is more evenly distributed throughout the population than before. That state of complete drunken stupor (*zapóy*) characteristic of Old Russia, which put a man out of action for days on end, is rarer now, if only because of stricter rules of work and discipline. Yet, judging by the increasing vehemence of the propaganda against alcoholism, millions of work-hours are still being lost because of drunkenness. And incidentally, the first onslaught on smoking has been launched; the Russians are notorious chain-smokers.

What makes the problem of alcoholism of even greater concern is its close connection with another acute problem, juvenile delinquency. When I arrived in Moscow in 1955, I was told of an incident involving two fifteen-year-old boys, Boris and Oleg. They arrived at a school dance drunk and, because of their improper behaviour, were escorted from the room by one of the students. On the staircase, Boris drew a gun and shot the student. The fathers of both Boris and Oleg were engineers, members of the elite.

A similar case was reported in the press. A gang of youths had made a country house the centre of their activities. They borrowed their fathers' cars and had plenty of money at their disposal. One of them had 1,000 roubles a month allowance. Finally, one of the young ruffians who became afraid and wanted to back out was murdered by the others. Again, the parents were all members of the elite: one of the fathers was a distinguished scientist, another an army colonel, and the mother of another boy was a university graduate.[8]

Many cases of *khuliganstvo* are reported, and frequently the parents are blamed. But if one asks a barman why he sells vodka to youngsters, he usually replies, 'I have to reach my sales target.' The police in the Soviet Union, too, often fail in their duty. They also want to 'fulfil their quota'—to close the gap between convictions and unsolved cases. They are apt to drop into the waste basket the papers of any case in which they see no prospect of quick success. Most people know this and don't even bother to complain to the police. The press reported the case of a young man who made a pass at a girl, was snubbed, and pushed her off a tram. Neither the other passengers nor the conductor did anything about it.[9]

Such behaviour is as old as the Soviet state. World War I, the Revolution, the civil war, and the anti-family measures introduced in the early days of the Revolution created an army of *bezprizórniye* (homeless children) millions strong—young vagabonds who roamed the countryside, begging, stealing, and murdering. In 1929, when I went from one end of the Soviet Union to the other for the first time, I came across them by the score. They were hanging around railway stations, begging on the trains, riding the rods under the rail cars, or organizing gangs of thieves in the side streets of Moscow.

At the beginning of the 1930's a strenuous effort was made to solve the problem. Many of the youths were rounded up and put into camps or organized in 'work communes'; the best-known of these was in Bolshevo, not far from Moscow. One of the last films shown in Moscow before the dead hand of Stalinism stifled imaginative creation in the Soviet film industry was called *The Road to Life*. It described the efforts of idealists to reclaim these embittered and disillusioned youngsters and transform them from outcasts into useful members of society.

Sometimes the results were astounding. One of my acquaintances was the sister of a teacher at Bolshevo. One afternoon, in 1931 or 1932, I was having tea with her in Moscow when there was a tremendous banging on the door, and her brother came in with a group of his young charges. He lived in the same hut as they did, and he tried to gain their confidence by showing confidence in them. For example, he never locked up anything in his room. But now his boots, his pride and joy, had vanished. As soon as he told his boys, they swore to get them back for him and, as the clues all pointed to Moscow, they had come to his sister's house to hold a council of war.

I found it difficult to follow their conversation, as they talked in underworld slang, but I gathered that they were going through a list of the thieves' markets in Moscow, places they had known themselves not very long ago, and were deciding which they would comb through first. The teacher did not go with them, as an adult would have been too conspicuous.

A few hours later the picture had not changed. From time to time scouts came back to report, there was a brief discussion, and off they went again. But at about ten o'clock three of the boys marched in triumphantly with the missing boots. First they had traced the boots, then the thief. All they would say about the thief was that they had 'given him the works, as he deserved'.

When the First Five-Year-Plan began, it absorbed those of the scattered younger generation who had not died of disease or in the camps. Even then, the problem of juvenile crime remained acute, and the measures adopted by the state became increasingly severe. From 1935 onwards, anyone over twelve years old who was accused of robbery, violence, sexual assault, maiming, or murder was tried in the ordinary courts instead of in the more lenient juvenile courts.

In the West, the favourite theme, and the most lucrative in entertainment—as provided by films, music-halls, cabarets, the theatre and magazines—is sex, which also plays a prominent part in many works with serious pretensions to literary merit. Sex is dealt with and analysed, too, in scholarly essays. But in the Soviet Union it has virtually no place in public discussion.

The Soviet press, which devotes little attention to court cases, rarely publishes reports of sexual crime. There are no pornographic works disguised as literature, and allusions to them are so rare that it is difficult to guess how much clandestine pornography exists.[10] In public, at least, the people are markedly prudish; as in Victorian England, sex is not talked about. Even films and film posters dare not break this taboo; a cinema poster showing a couple kissing which appeared in Moscow's Theatre Square early in 1956 caused quite a sensation. In a novel published in 1956, a period of forty years elapsed between a couple's first kiss and their second one, although for six years the lovers lived in the same village.[11]

Pre-marital and extra-marital relations are not entirely banned from recent Soviet literature, but they are treated with extreme reserve. Yuri Trifonov, in his novel *Students*, allows his young heroine only one phrase to define her relations with a boy friend: 'We were close to each other'. Equally—and typically—terse is the indication of marital infidelity in a book published in 1954. It says simply: 'And Julia went to Prosin'.[12]

Dudintsev, in his famous novel *Not By Bread Alone*, employs the same discreet and indirect method. Nadya, the idealistic wife of the careerist Drozdov, realises that her husband is plotting against Lopatkin, the inventor—an idealist like herself—and she decides to break with her husband and become Lopatkin's mistress. But it is only much later in the book that questions about their sexual relations are asked and answered unequivocally. Their relationship is not described by the author in his capacity as narrator; the information is elicited by an examining judge who is extracting evidence of Lopatkin's guilt. Even in this context such blunt language was unusual in Soviet literature—indeed, it would have been unthinkable a few years earlier. The erotic theme became more pronounced in the international film success *The Cranes Are Flying*, which in some of its scenes attempted to continue the great tradition of the 1920's. Here the young hero's fiancée and his brother succumb to temptation while he is at the front. But this scene does not receive the realistic treatment which one would expect in a Western production. Borís Pasternák's *Doctor Zhivago* frankly, though with restraint, depicts the extra-marital relations of the hero. Less restraint is shown by the authoress Natálya Davydova in her novel *The Love of Engineer Izotov*, in which she describes some scenes of high life among members of the 'new class'.[13]

Women are portrayed as they have always been in Russian literature, as much more sure of themselves in affairs of the heart than men. This may well be so in fact. In most contemporary Russian writing the heroes are ardent and conscientious fighters for world Communism; but as lovers they appear awkward and not too happy. Is this sexual reserve simply a social and literary convention, desired, perhaps even imposed by the state to conceal a very different state of affairs, or is it a true picture of things as they are? It is difficult to know. A group of experts from Harvard has carried out an exhaustive investigation into the working of the Soviet system, questioning thousands who emigrated during the 1940's and eliciting much important information[14]; but on sex questions, where Russians are always reticent, the information they gleaned was astonishingly meagre.

My own impression, which I put forward with some reservation, is that, compared with the West, the atmosphere in the Soviet Union is devoid of eroticism. Travelling through Russia, you hear plenty of vigorous and uncouth swearing, but you seldom hear a dirty joke. The worst I remember runs like this. Question: 'When should teenage girls go to bed?' Answer: 'At ten o'clock, because by eleven they should be at home.'

Prostitutes are rarely seen. In Arkhangelsk someone pointed one out to me, but added that she was really an agent, employed by the police to pick up information from foreign seamen. Americans who were in Soviet ports during the war, even during the peak period of Soviet-American fraternisation, have little to report on the subject. Among foreigners in Moscow men sometimes swap stories about the so-called *mózhno* ('you may') girls; but few have actually seen them.

As far as I have been able to discover, soldiers do not have the facilities which are taken as a matter of course in many other countries. The conditions which are notorious near Western military installations do not seem to exist in the Soviet Union. Once, when I was flying to Moscow, our plane was diverted from the civil airport to a military airfield fifty miles away, in the centre of a huge camp. We landed at night, but I saw nothing comparable to the activities near Western camps. The discipline enforced in the Red Army, which is stricter than in Western armies, made the outbreak of sexual licence on the part of many Soviet soldiers in defeated Germany the more violent; after years of bitter fighting and deprivation, the troops took women as the spoils of war.

During the stormy years of the Revolution, close family ties were considered an obstacle on the road to Communism. Marriage was condemned as a bourgeois institution, doomed to extinction. Stories of free love by the Bolshevik diplomat Alexandra Kollontai became best-sellers in the bookshops of Europe.

They were welcomed by some as a sign of the deterioration of the Bolshevik way of life and hailed by others as proof of courageous *avant-garde* thought. During those years, liberal and libertine Bolshevism and militant asceticism often overlapped. But whether the revolutionaries advocated some new form of marriage or favoured complete sexual freedom, they were all determined to smash bourgeois conventions, so that the energy hitherto absorbed by love, marriage, and the family might be used in the struggle for economic expansion.

Natural instincts, however, proved stronger than political theory. The utopian ideas and experiments were abandoned and replaced by new directives; a healthy emotional and sex life was to be integrated with the process of economic and political development. This imposed on Soviet literature in the 1920's that intolerably utilitarian form which even the Bolsheviks themselves later laughed at. As early as 1935, *Komsomólskaya Pravda*, the journal of the youth organization, poured scorn on an article in another journal in which love was described as 'a mighty incentive to productive effort'—a phrase much in vogue at the time. The writer in *Komsomolskaya Pravda* said:

> Our writers have hitherto shied away from writing about love. What sort of thing is it, this 'love'? Has anyone ever got anything out of it? Has it brought any author anything but kicks from the critics? Wouldn't the author be better advised so to fashion his heroes that the incidence of this 'socially dangerous emotion' is precluded, once and for all? Yet, in spite of all this, love has gradually begun to creep back into our literature, though admittedly only in very small doses and in a precisely defined form. . . . 'I love you madly, Manya, almost as much as I love my concrete-mixer. Let's get married.' 'I love you, too, Pyotr. Why shouldn't I? You keep your machine in perfect condition, you fulfil your quota of the plan, and you pay your subscriptions to the union.' 'And just think how wonderful it will be to be able to go to the union meetings together!'

In spite of such ridicule, the representation of love as an incentive to work is still found occasionally in literature.

It does not seem to me that these changes in the pattern of

literature are significant. They are ripples on the surface, but in the depths beneath very little has changed during the last four decades. A Russian I met when we were both in our early twenties was then in the throes of his first love affair, and he proudly introduced his girl friend to me. A few years later they were married; and when I next saw them, after nearly twenty-five years, they were parents of grown children and were still as devoted and happy as they had been at first.

If you stroll through a park in a Soviet city or go into the country for a Sunday picnic, you will see that the young people of today are as romantic as their fathers and grandfathers were, and that they, too, talk rapturously about the moonlight, the lilacs, a boat on the lake, the glory of a sunset. Writers, too, have begun to give romantic love its due again. For example, there is one recent story[15] which, although not of outstanding literary merit, does deal with the age-old theme of first love in a completely natural way, without any political slant. When the story opens, fourteen-year-old Tanya is visited by Fedya who is about the same age as herself. He is returning a paint-brush she had lent him. It is winter, and she will not allow him to come into the room in his snow-covered boots. He takes them off and then comes in and stands watching Tanya, who is busy with her school books. Fedya takes a sheet of paper and starts to make a sketch of her. She is aware of his glance darting from her face to the paper and back again, but dares not raise her head. Finally she shows him what she has been doing, and asks him if it is correct. The story continues:

> Fedya bent over the table, his dark hair brushing her cheek. 'Yes,' he said. Then suddenly his lips were drawn to those rosy cheeks and caressed them lightly, as a shower in early spring lightly touches the good earth. Tanya swiftly drew back and pushed him away. Both remained silent, abashed.
>
> At that moment Tanya's elder sister came into the room, her outstretched hands covered with soap. 'Take my watch off for me, will you, please, Tanya,' she said.
>
> The two youngsters heard nothing. In Tanya's breast something was singing, and the room was filled with a new glory. The sister looked from one bemused young face to

the other. 'What on earth is the matter with you both?'
she cried.

Only then did Tanya become aware of her sister's out-
stretched soapy hands. 'You want me to take your watch
off? There it is, then,' and she put it on the table. 'What
are you looking at me like that for? Go away! Go away!...'

There was such a desperately pleading tone in Tanya's
voice that her sister, about to make some caustic remark,
turned silently and left the room. Tanya threw a scarf
round her shoulders and ran out of the cottage and down
the hill, and hid herself in the thick reeds.

CHAPTER 4

FAMILY AND HOME

DURING A RECENT VISIT to the Soviet Union I travelled for several days across the monotonous plains in a third-class railway car. In the next compartment was a fourteen-year-old girl named Anna, known to everybody there as Ánnushka. I like talking to children on journeys, so she became a frequent visitor to my compartment. I gave her books and magazines, and every afternoon we had tea together. Another occupant of my compartment was a middle-aged war widow; like most of the long-distance passengers, she had her own tea-kettle, and at each stop her fifteen-year-old son Sergei fetched the hot water that was available free.

Annushka had just spent a year with her grandmother in a distant province and was on her way back to rejoin her parents in Tula. At least that was what I gathered, though she was a little vague about it. She told me about her school, about her favourite author (Pushkin), and about her favourite films (she was particularly fond of romantic stories, like the screen version of Lermontov's *Princess Mary*). She had no brothers or sisters.

'I'm sure you'll be very glad to be home again,' I said. 'Only three more days and you'll be back among your own people.' 'Yes . . . ', she replied, 'yes . . . ' But she made no further comment.

When the child had gone back to her own compartment, Sergei's mother said: 'From what I've heard from a woman in Annushka's compartment, the child is not going back to her parents. She has none.' At that moment Annushka appeared in the doorway. A look of horror spread over her face, she blushed deeply, turned and fled.

An hour later I met her in the corridor. She looked as though she had been crying. In spite of her protests, I drew her into my compartment, which happened to be empty. First there were more tears, then she poured out her story. Her father had deserted her mother when Annushka was quite small. After a time an 'uncle' came to join them, and all three lived together in one small room. The uncle did not like Annushka, and insisted that she should be packed off to her grandmother. But the grandmother was old, and the child had not been able to stay with her for long; now she was on her way to relatives in Tula.

I did my best to console her by telling her that I had grown up fatherless too. She was a good and clever girl, I assured her, and she would certainly make a success of her life. Gradually she calmed down, but the old intimacy between us had been destroyed, and she remained embarrassed and reserved.

'Why didn't she tell us from the start?' I asked Sergei's mother. 'Annushka felt too ashamed,' she replied. 'She didn't want you to know she had no family.'

Had such an incident occurred in the West, it would have been of little interest; but it was significant in the Soviet Union, where the government started its campaign against the family immediately after the Revolution. In one of the first decrees promulgated after they came into power, the Bolsheviks reduced marriage and divorce to formalities, and in 1926 citizens were absolved by law from having to register particulars of either.[1] The Kremlin directed that every woman should be entitled to have an abortion if she wanted, and special clinics were opened for the purpose, 'to ensure equal rights for both sexes'. All distinctions between legitimate and illegitimate children were removed; education was declared to be primarily the task of the schools and the political organizations. Educational authorities encouraged children to denounce their parents if the parents were rash enough to criticize the regime at home. A boy called Pavlik Morozov was cited as a heroic example because he had denounced his own father—an opponent of collectivization—and had, as a result, been murdered by wicked kulaks, thus becoming a martyr to the cause of denunciation. When, forty years after a state has come into being with such sociological portents, a child weeps with shame because she has no family to call her own, it seems to me a symptom that cannot be ignored.

It was at the beginning of the 1930's that I saw the first signs of the gradual rebirth of family life in a youth commune.[2] The young members were all children of the Revolution who had enthusiastically accepted the precepts of Communism. Like many other communes at the time, this one was made up of members of both sexes. Its statutes contained the following paragraph:

'We are of the opinion that no restrictions should be placed upon sexual relations (love). Relations between sexes should be open. We must adopt a serious and responsible attitude towards them. Uncomradely relations will result in a desire for secrecy and dark corners, flirtations and similarly undesirable phenomena.'

After a while, admittedly, the commune members did discover that when a couple wanted to be alone it was by no means necessarily a sign of uncomradely relations but was simply inherent in the nature of things. It was in such situations that the lack of adequate living accommodations was most painfully felt. Every room was always overcrowded. Where could relations —however 'comradely'—find room to exist? There arose in communal life innumerable problems which no one had thought of when the commune was founded. The commune assembly attacked the problem with a stop-gap measure, making the following addition to the statutes:

'Sexual relations between members are not deemed desirable during the first years of the commune's existence.'

According to the commune minutes, at least, this ruling was enforced for two years. But at the beginning of 1928 one of the members, Vladimir, announced at a meeting that he intended to marry Katya, who was not a member, and asked that she be admitted to the commune. The record of the meeting shows that conflicting views were expressed.

Misha: 'We are now facing a crisis in the commune. A marriage would mean the formation of a group within the commune and would further shatter our unity. I am therefore against the motion.'

Lolya: 'If we don't accept Katya, we lose Vladimir. We have almost lost him as it is—he's hardly ever here. I vote for the motion.'

Decision: Katya will be accepted as a member of the commune.

And another bed was set up in the girls' room.

Having agreed to the marriage of a member the commune then had to turn its attention to the probable consequences. After a long debate, the following ruling was adopted:

'Marriage within the commune is both possible and permissible. But in view of the shortage of accommodation, the unions must remain childless. However, abortions may not be performed.'

Not all the members of the commune agreed with this ruling. Some of them thought it was both unwise and unhealthy, but they all apparently obeyed it at first. Then, only a year later, a further resolution was adopted: 'The commune sanctions the birth of children.' On one point, however, the members remained in unanimous agreement. Neither marriage nor children could be allowed to make any difference to the basic principle that in the commune everything belonged to everybody. The children of members were to be regarded as the children of the commune and would be brought up at communal expense.

A little later Stepan and Tanya, both members of the commune, were married; six months after that, Anna, who was not a member, married Andrei, who was. Anna introduced a new note into commune marriages. She maintained her bunk outside the commune, explaining: 'In my opinion it is not necessary for married couples to live together. I will not therefore apply for membership in the commune.'

By this time five of the eleven members had married. But since no more accommodation was available, the commune had to remain divided as before into men's and women's quarters. This naturally had an adverse effect on the relations of the young couples. In despair Tanya wrote to her husband:

'What I long for is personal happiness—a quite simple and quite legitimate little world of my own. I yearn for some peaceful corner with you alone, where we can be together whenever we wish, where we no longer need to hide from the others, and where our life together can blossom into a fuller and freer happiness. Surely the commune can understand that this is a human need.'

A few months later more accommodation became available, and the families began to turn from the Communist experiment to the old, established form of married life; human nature triumphed over ideology long before the Party revised its attitude toward the family. It was not until 1935 that the official change first became apparent. At that time I was living in Moscow as a foreign journalist. Out of the blue, the papers suddenly began to print so much about family life that I had to start a new file on the subject. Previously the word 'family' had hardly ever been mentioned in the press; now items on family problems began to appear. For example: 'In the town of Serpukhov a socialist competition has been organized to decide which parents are providing the best upbringing for their children.' The standards by which the competition was judged were: has each child his own toothbrush? how often does he have his hair and nails cut?—and so on. Other towns followed suit. At Party gatherings the *tovarishchi* were called upon to give an account of how they were raising their children. In the minutes of one Party meeting I read:

> Having heard what *tovarishch* Dobrovolsky has to say about the upbringing of his son, the meeting decided that *tovarishch* Dobrovolsky and his wife have been taking adequate care of their son Volodya. But the meeting does not regard it as normal that Volodya goes to bed so late, that he does not brush his teeth regularly, and that he reads few good books. The meeting, therefore, directs *tovarishch* Dobrovolsky: first, to ensure that Volodya goes to bed at the proper time; secondly, to provide him with a toothbrush and tooth-powder and see that he uses them regularly; and thirdly, to make Volodya join the factory library and obtain the following books as soon as possible. [A list of book titles followed.]

Having spent years trying to turn women into men, one suddenly began to demand the cultivation of feminine graces. At a Komsomol meeting in one of the Leningrad high schools, a speaker said:

> A girl's appearance should be such that it is a pleasure to go for a walk with her. [*Applause*] Far too many of our female members have lost the qualities of charm which every woman must have. It is high time eau-de-Cologne and face-powder were declared indispensable adjuncts of every woman in the Komsomol. [*Applause*]

From about this time onwards, the policy of the government went hand in hand with the healthy common sense of the people.

In 1936 divorce was made more difficult; the state imposed a fee of 50 roubles, which went up to 150 for a second divorce and 300 for a third. Abortion was made a punishable offence.[3] In new publications on domestic law, the family was praised as a truly socialist form of home life. In 1941 a special tax was levied on childless couples, followed in 1944 by the granting of decorations, awards, and monetary grants to mothers of large families.

These developments in domestic legislation reached their peak in the last year of the war.[4] Recognition of common-law marriages, which had hitherto enjoyed equal status with legal marriages, was withdrawn, and since then only officially registered marriages have been recognized by the state, the father of an illegitimate child being relieved of his obligation to pay a maintenance allowance; the mother either receives a state subsidy for her child or, if she prefers, may leave it free of charge in a state-owned children's home.

To discourage husbands or wives contemplating divorce, it was decreed that they would henceforth have to give notice of their intention by inserting an announcement in the local press at their own expense. The courts were directed to do everything in their power to prevent divorce, and to grant it only when there was not a shadow of doubt that the marriage in question was an irretrievable failure. And to make things even more difficult, the cost of a divorce has now risen to 500 roubles or more. It is only recently that any objection has been made to these marriage regulations; and then only the harmful effect of the legislation on unmarried mothers has been criticized. Since the 1930's the strengthening of family ties has been continually urged. Until recently, sex could be mentioned in novels only in relation to engaged or newly married couples, and even then with the greatest possible restraint; once the marriage was established, sexual problems were regarded as non-existent. Anyone interested in advancing his career did his best to avoid divorce. In a novel published in 1956 which tells the story of a broken marriage, the man asks his wife, who has already left him, to return, supporting his plea with these words: 'You know very well the view taken nowadays about broken families, especially when a Party member is involved.'[5]

Parental authority, which was rejected during the early years of the Revolution, has also been restored. In the *Twenty Rules for Children* issued during the war, which all schoolchildren had to learn by heart, Rules 13 and 17 read:

'Be polite to your parents and behave modestly and obediently in school, in the street, and in public generally.'
'Obey your parents and help them to look after your younger brothers and sisters.'[6]

The state has also taken great pains to strengthen the position of the mother. Court decisions are made public only when they establish a desirable precedent. In a divorce case in 1944, for example, the father was granted custody of the child because the court declared that as a professor and the deputy director of a school he was better fitted to ensure a responsible, Communist upbringing for the child than was the mother, a student at the same school. A higher court revoked the decision and awarded custody to the mother. 'The father's more advantageous material position,' it said, 'does not constitute a good and sufficient reason for removing a two-and-a-half-year-old child from its mother.' This ruling was published.[7]

An authoritative Moscow newspaper carried an article entitled 'The Young Mother', which stated: 'The mother is sacred and must be treated with great respect by the family, particularly by the father. In the family the mother's word is law. Her authority is unassailable.'[8]

There were several reasons for this *volte-face* in state policy towards family life. The pragmatists among the Party leaders, with Stalin himself in the vanguard, must have been worried by the chaos resulting from the marital regulations in the early days of the Revolution; a chaos whose most striking features were a declining birth-rate, an appalling increase in the neglect of children, and a deterioration in the health of women as a result of numerous abortions. Moreover, the need for well-regulated family life was deeply ingrained in the Russian character, especially in Russian women. But we cannot assume that this applies equally to Russia today. Jobs which used to be done by men and are outside the scope of family life are being done more and more by women, to an extent unparalleled in history.

It is true that throughout the western world millions of married women, including many mothers, are compelled to go out and work in order to earn money. But most of them are either wives without children or mothers whose children have grown up. In the west, too, women rarely do jobs which are regarded as men's work because of the physical demands they make. But in the Soviet Union things are quite different. Nearly half the labour force of the country consists of women,[9] and little attention is given to the normal limitations of the female physique.

I shall never forget the women I once saw working in coal mines not far from the Chinese border. They were not actually digging the coal, admittedly, but they tended the machines, drove the coal trains, and pushed heavy, loaded trucks along the rails. I was appalled to see these women in their shapeless clothes, their heads covered with a hideous combination of a miner's cap and a scarf, their faces as black as the coal they were handling, hard at work in this arduous and dangerous task. It was obvious that they were out of their element; they looked disgruntled, and their voices were strained and tense when they answered the overseer's questions. Whether women should work in, say, a textile mill or a paper plant may be open to argument; but it would be, at best, theoretical since millions of women in the West either support themselves or supplement the family income through manual labour. But they are as much out of place in a coal mine as in the other branches of heavy industry in which they are compelled to work in the Soviet Union.

Only recently have there been indications that at least a partial and gradual withdrawal of women from these occupations—but not, of course, from the labour pool as a whole—was being considered. Nothing has come of it. In view of the great number of women working in industry, even the cutting in half of working hours for women would cost the state more than 20 billion working-hours a year. Official propaganda still urges women to work, including those who do not need the money.

Women who do not attempt to work are regarded as frivolous parasites. There was a story in *Ogonyók*, the most widely read Russian magazine, about a woman who had no job and only one interest in life—to preserve her figure. The reader follows her as she drives in her husband's official car from one doctor to another in her quest for a reliable diet until one day her husband, having fallen into official disfavour, loses his car. Now his wife, like most Russian women, is compelled to go everywhere on foot—with the result that she quickly loses her excess weight.[10]

Soviet women have to work far harder at home than most women in the West. Only a few of them can afford the luxury of domestic help, and there are as yet few of the labour-saving devices which we take for granted. Nowhere else in the world is the business of shopping so oppressively complicated as it is in Russia. Not long ago I saw women in one shop crowding madly round a small counter where a few chamber pots were displayed. When they noticed that a man who had already managed to buy one of these precious items had rejoined the line to buy another one—probably with the idea of selling it in the black market—they nearly tore him to pieces. It is no wonder, then, that Russian women visiting Western countries enjoy shopping more than anything else.

But undoubtedly the Russian women's greatest burden is the living conditions they have had to endure for decades. In recent years, whenever I have passed the house my wife and I lived in for a few months in 1934, I have glanced at the board listing the occupants to see whether the number of people living there had at last decreased. But in 1959, there were still seven names listed as occupants of the six-room flat in which we once rented one room. One day I went inside, for old times' sake, and was again assailed by the old familiar musty smells—a mixture of kerosene burner, cabbage, tobacco smoke, and damp washing. I retreated rapidly, but my mind was suddenly filled with vivid recollections of those months we spent as sub-tenants of the engineer Ivanov, who had temporarily been transferred elsewhere.

Our very first night there was chaotic. Again and again the front-door bell rang wildly. Everyone awoke, except, of course, the tenant for whom it was intended. Once I was jolted out of a deep sleep by three rings—our signal, inherited from Ivanov. It was half-past two in the morning, and I thought something world-shattering must have happened. At the door stood a complete stranger. He had pressed the bell the wrong number of times. Another night our sleep was wrecked by a loud argument in the next room. 'That lamp,' yelled an excited female voice, 'belongs to me! It's the one my aunt gave me and I'm going to keep it. Do you think I'm going to sit in the dark?' A man's voice answered, 'You won't have to sit in the dark. Your boy friend will buy you a new lamp; he's got plenty of money.'

'That's not true!' the woman screamed. 'He hasn't a rouble!' 'Not much, he hasn't! I took the trouble to find out. Sometimes he even has butter!' This time the woman had no retort. The butter seemed to have clinched the argument. It was obvious that this couple was preparing to separate and had probably reached that most difficult stage of a divorce, the division of possessions. The row went on for days, and whether we wanted to or not, we had to hear it all.

The most astonishing room was the kitchen, which was always overcrowded. One day our tomato soup tasted of soap; a neighbour's washing on the adjacent burner had overflowed into our saucepan. There was a silent but unending tussle over the three gas burners (the fourth had long since stopped functioning). Everybody wanted a gas-ring at the same time—to cook, to boil water for tea, to heat water for washing, or to heat an iron or curling tongs. The constant pressure of so many eager tenants had worn a hole in the floor in front of the stove, and one day I nearly broke my ankle in it.

For a number of people, particularly the two couples who lived in the windowless rooms beside the entrance, the kitchen served as their living room, while the children used it as a playroom. Yet it was always astonishingly clean. Each family, in turn, was responsible for maintaining the kitchen for as many days at a time as there were members in the family.

At one point, in order to establish my tenancy in the house, I had to go to see the chairman of the housing committee. His office was in the courtyard at the back of the house, and to reach it I had to go through the cellars. Here, too, every possible inch of space was occupied. Even in a recess, probably originally intended for the furnace, a white-haired old woman lived like a mole. When I reached the office, there was a violent argument in progress. A woman was complaining that so many things had been dumped in the corridor outside her room that she couldn't open her door, and she was demanding that a ladder be set up in the courtyard so that she could enter through the window.

The house had a communal telephone. The first time it rang it was ignored; at the second ring, occasionally (though rarely) somebody would answer it. At the third ring everybody sat up and took notice, but if you heard footsteps in an adjoining room you stayed where you were. At the fourth, despairing ring, everybody came to a decision at once, and there was a wild rush, with three or four people colliding in the corridor.

Since the end of the war there has been a great deal of construction; but it has taken years to repair the heavy war damage. It is really only since about 1955 that housing construction has been pushed vigorously and with mass-production methods, much to the delight of the Soviet population, which is more than happy to leave the overcrowded houses of pre-Revolutionary days and to move into the new ones, even though, because of their hurried construction, they have many deficiencies.

The housing problem is still one of the favourite themes of satirists. A few years ago, while in Moscow, I asked someone if he could recommend an amusing, topical play, and he advised me to see a revue which took its title from the first line of a song, 'Where is the street? And where is the house?' The theme, which ran like a thread through the loosely connected scenes, followed the adventures of a young bridegroom looking for a place to live on the eve of his wedding. He went to inspect a room which had been offered in exchange for his old one. This turned out to be a poor bargain because the room was in a newly built block, and there was much hilarity at the expense of its flimsy walls and its remarkable acoustic qualities. The comedy reached its climax, amid appreciative audience laughter, when the neighbours on both sides of the room, as well as those above and below, took part in a kind of tenants' committee meeting without leaving their own rooms.

Even when a family is united, family life in the Soviet Union is difficult because of the conditions that exist. The members of the family have less time to themselves than people in the West. As the claims on their time are not limited to working hours, but include factory gatherings, committee meetings, preparations for political holiday observances, all kinds of 'voluntary' social and political activities, and a great deal of more or less voluntary overtime work, it is usually rather late in the evening before the family can gather together at home. Time and again, when friends have invited me to spend the evening with them, they have added the warning: 'Don't come before half past ten; we want to be sure we'll all be at home.' In the autumn of 1953 Stalin's successors, anxious to appear in a more favourable light, put an end to the long hours of night work which had been the normal lot of state officials. One comment I heard on this reform was 'That ought to increase the birth-rate!'

The women of the Soviet Union have coped with all these problems astonishingly well. Soviet literature rarely deals with this negative aspect of Soviet life. One exception I remember is a story in which an ageing woman scientist wonders whether her professional career has been worth while, since all she has to show for it is much hard work and, as the result of her constant absence from home, a badly brought up daughter.[11] The idea that women are the weaker sex is less justified in Russia than elsewhere. The Russian woman has shown unusual physical stamina (one only has to recall the sensation caused in the West by the success of Russian women athletes), and she is— at least in my opinion—morally superior to the Russian male, more sure of herself, more stable emotionally, more vital. The Russians have a word for it—*tselnost* (wholeness).[12]

A Western sociologist has evolved a theory that the Soviet woman, product of a transition between two eras, possesses the stronger qualities of both, and that the basic conflict arising from her dual inheritance will develop only in later generations. On the other hand, the Soviet male, he suggests, has inherited the weaknesses of both eras.[13] But the strength of Russian women is by no means a phenomenon unique to current history; it is vividly portrayed in many of the Russian classics, from Tatyana in Pushkin's *Eugene Onegin* and Yekaterina in Ostrovsky's *Storm* to Tolstoy's *Anna Karenina*. This inherent strength, however, was stimulated through the new opportunities opened to women by the Revolution. They proved themselves equal to the heavy sacrifices and burdens of that stormy period. The Russian woman has emerged from those crushing years with her self-assurance firmly established. Of course the Revolution opened new professions to men as well, but the limitations imposed by state and Party meant, if anything, a narrowing of the opportunities previously open to them, whereas for women a professional career was something quite new in itself, offering a new range of activities and a challenge to their capabilities.

In view of the great gains made by Russian women in both family and economic life, it is perhaps surprising that they still play only a minor role in politics. Perhaps the Russian woman's instinct tells her to leave this dubious field to men. At any rate, among the Russians the idea of women in politics is still unusual. There is an anecdote, probably apocryphal, about Lenin's widow. Trading on her late husband's stature as a Soviet hero, she liked to give Stalin unsolicited political advice. Finally exasperated, Stalin is said to have threatened her: 'One more word from you and I'll appoint somebody else Lenin's widow.' As a matter of fact, only recently has a woman appeared on the scene in a high state office—Yekaterina Fúrtseva, who joined the Presidium of the Central Committee of the Communist Party in 1956. And only in 1959, during Khrushchev's visit to America, did his wife reach the limelight which in the U.S.S.R. she had never experienced.

The Soviet family, too, has emerged from the conflicts of the last few decades in a much healthier condition than one might have expected, although there have, of course, been drastic changes. In the old Russian family the father or grandfather was regarded as a complete autocrat. The wife, who came as a stranger into the fold, was treated as the lowest of the low. This patriarchal system has disappeared. The woman who earns part of the family income—sometimes more than her husband—is in a much stronger position than before. The mother's prestige has grown, while the father has lost his dual monopoly of power in the family as wielder of authority and sole breadwinner.

For a working mother, this increased domestic authority helps to counterbalance the disadvantage of increased absence from home. But her absence would have a more adverse effect on the family were it not for the second woman in the house, the *bábushka* (grandmother). Except among the postwar generation, there is a considerable surplus of women of all ages in the Soviet Union. Two world wars, civil war, Stalin's reign of terror—all caused far greater casualties among men than women; and the surplus is especially marked among the elderly, with three women to every man in the sixty-year-old group, for example.[14] Moreover, life expectancy in Russia has been increasing steadily. At the end of the last century it was thirty-two years; it has now risen, according to Soviet statistics, to sixty-four for men and seventy-one for women.[15] Hence the huge number of *babushki*.

With so many mothers going out to work, the *babushka's*

stock is higher than ever. The harder it became to get domestic help, the more popular became *babushka*; millions of families simply could not imagine life without her. It doesn't matter whether *babushka* is the father's mother or the mother's—she enhances the feminine influence in the family, and it should be said also that she keeps alive tradition through the legends and fairy tales she tells to the children, and even through religion. It would hardly be an exaggeration to say that in all Soviet families where there is a grandmother, it is she who has the most influence over the children, especially during the impressionable early years. Since the care and bringing up of children is primarily in the hands of women—completely in the nursery and kindergarten, and predominantly in the schools (90 per cent of the teachers in the elementary classes and 70 per cent in the upper grades[16])—one must inevitably conclude that the influence of men and the state on children is far outweighed by that of women. The role of the *babushka* is probably one of the reasons for Khrushchev's drive toward boarding schools for the young and communal homes for the old people.

Only a family in which both parents are wage-earners can afford the luxury of paid help. More than any other, it is the fatherless family that cannot carry on without *babushka*, and although no statistics are available there are obviously many fatherless families—deportation, for example, has torn millions of families apart. Men with, at best, the prospect of indefinite exile before them often set up housekeeping with fellow victims of misfortune or with local women in the region to which they have been sent. (The modern Russian still enters into mixed marriages with women of other racial groups with little inhibition.) But even families spared this cruel fate were subject to other misfortunes. Men took far greater advantage than did women of the opportunities for independence offered by the immediate post-Revolutionary legislation. They often took mistresses, with the natural consequences of children, though not with any deliberate intention of founding a family. Then again, many men who found their status raised by the Revolution abandoned their wives (and children), taking younger and better-educated partners, better adapted to their new social standing. This still happens quite frequently, although the regime views it with disapproval. In 1956 the divorce rate in the Soviet

Union was seven for every 10,000 of the population.[17] (In Britain the figure was six, in the German Federal Republic eight, and in the United States twenty-three per 10,000.) In 1957 it had risen to nine.[18] No divorce figures have been announced since. Divorced men remarry much more frequently than divorced women. ·When the political pressure on novelists was relaxed slightly after Stalin's death, the woman alone in the world quickly became a favourite theme.

The decline in the Soviet birth rate has been attributed to the weakening of family ties, but this is only partially justified. More potent causes have been the twin processes of industrialization and urbanization. This is clearly shown by the fact that it was not until immediately after the catastrophic years—including the period of famine that followed collectivization—that the birth rate began to fall steadily and continued to fall thereafter at an increasingly rapid pace. Except for the civil war years and the World War II period, the birth rate has been lowest when the economic situation has been relatively favourable—that is, from 1950 onwards. According to official statistics the birth-rate fell from forty-seven per thousand in 1913, to forty-four per thousand in 1926, to thirty-one in 1940, and to twenty-five in 1959—despite the special allowances granted to large families since Stalin's time.[19]

The Russians' love of children was well known before World War I, and today's visitors to the Soviet Union agree that it still exists. In the little quarrels that arise between adults and children in parks and trains and other public places, the sympathies of onlookers are invariably with the children. Anyone who hits a child, whether his own or someone else's (and this is a sight rarely seen), incurs disapproval from bystanders. I have seen no trace of the harsh family discipline reflected in many old Russian proverbs and sayings. On the contrary, the press seems to feel an increasing need to warn parents against coddling and spoiling their children. The director of a Moscow school wrote:

There are some parents who have a quite erroneous idea of what constitutes happiness for their children. They think it is primarily a question of material well-being, which they try to ensure by providing their children with as much amusement and pleasure as possible. Such parents spend the bulk of their income on the children; they buy them expensive toys, clothes, and shoes, and give them money for entertainment whenever they ask for it. In such families the children are not being brought up to be self-reliant; mother, grandmother, and the maid relieve them of the obligation of doing anything for themselves.[20]

Soviet family life has suffered not only through the absence of the mother but also as a result of the reign of terror, which struck arbitrarily at everyone, compelling extreme discretion in conversation, even in the intimacy of the family circle. To some extent this anxiety still persists, despite relaxation of controls. In 1956, when de-Stalinization was at its height, with the dead dictator being branded as a tyrant, I observed the following incident. In a rather crowded restaurant, I was seated near a young couple with a small boy of about five. Suddenly his clear, piping voice rang out: *'Stalin samy dobry!'* ('Stalin is the best man in the world!') The parents blushed, fidgeted nervously, and tried to divert the child's attention to another subject.

But persecution can also draw a family closer together. A recent American investigation showed that in Soviet families affected by the state's reign of terror a greater sense of solidarity had grown, while other families which suffered only from material hardship had become less closely knit. Terror and injustice may cause upheavals in a family, but at the same time they compel its members to show a united, defensive front, if only because a family on which the wrath of the state has fallen finds itself shunned by other people and must thus fall back on its own resources. Lack of the material necessities of life, on the other hand, often leads to bickering and conflict.[21]

Family life in the Soviet Union, then, is still very much alive and flourishing. During the last twenty years it has changed considerably; the family has become smaller, less patriarchal (more 'democratic', so to speak), and less religious. It has also had to surrender many of its former functions to schools, to outside activities, and to organizations of all kinds; and in so doing it has had to sacrifice some of its cohesion. There is also an unmistakable trend towards standardization; the extreme differences once found between a Great Russian peasant family and a Kazakh nomad family or among the families of the great landowners, the urban middle classes, and the villagers are disappearing.[22] But such transformations occur in every country undergoing industrialization and urbanization; actually, the family in the Soviet Union has retained much more stability than those in some Western countries.

In conclusion, it might be useful to try to define the relations between family and state. The Party's *volte-face* in mid-1930, from open hostility towards the family to effective support of it, could lead one to think that there was a change of heart. But I cannot go along with this assumption. The Communists simply realized that, for the time being at least, they could not do without the family; therefore, they have made use of it just as they make use of many other unavoidable things. This does not mean that they approve of family life; its basically conservative characteristics are a constant irritation to them. Moreover, because it is an independent, self-contained entity, and the only institution not entirely controlled by the authorities, the family constitutes a 'foreign body' within a state that controls everything else. For obvious reasons the family cannot be dispensed with. But the blueprints for the Communist future indicate that its role is practically to be reduced to its biological function.[23]

Khrushchev's campaign for the creation of boarding schools for millions of children, which he initiated at the Twentieth Party Congress in 1956, and his school reform of 1958 strike me as a Party vote of no confidence in the family. The history of the 'October Children' points in the same direction. This organization for children of about nine or ten was disbanded twenty years ago, ostensibly because there was no longer any need for it. But it exists again today, presumably because the authorities found after all that they could not get along without it.[24]

The Bolsheviks assumed that parents who grew up before the Revolution would influence their children to be hostile to the new regime; accordingly they set out to weaken family and parental authority in every way they could. Twenty years later, when most of the parents belonged to the generation that had grown up under Communism, the regime felt it could afford to be more tolerant and to promote parental authority. But then, after another twenty years, the children of those parents began to have families of their own, and it soon became apparent that their offspring were not being imbued with the right spirit towards Party and state. Faced with the danger that the rising generation might well grow up with a negative and critical view of the state, the authorities could think of no better remedy than the establishment of quasi-governmental youth organizations and boarding schools resembling military academies.

Symptomatic of the basic conservatism of the Russian family is the choice of names. After the Revolution many parents vied with each other in demonstrations of originality or loyalty to the Party line—or both—through the names they gave their children. Biya, from the Greek *bios* (life), was one example of a scientific-progressive girl's name. I knew a man born during this period who was named Spartak, after the leader of the slaves' uprising in ancient Rome. Another man introduced himself to me as Rem. When I remarked that it was an unusual name, he said wryly that it was made up of the initial letters of the Russian words for revolution, electrification, and world. Another name I came across was Vladlen, a combination of the first syllables of Vladimir and Lenin.

After a time, though, the Russians abandoned these affectations and reverted to the traditional names. When I was in Moscow in the autumn of 1957, I visited a Soviet Registry Office. A girl in her early twenties greeted me cordially, handed me a form, and eyed me expectantly, thinking I had come to register a birth or give notice of marriage. I apologised for interrupting her, explained who I was, and said that I wanted to learn something about how a Soviet Registry Office functioned. After she had explained the system to me, I asked, 'Tell me, what are the most popular first names now being chosen for children?'

'That's easy,' she replied. 'They always choose the same ones. For boys it's Andrey, Sergey, Vladimir, Alexey, or Alexander, and for girls Tatyana, Olga, Yelena, Irina, or Natalya.'

'Don't you ever get more original names, names with a political flavour, for example?'

'Very seldom. The only case I can remember offhand was about a year ago, when a mother registered her new baby daughter as Yazamir.'

'A rather awkward-sounding name for a girl,' I commented, 'but the sentiments it expresses are most praiseworthy.' (The Russian *Ya za mir* means 'I am for peace'.)

The 1956 edition of the *Great Soviet Encyclopaedia* (the source of all current official definitions) contains the following entry under *semyá* (family):

> In socialist society the family constitutes a cell for the Communist upbringing of mankind. The relationship among members of a family is based on mutual affection, equal rights for husband and wife, the corporate interests of the individual and the community, co-operation and mutual help in life. In the Soviet Union the family enjoys universal consideration. Care of the family and the strengthening of family ties have always been among the most important tasks of the Soviet state.[25]

This idyllic picture of the role of the state hardly corresponds with reality. But the fact that it is found in the *Encyclopaedia* is important and shows that the fundamental conservatism of the Russian people has survived in the family more than in any other sphere of life. The Soviet citizen is still a long way from being able to say 'My home is my castle', but the first assault of Communism on the private life of the individual has been repulsed.

THE MATERIAL WORLD

CHAPTER 5

PROSPERITY

ONE DAY IN 1932, I read in a Moscow newspaper that Comrade Ordzhonikidze, People's Commissar for Heavy Industry, had summoned directors and chief engineers from all over the U.S.S.R. to a conference. The opening of the proceedings had been delayed, the paper reported, because the People's Commissar had had to order one of the engineers back to his hotel to shave and put on a clean shirt and a tie.

This brief announcement brought about a revolution in manners and habits. The same men who had gone about collarless and unshaven to show that they belonged to the ruling class and were indifferent to bourgeois refinements now began to shave and to wear ties. Nor was this simply the result of Comrade Ordzhonikidze's order. Conditions themselves had changed; it now paid off to do better than the next person and to have one's appearance reflect this success.

This metamorphosis took place practically overnight. Two humorists writing under the name 'the Brothers Tur' published a satirical history of the collar since the Revolution. The collar began, they wrote, as an odious attribute of the degenerate *bourgeoisie,* and anyone who dressed with conventional neatness showed himself to be a class enemy. Then the first timid collar-wearers began to emerge, claiming that a man with a collar was no longer necessarily a counter-revolutionary. Next came a period in which it was possible to wear a collar without fear of abuse. In the following phase, the collar became, if still not absolutely necessary, at least desirable. Finally, it was not merely desirable but indispensable—until a point was reached when, according to the Brothers Tur, it became *de rigueur* to wear not just a collar, but a clean one.

The same thing happened with evening dress. Tails, once regarded as an absurd adjunct of capitalism, were suddenly tolerated. When my wife and I attended a reception given by Litvinov in 1935, we witnessed a little incident: some of the foreign journalists were in difficulty because they were wearing 'only' dinner jackets. A few days later, I noted that full evening dress was included in a display of new fashions in Gorky Park. And it was about then that Russian friends began asking us to let them have a surreptitious look at foreign fashion magazines.

This counter-revolution in dress took place in the winter of 1934-35. At the same time I became aware, during a visit to Leningrad, that the word 'equality' seemed less popular. Leningrad is a city of bridges—nearly 100 of them span the streams and canals which run in every direction through what was once a swamp. This proves most convenient when the question of honouring some member of the Bolshevik elite arises. It seemed more than pure coincidence to me that the old Bridge of the Holy Trinity, optimistically renamed Equality Bridge by the Bolsheviks, was suddenly changed again to Kirov Bridge, for the local Party secretary who was assassinated in 1934. Could it be that the word 'equality' had become as distasteful to the Communists today as the Holy Trinity had been to them fifteen years earlier?

A new catchword began to emerge, replacing equality, and at first I was rather baffled by it. One of the periodical (and at that time bloodless) Party purges was in progress. A few booths had been erected in Gorky Park where anyone could present himself for a sort of preliminary examination on current political questions—a trial run, as it were, for the purge examination to which he might soon be subjected. I thought I would try it, out of curiosity. All went well, except for one question, which I failed completely. I simply did not know what to say about the political significance of the word *zazhítochnost'* (material well-being, or affluence). If I had taken my preliminary test a few weeks later, it would have been easy; the new catchword had by then spread all over the country as a symbol of the importance material prosperity was assuming in Soviet life.

These significant changes had their origin in one of Stalin's most important speeches: on 23 June 1931, he sanctioned the shift from equality to wage differentials and inequality. He described the low level of labour productivity, the absenteeism, and the enormous drift of workers from factory to factory—blaming them all on the wage system under which most workers were paid the same exceedingly low wages, with no material incentive for greater productivity. The speech was an admission of ideological defeat. This swing away from equality—an ideal which Stalin described contemptuously as *uravnílovka* (the equality racket)—was not just a sudden whim of Stalin's; it was forced on him by the realities of the situation. Experience had shown that without incentives most people would not work purposefully. The fires of the Revolution had burnt low; equal pay had led to an equal but very low standard of productivity. Now, also, the time had come for factories built by foreign experts and equipped with foreign machinery to be taken over and run by the Russians themselves. In the first period of expansion the Russian workman did not have to learn anything new; he dug foundations, set up scaffolding, mixed concrete, and made bricks. But in order to work in the new factories and blast-furnaces, the workers needed more than mass enthusiasm—they needed knowledge and skills that could only be acquired through personal zeal and study. The romantic personification of the First Five-Year Plan was the ordinary soldier of the labour force, willing, undemanding, and imbued with the spirit of collective service. Now a new national hero appeared—the engineer, the director, the inventor who stood apart from the masses; in other words, the officer of the labour force. Almost anyone can be turned into a soldier of the ranks and given a humble task, but men must be trained to become officers—or rather they must be given the chance to develop their own potential. This presupposes a certain standard of living—in other words, a higher income—which permits such development.

Thus money once more became an incentive to better work and higher qualifications. Poverty became a social stigma. Girls, feminine again and increasingly concerned with their appearance, preferred well-dressed young men to drab proletarians. In 1934 an eager young workman admitted to me that his great ambition was to earn enough money to buy a new suit because he was ashamed to be seen in his old one. A few years earlier, such an admission would have been unthinkable.

It has often been noted that Soviet industrial planning is apparently illogical because it stimulates production by promises of material prosperity, and at the same time boosts heavy industry and restricts the production of consumer goods to a minimum. This contradiction is usually attributed by Western observers to the fact that the Soviet state is not particularly interested in its population's living standard, but is vitally concerned with the growth of heavy industry—which is only part of the answer. Low living standards exercise effective pressure on the population, driving the workers to make special efforts to avoid starvation and cold. The authorities seem to have come to the conclusion that the norm—the standard level of output per man-hour—can be a useful target only when every worker realizes that failure to reach it and to fulfil the state-imposed plan will result in extreme personal hardship. They have therefore evolved a system in which the basic wage is very low, and every step above subsistence level has to be earned by special, additional effort.

From a sociological point of view, the introduction of the piecework system was the most important measure that Stalin enforced during the decades of his dictatorship. By basing the whole wage system on the principle of payment for labour performed, he exploded the theory that once a revolution had been accomplished people would work happily and to the best of their ability because they were working for themselves instead of for some capitalist. Stalin realized that equality was possible only in a primitive agrarian society or during a period of famine, such as the years of the Revolution and the civil war, but not in a modern industrial state, which must have directors and chief engineers as well as factory hands and administrative personnel. He accordingly turned the rudder and changed the course to take advantage of the more dependable wind of individual self-interest.

Stalin's policy led to an ever-broadening application of the piecework system and thus to the rapid growth of wage differentials. Hitherto the difference between low and high wages and salaries had been roughly in the ratio of one to two; now it rose first to one to ten, then one to twenty, next one to thirty and even higher.

At the beginning of the 1930's wage differentials were also introduced into the rural areas, and there, too, payment was for labour performed. Wages were calculated in terms of so-called 'working days', which were a measure not of time but of performance. Even the grants made to students were based upon achievement—that is, according to the grades obtained in examinations.

Even scientists are spurred on to greater effort by such incentives as awards for inventions or other special contributions to the needs of the state. These awards are determined on the basis of the invention's value in savings for the state: for instance, if it results in a saving of a million roubles, the inventor receives about 40,000 roubles; the maximum award is 200,000 roubles for each invention. In some fields (atomic research, for example, or the discovery of synthetic substitutes for the rarer minerals) such awards may even be doubled.[1]

In addition to the piecework system with its broad differentials for special efforts, there is an infinite variety of merit awards. The chief conductor of a train in which I travelled to Moscow, for instance, told me that every time the train arrived in Moscow on time he and the engineer each got a bonus of 150 roubles. In the higher-income brackets these bonuses amount to a great deal. For the intermediate ranks in industry, and even more effectively for the higher ranks, they furnish the same incentive that the piecework system does for the ordinary workers. The size of the bonus depends on a complicated system of plan fulfilment—the fulfilment, that is, not only of the general production programme, but also of a host of subsidiary plans such as savings on fuel consumption, wage bills, or raw materials.[2]

For example, the basic salary of a director is calculated on the assumption that 80 per cent of the planned programme will be completed in the allotted time. For each additional 1 per cent above this, he is entitled to a bonus of 5 per cent of his basic salary. Thus, if he completes 100 per cent of the programme, he receives, in addition to his basic salary, a bonus of twenty times 5 per cent of that salary; in other words, he doubles his pay. Then, for each 1 per cent over the total programme, he receives a further bonus of 20 per cent of his basic salary. If, therefore, he produces 5 per cent more than the official target, he receives another five times 20 per cent, thus tripling his salary.

The chief engineer usually works under these same terms. The lower grades of the managerial staff receive a little less, and their bonuses are calculated differently—not on the basis of the fulfilment of the programme as a whole, but on the fulfilment of that part of it for which their department is responsible.

From the state's point of view, this bonus system has the advantage of offering a powerful incentive to the personnel concerned. But it also has one great disadvantage: the interest of all potential bonus-earners tends to concentrate on those activities which will yield a production bonus. Therefore the director of a plant that has a quota of fifty machines a month will do his utmost to exceed it. To produce a fifty-first and a fifty-second machine, he will skimp on materials for the first fifty. For instance, he might fail to provide an adequate number of spare parts to service the machines, thus conserving both labour and materials for the production of the bonus-earning extras. The director will receive his bonus, but the quality of the machines will have suffered. Economizing on fuel consumption has similar results. The director will ask for a maximum coal allotment at the outset of a project. Should this be granted, he is practically assured of having a surplus of coal which will yield another bonus. The entire industry suffers because the idle fuel could be used where there might be a shortage. Occasionally the bonus system creates utterly farcical situations. Because restaurant employees receive bonuses in proportion to the care with which they collect leftovers, they have a vested interest in serving poor food, since this naturally results in more leftovers.

Why does the state cling to the bonus system in spite of its obvious drawbacks? The answer is simple—it cannot do without it. When the Bolsheviks abolished private ownership in all branches of production and thus deprived enterprise of the profit motive, they hoped the 'new man' would work for the greater glory of the state instead. This hope was rarely fulfilled. The bonus system is simply the necessary Russian equivalent of the profit motive. To sustain its abolition, I believe, would be more difficult for the Soviet economy than the abolition of private profit would be for capitalism.

The desire to profiteer in the manner of the nineteenth century is by no means extinct. Many Soviet citizens buy articles in short supply and sell them at a quick profit. Automobiles are a favourite commodity. In an attempt to curb such practices, the state decreed in 1954 that no one was allowed to buy more than one car every three years. But the 'car dealers' were not worried; they ordered a number of cars—one for each member of their family. Some entrepreneurs hold on to their fleet and use it for private business ventures. They transport the first cherries from Vladimir to Moscow, the first grapes from Tiflis to Ivanovo, the first peaches from Yerevan to Sochi, the first apples from Gomel to Kiev, or the first apricots from Fergana to Tashkent; they fetch and carry anything and everything that shows a profit—geese before Christmas, eggs at Easter.[3] Wherever the state buyers are idle, the private dealers take over.

Paraphrasing the title of a well-known American novel, one might ask, 'What makes Ivan run?' The answer is quite simple. His strongest motive is, to use the official Soviet term, 'material self-interest'. The supposedly socialist Soviet state which asserts that its goal is Communism spurs on the self-interest of its citizens and creates a climate in which the unscrupulous operator thrives. It is departing further and further from its proclaimed ideals. In fact, it seems to me that after forty years of indoctrination with collectivist ideas, Soviet man has become more, not less, egoistical.

Although it is being vehemently denied in the Soviet Union, I am sure that anyone who has studied recent Russian history, and has been able to make comparisons based on personal observations, must conclude that Russia has entered its bourgeois era. The 'new class' does not constitute a *bourgeoisie* in the Western sense of the word. It is a state *bourgeoisie*. All its members work for the state and are dependent on it. The difference should not be underestimated. Nevertheless, the way of life of the present-day Soviet bourgeois amazingly resembles that of his flourishing Western counterpart during the Victorian era.

The word *bourgeoisie* comes to mind the moment one has contact with Russia's 'new class'. One sees homes filled with plush-covered furniture, adorned with lace antimacassars. Embroidered cushions are piled high on sofas. Pictures (often petit-point) with sentimental motifs line the walls—the prince and princess riding through the forest on a wolf, or Shishkin's 'Bears at Play in the Forest' for example. The satin mats and runners on the tables, the small vases and figurines, the pink lampshades have not been inherited but are the products of modern Soviet industry.

That the hotels of Tsarist days have been preserved exactly as they were—*art nouveau* bronze figures and all—might be attributed to an act of piety. But a Moscow hotel recently built to accommodate guests of the state represents, with its *portières* and tortuous glass ornamentation, a reproduction on a monumental scale of the style of the turn of the century. Forty years after the Revolution, the nation that supposedly marches in the vanguard of human progress has been unable to create a style of its own. It still copies the tastes and fashions of the pre-revolutionary aristocracy and bourgeoisie—with only one difference: formerly the quality of furnishings and decorations was excellent; now it is flimsy and poorly finished. Only very recently have there been signs of improvement.

Another manifestation of bourgeois values is the desire to marry into a 'good family'. *The Return of Vasíly Ivánovich,* a play by Yevgeny Bermont that I recently saw in Moscow, illustrates this aspiration. The play is set in a furniture factory. The antagonists are Lobásov, a junior executive, and Giatsíntov, an interior decorator who tries to apply the tenets of art to the production of furniture. At first I assumed that the author intended to portray Giatsintov as the real hero. Not only does Giatsintov sacrifice his artistic creativity to devote himself to the beautification of Soviet furniture, but he also believes in the increased production of consumer goods, an aim which has been fervently proclaimed, though less fervently pursued, since Stalin's death.

Lobasov, on the other hand, has only one concern—to increase mass production. His character crystallizes in his attitude towards Nadya, his fiancée. Her landscapes elicit no response, and he advises her to consult textbooks on forestry.

When it is revealed that Giatsintov has exceeded his gasoline allowance on private trips, the audience is inclined to condone this transgression because it has been inspired by love and a desire to help Nadya. But it soon becomes clear that Giatsintov has been paying court to Nadya not so much because he is in love with her, but because he has discovered that her father is about to be made a member of the government. Giatsintov wants above all to marry into her family and thus assure himself of membership in the 'new class'.

Giatsintov is exposed by Nadya's father. In order to test the suitor's love, the father informs his daughter that he has been reprimanded by the Party and has not received his promotion. No sooner does Giatsintov hear this than he decamps precipitately. The play ends with Nadya's disenchantment and tears. These, the audience realizes as the curtain falls, will soon be soothed by the stout-hearted Lobasov.

Another symptom of the whole-hearted acceptance of bourgeois standards is the fact that contemporary writers in most cases set their stories in an upper-class milieu. When they depart from this setting, their readers complain. The Soviet writer K. Mintz, for example, wrote a film script in which the principal character was a bank clerk. The producers of the film protested that it was impossible to make a convincing hero of such a person. The script was altered; the hero started as a bank teller, but ended as director of the bank. The following paragraph appeared recently in a literary periodical:

> The trouble with our writers is that they write too much about the *nachal'niki* (the bosses) and pay too little attention to those who do the work. There are very few plays or films in which the man in the street is given a leading role; for the most part he merely provides background and local colour for the principal characters. If a play is about industry, the audience generally sees the director in the leading role. . . . If the play has a rural setting, the hero as a rule is the chairman of the *kolkhoz*.[4]

In one play, *Dangerous Partners*, which I saw in Moscow, there were two pairs of lovers from different social strata. The love of one couple was earnest and exalted—love on the engineer level. The other couple, on a lower social level, spoke in uncouth, semi-educated dialogue—in short, proletarian love.

The question of whether the primacy of material self-interest can be regarded as a constant and continuing feature of Soviet life remains unanswered. Do recent personal observations of a period during which bourgeois values have been on the ascent justify the conclusion that the country will continue to develop along these lines?

One day, in conversation with a Soviet manager, I asked him what would happen if the Soviet state were to lay aside the whip of the norm and the carrot of piecework rates and bonuses. He looked at me in surprise. Here was something to which he had evidently never given a thought.

'Such a thing just couldn't happen,' he said.

'All right,' I replied, 'but try and imagine it has. What do you think would be the result?'

'Well, the process of rapid expansion would stop, and things would begin to deteriorate; we need these incentives.'

'But,' I persisted, 'Soviet citizens are far more industrious today than they were in 1900 or 1850. Work has become more of a habit with them. In the West many people work because they are interested, because they feel they ought to, and because they enjoy doing a particular job well. I admit this is the attitude of a minority, but of an exemplary minority. These people don't need the incentive of exceptional pay or profit; they work in response to an inner urge. Don't you think that in time something like this might happen in the Soviet Union?'

He remained sceptical. 'Perhaps,' he said, 'though I can't imagine it. But in any case we are still a long way from anything like that. I certainly couldn't afford to treat my workers that way; we'd never even begin to fulfil our quota.'

It is theoretically possible that some Soviet leader might stand up and say: 'The era in which we appealed to man's self-interest has ended.' Such an appeal might resemble those made in the stormy year of 1917, during the initial years of the First Five-Year-Plan (in the early 1930's), or during the bitter days of 1941–42.

Can the people of the Soviet Union, after all the privations and disappointments they have suffered, be expected to respond to such an appeal? If it were launched in trenchant terms, in a way that commanded belief, the people (particularly the 'Great Russians'), confronted with truly exceptional circumstances, would probably show themselves capable of selfless achievements. Communism's greatest chance of success, after all, lies in the exceptional capacity of the Russian people for self-sacrifice and suffering.

But the circumstances would indeed have to be extraordinary —a state of real emergency, in which men are prepared to make sacrifices on a grand scale. In normal times, when it is a question not of an all-out effort but of steady, day-to-day slogging, material incentives are needed. The increasing material demands made by Soviet man have, of course, been violently interrupted from time to time—in 1917, in 1930, and in 1942; but these interruptions have failed to halt the increase. And I am inclined to predict that this will not change in the foreseeable future.

CHAPTER 6

PROPERTY

IN THE CONFUSION of the Revolution, disregard for private property reached its height. Law and order vanished. Under the slogan 'Expropriation of the expropriators', private possessions were at the mercy of every wanton impulse. The expropriations, accompanied by appalling brutality towards the landowners especially, were not confined to the estates but extended to all possessions. During the period of 'War Communism', up to 1921, the idea of communal ownership was interpreted in the most sweeping way; 'what's yours is mine' was the order of the day. The basic principle of the communes, as we have seen, was that everything belonged to everybody. A second wave of violent and bloody expropriations swept over the country during the process of collectivization in the early 1930's.

The atrocities associated with these events engraved them indelibly on the consciousness of the world and were responsible for Western misgivings about the Soviet Union's attitude towards private property. But this view is no longer correct. As early as 1920 the Communist leaders began to impose a semblance of order. They impressed on the people the Marxist distinction between two types of ownership: ownership of the means of production by the state (or collective), and ownership of consumer goods by the individual.

At first not much more than clothing, food, and cooking utensils were included among consumer goods. Later the list was extended to furniture, household appliances, books, automobiles, savings accounts, state bonds, and homes. In Articles 7 and 10 of the Soviet Constitution of 1936 such goods were specifically described as 'personal property'; the term 'private property' was avoided. This was the inevitable result of the piecework and bonus policy described earlier. Unless the state protected personal property, it could not exhort its citizens to work harder.

Changes in the inheritance laws have been particularly interesting. At first the right of inheritance was abolished altogether; then it was limited to 10,000 roubles. It was restored in principle by Stalin and finally incorporated in the Constitution of 1936. This step was as logical as the protection of private property. Article 10 of the Constitution reads: 'The citizen's right to bequeath or inherit personal property is protected by law.' The safeguards are so stringent as to be propitious to fortune-hunters. One man, although already married, courted a wealthy woman who was seriously ill. Their marriage was registered seventeen days before her death. The man's previous marriage had never been registered. Under the marriage law of 1944, only registered marriages are legal. The court had no option but to recognize the man as the dead woman's heir.[1]

In 1943 the inheritance tax was abolished; all that has to be paid now is a fee amounting to no more than 10 per cent of the inheritance.[2] The graduated inheritance tax, which in the West favours the small income groups, does not exist in the Soviet Union. Since the Soviet citizen may not own means of production, he can only bequeath personal possessions. But these include money, government bonds, works of art, houses, and personal effects of every kind.

Reaction to the categorical ban on private ownership of the means of production has been varied; it depends on whether it is applied to industrial or agricultural property. Anyone familiar with capitalist industry in pre-Revolutionary Russia could not expect the Russian worker to cherish the memory of it. Industry in those days had not yet emerged from the early stages of capitalism which Western Europe had outgrown several decades before. Even in the new factories some practices persisted which had been discarded long ago in the West. I remember the painful embarrassment I felt when, as a small boy visiting my grandfather in Moscow, I watched the stream of workers emerging from his nearby factory at the end of their shift and saw them being searched to make sure they had not filched anything. When people in Russia talk about the 'good old days', they don't mean the factories.

Whatever reasons the Soviet worker has to dislike or even detest Bolshevism, the nationalization of industry is not one of them. In my conversations with workers I have been impressed by their acceptance of the regime's thesis that the means of production must belong to everybody and that state ownership is the obvious and natural solution. The Russian worker is proud of his country's social legislation. It has provided old-age insurance and free medical care. He believes that these accomplishments are Soviet innovations and is surprised and a little incredulous when the evolution of welfare legislation in the West is described to him.

As far as I can make out, the Soviet worker still remains indifferent when the question of the transfer of the ownership of a plant to its employees is raised. Nevertheless, news of the Yugoslav factory councils and their quasi-ownership of the plants may eventually find its way into the Soviet Union. It has probably been the Soviet worker's lack of self-confidence which, until now, has made him feel incapable of running a modern industrial concern.

What is the attitude of the elite, or managerial class, to state ownership of the means of production? Will it, as some Westerners believe, eventually demand the ownership of the concerns it directs? In feudal times, princes rewarded their supporters with fiefs of land which eventually passed into the permanent possession of their heirs. Will the Soviet 'princes' someday emulate these practices?

On two occasions, when I had the chance to talk to Soviet factory directors at some length, I asked the crucial question: 'Haven't you ever had the wish not merely to administer the factory for which you are responsible, but to own it?' The answer, of course, was 'No'; what else could it be under the political circumstances? But I was interested in their reasons. These consisted first of a few quotations from the Leninist-Marxist catechism. But then it became quite clear that these men had realized long before James Burnham wrote *The Managerial Revolution*[3] that it was the control of the means of production which mattered, not the ownership. Under capitalism, too, a manager has infinitely more control of a business than the aggregation of shareholders who own it.

The Soviet manager of a state concern and his American or European counterpart who manages a business owned by a group of shareholders differ greatly in the measure of authority they exercise over their employees—to the advantage of the Soviet manager. The Western manager finds his powers everywhere curbed—by the board, by the trade unions, by labour legislation, and so on. The Soviet manager, on the other hand, is granted almost unlimited powers by the Party and the state to enable him to fulfil their extravagant plans. Absolute control of the means of production places enormous power in the hands of the state and its industrial leaders. This last point is brought out very convincingly by Milovan Djilas in his book *The New Class*.[4]

From my conversations with the two directors, I gathered that they had never considered owning the factories they managed. But inquiring a little further, I discovered that they did have misgivings about the system and their own positions in it. For instance, there was the ever-present danger of falling into disfavour and of losing their jobs; of not fulfilling the production quota and being severely punished; or even the lesser danger of an unwelcome transfer to a new district where they would have to start again from scratch. The Soviet state makes frequent transfers because it fears that too much intimacy among employees might lead to the formation of independent cliques.

Above all, members of the managerial class, like all Soviet citizens, suffer under the whip of the norm. But they do not realize that their complaints are directed against the system itself; they seem to assume that its disadvantages and inconveniences can be removed without abandoning its basic principles. They do not want the additional risks and responsibilities which ownership entails, but they do want a reduction of the dangers to which they are exposed as state employees. Very late one night a manager said to me: 'I'm in charge of a great factory. I have a friend who is in charge of the corresponding department in the ministry. What more could I want?' Apart from this, Soviet managers do not differ much from their Western counterparts: they like to live well; they like to take care of their families; they like to think that they are doing a service to society.

In the rural areas reaction to the state's policy on private ownership differed. The peasants agreed with the first phase of the agrarian reform, the expropriation of landowners' property. They took part in it with zest, and the record of the atrocities committed in the process forms one of the darkest chapters in Soviet history. The unleashed *muzhik* was not a pretty sight. But the peasants were allowed only about ten years to enjoy unrestricted use of the land. The true Bolshevik agrarian reform followed. Under collectivization the peasants had to hand over their private property to the *kolkhoz*. A bitter and merciless struggle ensued. Many millions of villagers lost everything. Millions died violently, starved, or were deported. The *muzhik* preferred to slaughter his cattle rather than relinquish them to the *kolkhoz*; nearly a quarter of a century was to pass before the U.S.S.R. recovered from this large-scale extermination of cattle. The situation compelled Stalin to compromise. The Kolkhoz Statute of 1935 permitted each peasant to own a garden and one cow. Depending on the district and the nature of the soil, the private plot could be from five-eights of an acre to two and a half acres.

The peasants' historic craving for property, frustrated by the Bolsheviks, now concentrated on these gardens, on which the peasants lavished all their care and affection. Millions of *kolkhoz* peasants, particularly in the years when state pressure was lowering their standard of living, took infinitely more interest in their own little plots than in their obligations to the *kolkhoz*. *Krokodil*, the official humour magazine, printed many cartoons contrasting fat, sleek private cows with the lean beasts of the *kolkhoz*; in one, stalwart peasants work frantically among luxuriant vegetable rows in their private garden while a solitary member of the family, the grandmother, plods slowly and reluctantly to the arid fields of the *kolkhoz*, followed by shouts of 'Off you go, *bábushka*, to the *kolkhoz*. We'll manage here without you somehow!'[5]

The peasant has had to struggle to keep his cow. Khrushchev recently argued that if a peasant sold his cow to the *kolkhoz*, he could buy his milk more cheaply and would not be bothered with tending the beast.[6] To a townsman this might seem plausible, but not to the Russian peasant. He has been cheated too often. He knows that if he wants to have his milk, he'd better keep his cow in his own barn.

For decades the peasants have obstinately waged an unequal battle with the state to retain their personal property. The countryside has been decimated by the disappearance of the *kulák* (well-to-do peasant) and the continued migration to the towns of the more alert elements of the rural population. Though he may appear so to foreigners, the Russian peasant is no fool. His cunning enables him to take advantage of every opportunity in a field of activity in which he has been at home for generations. The struggle between state edicts and peasant cunning is unending. The chairman of a *kolkhoz* (a functionary ostensibly elected, but in fact appointed) once bought a thousand chicks with *kolkhoz* funds and gave them to the peasants. He explained that they were to return half of the grown chickens to the *kolkhoz* poultry farm, and would be allowed to keep the other half. The peasants did as they were told, raised the chicks, and in due course delivered one-half to the *kolkhoz*. Later, when the chairman inspected the poultry farm, he discovered that 90 per cent of the chickens returned were roosters.[7]

Although the Russian peasant is tenaciously defending his position, it may well be that sooner or later he will be reduced to the status of a mere wage-earner. The time may come when he will give in and abandon his struggle as hopeless. I have seen model *kolkhozes* which have been boosted by the state, and I have found that the private garden there has lost some of its former importance and has been neglected through lack of interest.

Once the *kolkhoznik* is transformed into a worker on a state farm, he will have taken a further step towards becoming an industrial worker. I have met tractor drivers who could no longer be called peasants. Some of them, particularly on the newly opened Siberian farm lands, were recruited from the urban youth labour pool.

The disappearance of the sense of property has some unpleasant results for the state. I well remember whenever anything was broken during my childhood, it evoked the comment: *'Bey posúdu, ne tvoyá!'* ('Smash it! It isn't yours anyway!') This attitude prevails more and more as the state continues to expropriate and uproot its people. One constantly hears of people appropriating state property for themselves or letting it simply go to waste. I remember a worker in a clothing factory who used to sew suits badly because he wanted to save thread. From four badly sewn suits, he could squeeze enough thread for a fifth suit (for a private customer).

I sometimes think of all the machinery, the building materials, and goods of every kind—probably worth billions of roubles—which are lost to Soviet industry every year because no one takes a proprietary interest in them and they are left to rot in the snow and the rain.

Perhaps in time, as acute poverty abates, this situation will change, and offences against state property will decrease. At the moment, however, there is no such trend. On the contrary, the state conducts a continuous and costly campaign against this kind of attitude. In 1932 the death penalty was introduced for the theft of state property.[8] When this law was repealed in 1947, one could assume that conditions had improved. But in 1950 the death penalty was re-introduced. Officially it applied only to traitors, spies, and 'enemies of the state', but the subsequent interpretation of this law indicated that theft of state property may be regarded as an act inimical to the state, punishable by death. In 1961, as we shall see on page 241, the application of the death penalty was further widened.

In spite of relentless indoctrination, large sections of the population have not been convinced of the sacredness of state property. The scant respect with which Russians have always treated state property has dwindled still further as a result of the state's confiscation of land and cattle. When the *nachalnik* (boss) is allowed to own a car, a villa, and a fine garden, while the peasant has to struggle to keep his one private cow and his little private garden, a confusion of values is inevitable. The violence done by the state to its citizens' sense of private ownership has resulted in a devaluation not only of private property, but of all property—and above all, of state property.

CHAPTER 7

SUCCESS

The desire to rise socially and amass power and fortune is as common to the Soviet Union as to the rest of the world. But the criteria of success in the field of industrial management differ sharply from those in the West. In the capitalist system it is primarily the competition on the open market that determines success or failure. In a state-controlled economy the state decides. Not only does it draw up the production programme, but it also distributes the end product. As a result the economic 'climate' in the Soviet Union bears no semblance to that in Western countries. Without a knowledge of this climate, it is impossible to understand the peculiar nature of Soviet man's struggle for success.

A chance encounter at an airport in Siberia was very informative. I had arrived in the evening, and my plane was not due to leave until the next morning. At the airport hotel the receptionist told me that no beds were vacant at the moment, but that one would become available during the night.

I settled myself in an armchair in the lounge. A little later a passenger carrying two suitcases arrived. After arguing volubly with the receptionist, he sat down beside me. He had sharp features, an intelligent face, and a rather glib manner. He offered to order cognac for both of us. I told him that when I was at home in the West, I liked cognac, but in Russia I preferred vodka. As soon as he realized that he was talking to a foreigner, he said it was a scandal that a visitor from the West should be kept waiting around like this without a bed. Having ordered the vodka, he plied me with questions about the economy. 'Let us take as an example,' he said, 'the Volkswagen plant in Germany. Let's say the programme for the year is 10,000 cars.' 'Last year the Volkswagen factory turned out well over 500,000 vehicles,' I said. 'Very well,' he continued, 'let's say it has an output target of 500,000 cars for the year. If you include one spare, then five tyres will be needed for each car, or a total of two and a half million tyres. Suppose the factory then finds it can produce 30,000 more cars in a year. It will then need

150,000 more tyres. What does the management do to get them? That sort of thing must happen, I imagine.'

'Not quite,' I answered. 'In the first place, Volkswagen works on the basis of expanding production and plans ahead accordingly; second, it would have no difficulty in getting extra tyres from the firm that supplies them, since that firm, anticipating such a situation, will always keep a surplus on hand.'

'I see. But let's suppose they can't get them like that—suppose the supplying firm just hasn't got them.'

'In that case Volkswagen goes to another tyre manufacturer.'

'Direct? Just like that?'

'Yes, just like that.'

'But suppose the second firm doesn't have 150,000 tyres either, and no other tyre manufacturer in the country has them? This could happen, couldn't it?'

'It's highly unlikely, but never mind. Just for argument's sake, if that happened then the firm would turn to a tyre company abroad.'

'Could they get the necessary foreign currency?'

'No difficulty about that. There hasn't been for years.'

'Then in your country,' he said with a laugh, 'I should be out of a job.'

'I find that difficult to believe,' I said. 'In the West you'd probably be a highly successful businessman.'

He asked me more questions while we emptied half a bottle of vodka between us. 'No, no,' he said after a pause, 'if what you tell me is true, I should be out of a job all right.'

'What do you do for a living, then?' I asked, although I already had a fairly good idea.

'Me? My speciality is eliminating bottlenecks and oiling the wheels of industry.'

'Ah!' I said. 'So you're a *Zis* man?'

He laughed. 'You know the expression?' (It is a play on words.) There is a car called the Zis, a product of the Zavod Imeni Stalina, the Stalin Factory (since renamed). But *Zis* also stands for *Znakómstva i svyázi* (connections and contacts).

I asked him, 'How do you go about it?'

'I'll tell you. Let's say a factory is short of tyres and can't get them anywhere. The director phones me. "Stepan Alexeyevich," he says, "get me forty tyres, will you? Our trucks are being held up, and our suppliers have let us down. The Glavk (the appropriate administrative department) can't help us, and the Ministry has let us down too. *Idí s Bógom!*' ' ('Go with God', the traditional Russian way of saying goodbye.)

'Does he really say "Go with God"?'

He laughed. 'It's a figure of speech, you know. . . . Well, I go to the chief accountant. "Maxím Ivánovich," I say, "the director told me to come to you. He wants me to get forty tyres. Give me the money!" The accountant moans and groans. . . . He always does—as though he already had one foot in prison!' (The accountant is not allowed to make money available for any purpose not provided for in the plan, and Zis men, with their fairly heavy expense accounts, are not, of course, included.) 'But he has to fork out anyway, because if we fall short of the target due to lack of tyres, it won't be any more amusing for him than for the rest of us.'

'So he overcomes his scruples and does something illegal?'

'What else can he do? We've got to complete the programme. But he'll try to cover himself by getting the director to sign and pretending he doesn't know what it's all about. So in the end he gives me my travelling expenses—first class, of course, because we're an important firm—with some extra money for gifts and entertainment.' He tapped his breast pocket. 'Before I set out, others let me know of their needs. One wants so much copper wire, another asks me to find him a skilled mechanic . . . That couldn't happen in your country. You wouldn't have to go scrounging round for a mechanic, with all your unemployment.'

'Don't you believe it!' I said. 'We too have bottlenecks in the labour market, and it's sometimes very difficult to find the right man. But you are helping us a lot. Every night a few hundred people flee from your zone of Germany to the West.'

'Then they must be capitalists who don't like conditions under the workers' and peasants' regime.'

'Not a bit. In recent years more than two million people have sought refuge in Western Germany, and there weren't two million capitalists in the whole of the Soviet zone to begin with. Most of them are ordinary working men, and young men at that. But don't let me interrupt your story. . . Incidentally, what does the Party secretary in your factory think about your mission?

Surely he considers himself responsible for your morals?'

'Him? Oh, he looks the other way. He's just as eager as anyone to see the plan fulfilled, and he has to think of himself and his family. It's much better for him, too, if the factory where he is Party secretary reaches its quota.'

'But surely, as Party secretary, he can count on being commended if he discovers irregularities and reports them?'

'Perhaps. But I know of one case where a Party secretary who had reported irregularities was reprimanded for being a bureaucratically minded grumbler. Still—let's assume he gets a pat on the back. It's the last he'll get, because from then on he won't be let in on any of the factory secrets. We're all equally interested in seeing that we meet the state's production demands. Director, chief cashier, Party secretary, staff, and the Ministry —everybody's on the side of the man who sees that the plan is carried out.'

'What about the Ministry of Inspection and Supervision?'

'That's different. They've got their own machinery. Fulfilment of their plan isn't a question of goods produced, but of wrongdoers handed over. That's what they get their decorations for. But there are limits even to that. Counter-intelligence measures—the police are first-rate at that. But bookkeeping, no.'

'So they all come to you with requests, and eventually you set off?'

'Yes. I travel here and there, visit people, chat with them, give them all kinds of presents, dine them, wine them, and promise them this, that, and the other, until at last I've got what I want.'

'A few years ago I saw a poem in *Krokodil* that gave a rather uncomplimentary description of people like you.'

'I remember it. Some of it was quite libellous, but the refrain kept repeating that we were indispensable, and it was quite right.'

'I agree. You should be made Heroes of the Soviet Union. Without you, the whole of your planned industry would grind to a halt.'

He was flattered and raised his glass to me. At that moment the receptionist came to tell me my bed was ready, and I left to get a few hours' sleep.

The successful contact man in the Soviet Union must have

knowledge, industry, and energy, as well as a flair for making friends by rendering all kinds of useful little services; he must be loyal to his own clique, but at the same time ready to drop them when his livelihood is at stake; he must combine a minimum of ethical fastidiousness with a maximum of political dexterity if he is to avoid disaster and be successful.

I have often met men of this type on planes, in first-class train compartments, and in hotels. I gradually became expert at spotting them. They are often mentioned in the press, always in unflattering terms, usually as *tolkachi* (i.e. pushers). It is probably realized that if men of this type did not exist they would have to be created. Without them, the industrial bottlenecks would become so numerous that everything would stop. In 1953 the oil industry alone sent 700 Zis men to the automobile works in Gorky to procure the vehicles it needed. One of their tasks was to make sure that the colours of the managers' private cars were suited to their individual tastes.[1]

Some Zis men are on the move for months on end, and they are always glad of an excuse to stay in Moscow. No wonder it is difficult to get a room in a Moscow hotel. The so-called decentralization of industry which Khrushchev has been pushing has had no effect on this problem, and complaints of this kind are still appearing in the press:

> All over the country crowds of representatives from various firms continually appear and travel about in search of raw materials to supplement the allocations made to their factories. They play havoc with the normal channels of supply.[2]

And the city of Yaroslawl has complained that the *tolkachi* 'have occupied all the hotels in town'.[3]

When a Russian begins to talk to me about the 'chaos' in the capitalist system, I react sharply. On one of my trips I talked to a casual acquaintance who turned out to be the chief engineer of a factory producing agricultural machinery. We argued about our respective industrial systems, and, as it happened, I knew much more about his system than he did about ours. He believed that our industrial organization was in the same state as Marx described in his *Communist Manifesto*. Such ideas, assiduously fostered by Soviet officials, are very widely held, despite the increasing number of contacts with foreigners.

When this engineer, too, began to talk about the 'chaos of capitalism', I said, 'To our eyes it's the Soviet industrial system that is really chaotic.' He brushed this aside with a laugh.

'I've been reading your newspapers regularly for thirty years,' I continued. 'Let me explain what I mean. All of you who control industry live under the constant menace of "the plan". The man who fails to deliver his quota pays the penalty.[4] Naturally, you try to cushion yourself a bit against the danger. In the first place, when next year's quota is estimated, every factory understates its productive capacity to give itself a better chance of fulfilling, or even exceeding the programme. You battle with the authorities to obtain the lowest possible quota. You fight because your very existence depends on your ability to carry out the programme eventually laid down. When you discover that because you deliberately understated your capacity you can, in fact, exceed your quota, you wonder anxiously whether you should risk disclosing this to the authorities or not. If you do, next year's quota is bound to be higher. The bonus you receive this year may not offset the future risk. Because your thinking focuses on the fulfilment of the plan, you are not particularly interested in new production methods. Innovations inevitably interfere temporarily with the smooth operation of the factory. You admit new methods only when you are compelled to do so by the authorities. That's another way in which your system is inferior to ours. Even a factory capable of exceeding its quota regularly will frequently decide to show a production deficit for a few months to avoid becoming too conspicuously efficient.'

My companion had tried repeatedly to interrupt me, but I was annoyed and determined to have my say.

'In spite of all this,' I went on, 'you still fail to meet your obligations and you try to fabricate some kind of a "target reached" report for the authorities. You even invented a term for this practice, which is constantly quoted in your press— *ochkovtirátel'stvo* (from *vterét' ochkí*, to throw dust in someone's eyes). Although there are hundreds of variations of *ochkovtirátel'stvo*, you have to go on inventing new ones, as each ruse is exposed. Moreover, to be ready for any eventuality, you have to hoard raw materials and equipment. No one knows exactly, a year in advance, what he is going to need to complete the quota, so everybody requests as much as possible. I read in one of your periodicals that nearly a third of all the delays in heavy industry are caused by late delivery of materials and spare parts. You never surrender any of the stuff you've hoarded, for then you would be open to the charge of having requested too much, and you would get less next time. Materials lie around in the open to rust and rot. Your own press cites hundreds of examples of all these aspects of your industrial life. Am I right or not?'

'Within the framework of our practice of self-criticism,' the engineer retorted primly, 'one can read a great deal in our newspapers. That is as it should be; therein lies our strength. But the point is that there are supervisory authorities in control who keep a very sharp watch. Whole ministries exist to root out deceit.'

'Come, come!' I protested. 'You know very well that you are all in cahoots. Everybody wants to work in an outfit that always completes its quota. If you work in a ministry, you naturally want to be responsible only for successful ventures. Take your distribution organization, for example. This used to be in the hands of the same ministries that administered the factories. Then, some time ago—I think it was in 1954—you took it out of the hands of the production ministries and transferred it to the Ministry of Commerce because the production ministries, as everybody knew, shut their eyes to the inferior quality of goods produced by "their" factories. Your government feels that it can ensure effective control only through an "alien" ministry.'

My companion tried a new tack.

'Capitalism,' he declared, 'is itself corrupt and leads to nothing but corruption.' He cited a few examples from Western countries which had been mentioned in the Soviet press. I let him have his say and then returned to the charge.

'You're right,' I said, 'there are such cases. They all come to light sooner or later. We do our best to expose them. In the West the opposition parties constantly scrutinize the government for mistakes. But where is the opposition in your country? If any firm in the West tries to gain an unfair advantage through bribery, it will soon be exposed by its infuriated competitors. In this way the public has some assurance that transgressions cannot be hushed up indefinitely—as they are in your country.'

As this was not the first conversation I had had with Communist acquaintances on their favourite topic of capitalist corruption, I did not have to search long for arguments.

'Tell me,' I asked, 'are you a Marxist?'

'Yes,' he replied emphatically.

'Then you believe in the Marxist thesis that the superstructure of ideas and modes of conduct alters when the economic basis changes?'

'Of course.'

'And to which, in your opinion, does corruption belong—to the base or the superstructure?'

'To the superstructure, of course.'

'Good. Then corruption changes its form when the base changes; but it doesn't disappear. In our economic system we have what we may call the private-enterprise type of corruption. Let me give you a typical example. A city government needs fifty new buses. It invites bids—that is, it makes a public announcement that it wishes to buy fifty buses. Let's assume that three bids are submitted, by firms A, B, and C. The representative of firm C invites the appropriate city official to dinner and tells him, "If I get the contract, the firm will give me a new car. But I already have a car, so I'll tell you what I'll do, I'll let you have the new car very cheap." If the official accepts the offer— and there are, unfortunately, quite a number who would—then you have a clear case of corruption; corruption, that is, on the private-enterprise level. Not a good thing, but why deny it? Now the Soviet Union has a different system, which you call socialism, and as a result you have socialist corruption. You can find examples of it every day in your own newspapers. A factory is short, say, of coal, or steel rods, or anything you like. It tries to get what it needs through legal channels, but fails. The factory must complete its quota at all costs, so it is obliged to try other means. To the firms producing the goods it needs, it offers its own products in exchange. Such bartering is not part of the state plan. It was illegal in Stalin's time and for some years afterwards, and was liable to heavy punishment, but it occurred hundreds of times every day. The directors knew all about it, as did the chief accountants, as well as half a dozen other members of the factory hierarchy, but they all stuck together and said nothing.

'If these illegal methods fail to produce the necessary materials, the factories must still fulfill their plan. Since they are not allowed to reduce the quantity of their production, it is the quality that suffers; the product lasts only six months, instead of five years. The state is the loser. To produce goods of inferior quality is still, I believe, punishable by minimum prison sentences of five years; but it's done all the time. The manufacturer knows that his customers have such urgent need of his products that they would rather receive inferior goods than none at all. I was told of a director who was having difficulty in reaching his quota. In the end he managed to produce the prescribed number of articles by reducing the scale of each below the original specifications: the punishment for delivering undersized articles is less severe than for delivering too few. From the economic and industrial point of view, such a ruling is nonsensical, but as long as it remains in force, every director will take advantage of it.'

Here my companion intervened. 'I admit,' he said, 'that such cases do occur. There would be no point in denying it since they are frequently mentioned in our newspapers. But that, surely, isn't corruption. The people who break the law like that are not doing it for themselves, but for their firms and in order to comply with the plan. There is no question of any of them taking a private car for his own use, like the city official you mentioned.'

'But there is,' I protested. 'If these people don't reach the target, they lose their jobs and the handsome official cars that go with them. When they reach their target by illegal means, they keep their jobs and cars and get a large bonus. When there is corruption in the West, where supply exceeds demand, it is invariably the seller who tries to corrupt a prospective buyer; in your country, where demand is greater than supply, the reverse is true.'

I don't think I convinced him with my 'Marxist' lecture on corruption, but I did, perhaps, give him something to think about. Shortly afterwards I read in one of the most popular Moscow periodicals about a minor inspector who was offered a bribe by the chief engineer of the works he was about to inspect.[5] The official, however, was a model of professional integrity; this gave the chief engineer the surprise of his life; he was obviously used to less scrupulous inspectors.

It is evident from the Soviet press that nothing is safe from the black market. There was even one case in Moscow where a fire engine disappeared and was later sold to a *kolkhoz* for use as a truck. It came to light recently that horse racing in the Soviet Union had succumbed to 'capitalist sin': jockeys were taking bribes from backers to fix the result.

The following case of 'socialist corruption' and nepotism occurred recently in the Kirghiz Republic: the Party secretary of a Central Asian province had brought about, by threats, a falsification of the provincial production statistics. Although this was known to his superiors, he was soon afterwards appointed Minister of the Interior of the republic.[6]

It would be unfair to consider the Soviet economic system solely from the angle so far revealed here. It has achieved extraordinary success in the industrial field. But the system's innate faults encourage certain human weaknesses. The stratagems I have described are not, of course, ends in themselves, but means to an end—the means by which success can be achieved. Their analysis helps to determine the mentality and behaviour of the people.

One weakness is deeply rooted in the Russian character. It is the reluctance to accept personal responsibility which makes it difficult to create the cadre of executives so essential to the development of any economic system. This reluctance was encouraged during the early years of the regime by its ideological drive to have everything done collectively. As many people as possible were made responsible for a project without defining the extent of their personal authority. This proved disastrous, and towards the end of the 1920's the principle was condemned as a 'leftist deviation'. Collective responsibility, the official 'line' now stated, led to *obezlíchka*—the elimination of the personal factor—and harmed the country's economy. In the future, individuals were to be more closely 'attached' to a specific piece of machinery or a specific process and given sole responsibility. *Yedinonachâliye*—individual authority—was to be the solution.

The ruthlessness with which the new principle of individual responsibility was applied when it was a question of finding scapegoats for the failure of the system of planned economy is well known. Artisans, mechanics, engineers, directors—all appeared before Soviet tribunals and confessed that they had brought about disasters through criminal negligence or treasonable sabotage on behalf of class enemies and foreign powers. The effect was deep and lasting. There exists today a noticeable desire for some kind of 'insurance'. A former Soviet expert on mining machinery reported the following experience—a typical one—to some American investigators:

As inspector I once arrived at a plant which was supposed to have delivered mining machines, but did not do it. When I entered the plant premises, I saw that the machines were piled up all over the place, but they were all unfinished. I asked what was going on. The director gave evasive answers. Finally, when the big crowd surrounding us had disappeared, he called me to his office.

'Now we can talk,' he said.

'Well,' I said, 'why don't you ship the machines? We are waiting for them.'

'Here is the story,' he said. 'According to the technical specifications the machines must be painted with red oil-resistant varnish. However, I have only red varnish which is not oil-resistant and green varnish which is oil-resistant. Therefore I cannot complete them. You see, if I send the machines with the wrong kind of varnish I shall not have fulfilled the technical requirements, and for that I shall get eight years in prison. But if I don't ship them this will come under the charge of failure to arrange for transportation. And what will they do with me then? At worst, they will expel me from the Party. Well, the hell with my Party card. So what do you want me to do?'

'But listen,' I replied, 'the mines cannot work, they are waiting for the machines and you are holding them up because you don't have the right kind of paint.'

'But I don't want to get eight years. Give me a written note with your signature and I shall have the machines ready in nothing flat.'

Well, I don't want to get eight years either. So what do I do? I cable the Ministry and ask for permission to use the green varnish. I should have received an answer at once. But it took unusually long. Apparently they did not want to take any chances at the Ministry either, and they wanted to cover themselves. Finally I received permission. I put this cablegram from the Ministry in my pocket and kept it for the rest of my life, and signed the note allowing the use of green paint, referring to the cablegram. In a short time the machines began to roll from the plant.[7]

This excessive caution is easy to understand. The Soviet manager must at all costs produce his quota. The fear of the consequences of failing to do this is, as a rule, stronger than the fear of being punished for the illegal practices without which the quota can seldom be completed. The directors know that the authorities depend on the fulfilment of the plan and are far more interested in its success than in the methods used. The Soviet executive knows that a dossier of every infringement is kept. He is liable at any time to be sent on a new assignment to the Arctic. He knows that in most cases the state is tolerant towards those who reach their quota; but the dossier is suspended above his head like the sword of Damocles. Leniency was greatest in the years following Stalin's death. The managers were encouraged during this period because their rapid rise to a managerial position was not followed—as it had been during part of the Stalin era—by an even more rapid descent to the GPU cellars and Siberian camps.

The question of responsibility is closely linked with that of inspection and control. The state has recourse to these inspections because it cannot depend on its citizens. When I visited a medium-sized factory near Moscow, I asked how many people there were in the technical inspection department. 'Forty-seven,' the director replied. I expressed astonishment at finding so many in a factory of this size. 'That's nothing,' said the manager, 'there are lots of factories with hundreds of inspectors.' Later I read in a newspaper that the Novo-Kramatorsk machine factory had 518 inspectors; in other concerns, the report added, there were even more—an inspector for every few workers.[8]

The Soviet executives' first considerations are the inspectors and bureaucrats at all levels of the economic structure, up to and including the Minister himself. The customer comes last. In the silent struggle between directors and inspectors, each tries to outwit the other. The advantage lies mostly with the director, because he knows more about his plant and its capacity than the supervising authority and its representatives.

Naturally the directors find the constant supervision repugnant. It dampens their initiative and enterprise. One director said in a typical newspaper article:

> We are convinced that the time has come to give factories and other industrial concerns a larger measure of independence. . . . It is essential that the superfluous and obsolete superstructure of the supervisory apparatus be dismantled. This does not mean that all supervision and inspection should cease, but that it should and can be carried out within the framework of the existing factory organization. We consider that directors should be given the right to decide the structure and personnel of the factory departments, and also, within the framework of the wage scale authorized for the plant, the right to increase or reduce the salaries of the senior grades.[9]

The antithesis of the enterprising manager is the bureaucrat, who prefers a minimum of risk and would rather indulge in intrigue than accept responsibility. This type is not confined to the ranks of officialdom, but is found at every level of the economic administration. He provides almost inexhaustible copy for the author and dramatist. In a state-controlled economy, which makes officials and dependants of its citizens, it is inevitable that conflicts will not be fought out in the open. They are transferred to the back room. It is there that success and failure are judged. Recognition, reward, and promotion belong to those who excel in intrigue.

The academic world, too, is not immune to the reproach of shirking responsibility. The press complains incessantly that students, instead of devoting themselves to significant projects, concentrate on out-of-the-way problems, thus avoiding the possibility of coming into conflict with the Party line.

My own impression, however, is that those on the higher levels of the industrial and Party pyramid are beginning to accept risks more readily. This is indicative of a growing self-confidence in the managers since the end of Stalin's reign. They realize that success is ultimately won through the acceptance of responsibility and risk.

Soon after the Revolution, the Bolsheviks appealed in a variety of ways to the natural desire for prestige. They publicized those they wished to honour on bulletin boards in schools and factories and in newspapers with mass circulations. They introduced uniforms, distributed decorations, and granted ranks and titles such as 'Meritorious Artist', 'People's Artist', and 'Great Master Catcher' (in the fishing industry).

For about fifteen years after the Revolution it was almost impossible to distinguish an officer—then called a 'commander' (to avoid the invidious, bourgeois word 'officer')—from other ranks. The only difference was a small badge on the collar. But gradually the officers' uniforms became smarter, and the old ranks, abolished in the first flush of revolution, were restored.

In civil life an elaborate system of ranks and grades has also been reintroduced. As early as 1930 a handbook listed 200 ranks and grades for officials alone.[10] But the classic example is the hierarchy of state attorneys, which consists of the following ranks: State Judiciary Counsellor-General; State Judiciary Counsellor, First, Second, and Third Class; Judiciary Counsellor-General; First Judiciary Counsellor; Second Judiciary Counsellor; Lawyer, First, Second, and Third Class. The decree setting out these ranks also indicates the corresponding army rank, from General to Lieutenant.[11] Since Stalin's death, this mania for titles has subsided somewhat.

From time to time new criteria of social status have been adopted. In the middle of the 1930's a new catchword suddenly became current—*znátniye lyúdi* (outstanding people). Among them were the members of the new elite, which included Stakhanovites and star athletes. *Red Books of Prominent People* were published. Elaborate social events were organized for this new elite. Since the days of Peter the Great, the rank of members of the Russian nobility had been determined by the nature and length of their service. In this respect Stalin and Khrushchev are the Tsar's successors. To emphasize the rewards for those publicly honoured, the regime simultaneously resorted to a system of public degradation. In factories and workshops, alongside the 'red board of honour' there was a 'black board of shame' for the names of those who had not worked hard enough or who had violated discipline. Caricatures and lampoons of these workers were often pinned to the board as well.

Since public expression of esteem or disapproval had been more prevalent in Tsarist Russia than anywhere else in the world, people did not find it difficult to accept them. They subsequently developed a keen awareness of the new differences in status. When I asked a Soviet major who had just fled via East Germany for his impression of the West, he said:

'For the first few weeks I was in an American army camp. What surprised me most were the informal relations among the various ranks. In the mess hall I saw a general and a lieutenant sitting at the same table! Although I am only a major, I would never have dreamed of sitting with a lieutenant. Differences in rank must be observed!'

The children of the elite take advantage of the status won by their parents. The younger generation regards it as a matter of course that the privileges their fathers earned should devolve automatically on them. I once heard a lad who was quarrelling with another boy shout: 'My father's a director! He'll soon show you what's what!' Not long ago a few rowdies were arrested in Moscow. They were most indignant when they were taken to the police station. 'My father,' one of them protested, 'is a member of the Academy of Sciences!' Another said, 'Mine is a colonel!'

At first the state satisfied the desire for social status by marks of esteem of a non-material character. But it soon supplied the social setting for which the careerists clamoured. In the early 1930's, hotels for foreigners like the Metropol, with their renovated pre-war *art nouveau* elegance, were rarities in a revolutionary and proletarian Moscow. No young Russian would have thought of setting foot inside one. Only once a Russian student came into my hotel with me for a moment, just to take a quick peep at a forbidden, degenerate world. But in 1934, almost overnight and without being changed in any way, the Metropol suddenly became an ordinary part of Moscow. Foreigners still went there, but the majority of the guests were Russians. The evenings before holidays were particularly gay. Theatre Square, in front of the hotel, was illuminated with big floodlights, and a stream of cars pulled up at the hotel entrance. Only a few of the cars, recognizable by their pennants, belonged to foreigners. Out of luxurious Lincoln limousines, imported by the thousand from America, stepped Russians with their ladies.

These were the *znatniye lyudi* who were parading for all to see the tangible evidence of the success they had achieved.

Another sign of status is residence in one of the great cities. The urban resident knows that he is materially privileged and feels vastly superior to mere provincials. For many gifted young Russians the goal of their professional endeavours is not so much to earn a higher income but to move out of the drab provinces into a big city. No one who gets a job in Moscow ever shows any desire to leave.

This flight from the provinces is one of the main obstacles to the economic decentralization Khrushchev is so anxious to achieve. If the Kremlin sanctioned complete freedom of movement, Moscow—already seriously overcrowded—would burst at the seams. By selecting, deliberately and for propaganda purposes, a small number of towns on which to concentrate their efforts to improve the living standards, the regime has created a gap between urban and rural conditions unknown in the West. The favoured towns lure more and more people.

Moscow and Leningrad are in a class by themselves. Leningrad has held its position remarkably well, in spite of the transfer of the Academy of Sciences to Moscow in 1935. As for Moscow, even to today's Russians the name recalls the old capital of the Russian Middle Ages and the almost legendary city of twisting alleys, of merchants and artisans; it is only in the past few decades that it has become the centre of a world power. But Leningrad was St. Petersburg, and St. Petersburg was the capital city in the eighteenth and nineteenth centuries. It is a symbol of the greatest epoch of Russian cultural history, filled with the glamour of Peter the Great and Pushkin. For many Russians it is still the true centre of cultural and intellectual life. In the second category, Kiev, the capital of the Ukraine, stands alone, towering magnificently above the Dnieper. Rich in culture and tradition, it is enshrined in the heart of every Ukrainian. The rest are merely provincial towns.

Much is being done to make life in the provinces more attractive. The rapid expansion of the television network is expected to play a big part in this endeavour. The provincial towns themselves vary greatly. There are beautiful towns rich in history, like Gorky (formerly Nizhny Novgorod) on the Volga, and Odessa on the Black Sea; there are big industrial towns that have sprung up recently and leapt into prominence as the result of industrialization, such as Magnitogorsk and Sverdlovsk (formerly Yekaterinburg); and there are towns cradled in the twilight of the frozen north, like Murmansk, and others scorched by the blistering heat of the desert, like Ashkhabad or Merv.

I shall never forget my first visit to Magnitogorsk in 1934. At that time the vast majority of the population (about a quarter of a million) were living in barracks. These were furnished with twenty or more cots, a table, and several chairs, and were lit by one or two naked light bulbs dangling from the ceilings. The families had a particularly hard time. In some cases ten to fifteen families with their children were housed in a single hut. Many of them preferred to leave the town and dig underground shelters in the fields. Only a few had a room to themselves, and this was regarded as the height of luxury. When I asked whether any of them would like to return to the villages from which they had come, I was greeted with derisive laughter. 'Not likely!' they said. 'We much prefer this!' 'Living in town', as they called it, gave them the feeling that they were on the first rung up the ladder of success.

In the Soviet Union, as elsewhere, the really successful men are ambitious and austere rather than easy-going pleasure-seekers. They have chosen a way of life in which self-indulgence has its perils. Alcohol makes a man talkative, and everybody has secrets. Love affairs evoke frowns from above and impede advancement. Carefree holidays are not for the man in charge of a big concern, whose head is at stake, even during his absence. Few traces remain of the joyous figures of the old Russian capitalism, revelling in the luxuries of life. In many respects the successful Russian of today recalls the puritanism of the seventeenth century, when, it has been suggested, the seeds of Anglo-Saxon capitalism were first sown.

But the man who has made good in the Soviet Union presents an image that has nothing in common with puritanical simplicity. The governing principle is that men must not only succeed but must be seen to succeed. Success must be made visible in the form of a higher standard of living. In a state in which, only a few decades ago, everything was turned upside down and everybody had to start all over again from scratch, the standard of living is to a very large extent the yardstick of success or failure.

The Soviet student who receives a higher scholarship and can afford smarter clothes is not merely better dressed than his fellow students, but he is also, demonstrably, a man of greater ability; his smart suit is tangible proof of this. The manager in the higher-income bracket is the more efficient manager; in a hotel on the Black Sea he and his family will occupy rooms that cost seventy-five roubles a day and more, and his wife will buy jewellery that costs thousands of roubles.

The man who, in the eyes of the Soviet state, is more useful is also the one who lives on a grander scale, has a better car and a more expensively dressed wife—and is, in fact, one of the country's elite. The insistent demand of the state that the principle of 'material self-interest' be constantly borne in mind as an incentive to high endeavour means, in reality, the exploitation of egoism. Everybody must be made to realize that he could be better off if he worked harder and were more single-minded in his devotion to duty. Some day in the distant future when 'transition to Communism' has been accomplished, the principle of material self-interest—so the Party ideologists claim—will no longer be needed; then—they tell us—everybody will work for the joy of it. But for the time being it is one of the most widely used terms. The stimulus for the workman is the well-rewarded *Stakhánov* status. For the ordinary *kolkhoznik*, the incentive is to become a model *kolkhoznik* and thus receive a much larger share of the yearly income.

The whole population's attention is drawn to certain focal points of prosperity, on which the searchlight of propaganda is then turned. The extravagant opulence of the Moscow subway, on which anyone can travel for a few kopeks, is designed to convince the Moscow masses and the visitors who stream into the city from the countryside that the whole Soviet Union, including even their own miserable homes, could be turned into palaces if everybody made the necessary effort. The gigantic buildings of Moscow University, the ornate railway stations in many towns, the deliberately low-priced television sets which give their owners a sense of being well-to-do (and which incidentally bring government propaganda into the home every evening); the constant stream of success stories in books and magazines, reminiscent in some ways of the American glorification of the self-made man—all these things serve one and the same purpose. They constantly stimulate the will to work and the urge toward making good. Success, prosperity, prestige, and power, attained through hard work; this is the order of the day.

What a long way from the egalitarian thinking of the Revolution! And along this way, the men who have made most progress are precisely those who differ most sharply from the common conception of a socialist. For their motto is 'The more you put in, the more you take out'.

CHAPTER 8

AND EQUALITY?

THE MOST widely discussed play of the early post-Stalin years was *Wings* by the Ukrainian playwright Alexander Korneychuk. The hero—another 'negative' hero—is the chairman of a provincial executive council (roughly equivalent to being governor of a province). His name alone is enough to indicate why he is the author's target: Gordéy (*gordy* means 'proud') Dremlyúga (from *dremát'*, meaning 'to doze').

With slight modifications, Dremlyuga might have been the Tsarist provincial governor in a nineteenth-century play. He is an autocrat and a tyrant. He makes his gardener, an ex-soldier with many medals, spend hours digging for worms so that he can go fishing. Dremlyuga justifies whatever he does by saying that he is 'building communism', just as the inefficient Tsarist bureaucrat used to hide his misdeeds behind a professed loyalty to the Tsar. One of the characters says, in an ironic description of conditions in the province, 'We always tell our superiors the solemn untruth'.

When the mayor's wife mentions to a visitor that the city park is an accomplishment of her husband's, Madame Dremlyuga says sharply: 'Indeed? And where, may I ask, was Comrade Dremlyuga at the time? On tour, I suppose?' Whereupon the mayor hastily intervenes. 'My dear,' he says reproachfully to his wife, 'surely you haven't forgotten that we laid out our park under the personal supervision of Comrade Dremlyuga?'

Even on Sundays Dremlyuga has people working for him, building a garage for his car. 'How much longer are you going to loaf around?' he says to two women carrying tiles. 'If this garage isn't finished in two days, I'll fire you . . . Understand?' When one of the women ventures to answer back, Dremlyuga's secretary cuts in: 'Who do you think you're talking to? This is Comrade Dremlyuga, chairman of the executive council.'

Dremlyuga, who assiduously and arrogantly plays the part of 'father of the province', in fact hasn't a clue about what is going on around him. When he has to submit a report to the new Party secretary, he hides his personal assistant in the bushes

103

to be prompted by him when he doesn't know the answers.

When a preliminary conference is held to prepare for an important council meeting, Dremlyuga asks for drafts of all the speeches to be made. He deletes from them anything that might be construed as criticism of his regime and even writes some of them. When he is asked how many speakers are to take part, he replies: 'I've telephoned Kiev, and they tell me thirty-five speeches were made at their meeting. At Odessa there were also thirty-five. That seems to be the norm. So we'll have thirty-five, too.'

His wife is vain, incompetent, and ignorant. One of her guests, admiring the city park, says, 'The view reminds me of Levitan' (a reference to one of the most famous Russian landscape painters, who is still a great favourite). 'Levitan?' asks the chairman's wife, 'what province is that in?'

The author also ridicules other members of the bureaucratic ruling class in the provincial capital. The man in charge of vegetable supplies, an old Party member like Dremlyuga, is lazy, unreliable, and frequently drunk. The director of the tractor station is far less interested in his work than in duck shooting and his dog, Tarzan. In the end, of course, the play depicts the triumph of the good Communists.

When I saw *Wings* at the Little Theatre I overheard a lively exchange in the cloakroom during intermission. Three young factory hands were expressing their dissatisfaction in no uncertain terms.

'It's a bloody shame,' said one of them, 'the bosses having a great time down in the best seats, while we're stuck up there under the roof where we can't see or hear a damn thing. At least the play gives them hell. I hope our boss has taken it in. Anyway, I don't see the point of staying any longer . . . Let's go home.'

'I'll tell you what really got me down,' said another, his face red with anger. 'I had to lean over a lady (*dámochka*) in front of me in order to see the stage and she said "Somebody smells of sweat around here". That was too much for me!'

Similar incidents occurred on my trips around Russia; they show that there is a certain amount of resentment among the lower classes against those who have become their 'betters'. When all the emphasis is placed on success, those who remain on the lower rungs of the ladder inevitably feel animosity towards those who have reached the top. Letters demanding the abolition of the present inequality in wages have begun to appear in the press,[1] and Khrushchev has taken up the theme.

It would be unwise to exaggerate the importance of this unrest, but surely many Soviet citizens, when they contemplate the privileged few, must think to themselves: 'Why *them*? We're always being told we live in a socialist state. Why should the *nachál' stvo* (the bosses) live so much better than the rest of us? We want what they've got.' In other words, the Soviet state is creating a new frame of mind among its subjects—the urge to 'keep up with the Joneses'.

This outlook is also found among women. In the Kuznetsky Most, one of the principal shopping centres of Moscow, there are two women's shops opposite to each other. One is a fashion salon. Elegant cars draw up, chauffeurs hold the doors open, and the wives, daughters, and fiancées of the *nachal' stvo* step out to spend thousands of roubles on evening dresses made especially for them of imported materials. Across the street is an ordinary clothing store, where dresses can be bought 'off the rack'. During my last visit I spent some time in one department of this store, observing women buying dresses. The corner where the selling was done was separated from the rest of the room by a wooden barrier, outside which women were standing in long lines. Inside saleswomen were taking care of the customers. As soon as one woman had been dealt with, she left the enclosure through a small gate and was replaced by another. 'Size, Comrade?' the saleswoman asked the next customer briskly and, on being told, pushed her towards the appropriate rack. There were only three or four colours and styles from which to choose.

If a customer—perhaps undecided, but nevertheless conscious of the impatience of those behind her—so much as fingered a garment, the saleswoman whipped it off the hanger and directed her to a cubicle. A moment or two later the customer emerged and stood before a mirror, amid the approving or critical remarks of the husbands gathered in a tightly packed group in a corner beyond the barrier. If the customer ventured to murmur, 'Could I try another?' the saleswoman interrupted brusquely with 'Make your mind up, comrade ... There are others waiting'.

Few of the customers had the nerve to try on a second or third dress.

As I left the shop a couple came out into the street beside me. The woman had bought a dress, and her face still bore traces of the excitement and effort. At that moment a large car drew up outside the salon. The woman glanced across at it. '*Im légche*' (It's easier for *them*!), she muttered, and then, as though shrugging off an unwelcome train of thought, she tucked her parcel under her arm and hurried off.

I was constantly overhearing remarks like that. Once, on a train near Moscow, I was passing a group of huge new apartment houses. It was the first time I had been in that district, and I turned to the man sitting next to me. 'What a lot of new flats!' I commented. 'Sure!' he replied, 'and all for the *nachal'-stvo*!' (Since then building has greatly increased, and the circle of people who benefit from it has been enlarged.)

One evening I went to see the film *The Lesson of Life* because I had read in a review that it dealt with the new elite. The story opens in Moscow University. The life of a group of students, and of one girl in particular, has been disturbed by the visit of a young engineer—the personification of the current Soviet hero, a broad-shouldered, handsome, energetic young man, his whole personality glowing with health and vigour. Although the girl already has a boy friend, the newcomer sweeps her off her feet.

They marry, and the husband goes from success to success. After a few years, he has become chief engineer for the construction of an important dam; they are quite prosperous, and they have a four-year-old son. But it is apparent that the marriage is not a happy one. The young wife is disillusioned with her husband because he is so completely absorbed in his work that he neglects her. She feels that his attitude toward her and his work is wrong. He has become a despot, like an old-time capitalist business executive. Everybody has to dance to his tune. Objections, even those of his closest colleagues, are brushed aside with an autocratic 'We are building communism, and we can't afford to be fussy.'

An apparently trivial incident brings things to a head. In an effort to counter the growing hostility of her husband's workers, the wife tries to improve the atmosphere by organizing an outing for them and their families. Her husband promises to provide transportation. The day of the outing arrives. Everybody is there, looking forward to it. But where are the trucks? Half an hour passes . . . an hour . . . and still no sign of them. Finally the wife phones her husband, who is in conference. He is impatient with her.

'What trucks?' he snaps.

'The trucks for the outing. You promised to let us have them. I reminded you only last night.'

'Oh, those . . . I'm afraid we really have more important things to think of. We're building Communism, and the trucks are needed for more serious work.'

'But what am I to do? There are hundreds of men and women here. I counted on you to provide transportation. They've been looking forward to this treat for days. I can't just tell them to go home!'

'Yes you can. Tell them they'll have the trucks next Sunday!'

This is the last straw. The young wife's self-respect is deeply wounded. Her husband realizes this when he comes home in the evening and finds no dinner ready. Angry, he goes to her room, where she sits with her back to the door and hardly deigns to answer him. 'I see,' he says with heavy irony, 'diplomatic relations have been broken off!' Banging the door behind him, he strides off to the kitchen.

After this scene, a middle-aged woman sitting next to me turned to her companion and said: 'It's easy for them to break off diplomatic relations in an eight-room apartment!' Like most people in Moscow, she probably lived with her family in a single room and could ill afford such defiant gestures.

This, then, is another obvious dilemma facing the regime. It realizes that many resent the arrogance and opulent life of the upper classes. It tries, by critical comment in the press, theatre, and cinema, to disassociate itself from both and to improve the behavioural attitudes of the *nouveau riche*. At the same time, by giving everyone the chance to see such films and plays, the regime encourages resentment. The feelings of the audience are exacerbated, their anger at the elite's lack of consideration is increased, and the demand for equality becomes an audible protest.

The disillusionment of those who still believe in social equality can have far-reaching repercussions. A few years ago I spent two days in conversation with an intelligent young Russian who had recently fled from the Soviet zone of Germany. I tried to discover just when his loyalty to the regime had first been seriously shaken, when the idea to flee had occurred to him. He told me that the re-introduction of school fees, which had compelled him years ago to give up his studies, had shaken him to the core and had been the seed of his later decision. School and university fees had been abolished after the revolution, but in 1940 fees for the senior classes in schools and for the universities were restored. This was regarded by the majority of the people as a device of the elite to reserve admission to universities for their own children. A few hundred roubles here or there were of no great importance to them, but many children from the lower social strata had to abandon hope of higher education.

By the time fees were abolished again, in September 1956, the situation had changed: the number of young people graduating from the schools was far greater than that of the openings in the universities. Now the richer families found various ways of ensuring the admission of their children to the university, even of those not particularly gifted or industrious. They made full use of their personal contacts with members of selection committees, directors, and professors, and judging by the number of cartoons of well-dressed mothers gushing over university officials, this must have incensed the masses.

Among the leaders of the post-Stalin era, Khrushchev has shown the greatest sympathy for and understanding of this feeling among the people. It was he who announced that the minimum wage rates should be raised.[2] He also increased the prices of luxury goods to decrease the spending power of the upper class.[3] And it was he who announced the abolition of school fees at the Twentieth Party Congress.[4] In his speech to the Thirteenth Komsomol Congress he inveighed against parents who resorted to any and every means to get their children into the universities. He castigated particularly those parents who threatened their children with a life of manual labour unless they gained admittance to a university.[5] This marked the beginning of his drive towards reform of the educational system.

Perhaps the emphasis on the eventual 'transition to Communism' can be explained in part by Khrushchev's desire to promise equality—in a period of extreme inequality—at least for the distant future.

The high-handed tone adopted towards them by some of their 'betters' angers the masses more than their lower standard of living. For a socialist state, there is a noticeable lack of friendly interchange among the different social groups in the Soviet Union. Social distinctions are greater there than in the United States. The man who is determined to succeed cannot be too scrupulous. A ruthless system creates ruthless men to serve it. Successful men are inclined to look down on the rest and say, 'The man who remains at the bottom of the social pyramid lacks qualifications—he must be lazy as well, otherwise he wouldn't still be there!'

A few years ago, when I went to Gorky to see the automobile plant, an executive took me for a short drive. The road was bad, and we got stuck in the mud. A passer-by, very poor and shabby, helped us to get clear. As we drove off, I said to my host, 'Don't you think we might have offered him a lift?' My companion raised his eyebrows in astonishment. 'Him?' he exclaimed, 'why, he's a good-for-nothing! Surely you could see that from his rags.'

Contemporary Soviet literature offers many examples of the widening gap between the classes. There is an episode in *The Fate of a Comrade*, a recent story by Parkhomov, in which a *nachal'nik* named Mezhevich greets a new subordinate, Odintsov, with marked coolness. It seems that Odintsov has earlier, quite by accident, met Mezhevich socially at the latter's country house.

> 'With every word and gesture,' Parkhomov writes, 'Mezhevich emphasized the gap between Odintsov and himself, and made it quite clear that he regarded the previous meeting as entirely fortuitous. If he, Mezhevich, had any say in the matter, he would make it a rule never to meet socially any subordinate who did not belong to his circle of personal friends.'[6]

That there are writers who literally set up barriers between themselves and the people is illustrated by Nikolai Virta, who built himself a two-storey villa surrounded by a blue fence. To build it, he mobilized the Komsomol members of the village and asked them to do the work without pay, explaining that the task was a *subbótnik* (a 'Sunday', or voluntary, chore, an institution introduced during the revolution and hallowed by it, whereby men could be called on to work in their free time and without payment on any urgent task for the good of the community).

In the morning, when the *kolkhoz* women went to work in the fields, they used to see Virta's wife taking her morning ride, dressed in a gaily coloured cowboy shirt and well-cut riding breeches. As his wife was fond of ice skating, Virta had a skating rink built (again by the *Komsomoltsy*). Small wonder that the villagers referred to him as the *bárin* (the lord), as they had called the great landowners of the past.[7]

Virta was a spoilt darling of the regime; for his works, which adhered rigidly to the Party line and some of which were anti-western in tone, he won a number of Stalin prizes. And he is not an isolated example. Many, though certainly not all, successful artists live a life of their own in a milieu of their own. They are often privileged guests at state receptions. Outside Moscow they have their own settlement. Its name, Peredélkino, is particularly apt, since it is akin to the word *peredelat'* (to remodel). Many a writer has had to spend a lot of time 'remodelling' his work to conform with the ever-changing Party line.

Nevertheless, whatever most of the Soviet people may feel, their attitude towards their 'betters' is, as a rule, polite, cooperative, and even a little devout. By and large, their respect for those above them is stronger than their envy. And this in a land where the contrast between the proclaimed classless society and reality is so blatantly obvious, where the gaping chasm between top and bottom must strike every Soviet citizen—a land whose official 'bible' is the *Communist Manifesto*, many of whose ten points demand that the economic differences and privileges dividing the social classes be eradicated.

The people of the Soviet Union are obviously as conscious of class distinctions as the people of Tsarist Russia were. They 'know their place'. This has often been portrayed in Russian literature, a classic example being Gogol's *Inspector General*. Readers may also recall the brilliant short story by Chekhov entitled *The Death of an Official*, first published in 1883. A civil servant of medium rank, Chervyakóv (from *cherv'* meaning 'a worm') unfortunately sneezes at the theatre over the bald pate of a high-ranking official sitting in front of him. Chervyakov at once apologizes profusely. He repeats his apologies during intermission. The next day and the day after he presents himself at the great man's office and renews his apologies. In the end, the official, who attached no importance to the incident, becomes exasperated and tells him to clear out. Chervyakov is so distressed that he goes home, lies down on his sofa, and dies.

Two generations after the publication of Chekhov's story, when the allegedly Socialist state was already thirty years old, a ship under the command of a Captain Vinográdov was steaming up the Moskva. A launch came too close to the steamer and the clothes of the Deputy Director of Inland Water Transport, who was aboard the launch, were splashed. Although it was entirely the fault of the pilot of the launch and Vinogradov was in no way to blame, the Deputy Director insisted that Vinogradov be reprimanded for disrespectful behaviour and that a bonus already awarded to him be withdrawn.[8] Thus a socialist official displayed far less tolerance than his fictional Tsarist predecessor.

Their long history of subservience makes it easy for the Russian people to slip back into the habits of servility when the occasion demands it. They have been denied the opportunity, enjoyed first by the middle classes and then also by the working classes in the West, to develop a sense of self-assurance. This, and the fear of reprisal, seem to me the primary reasons for the attitude of the Soviet masses. After all, the boss represents the power of the state and can be far more dangerous than his Western counterpart.

However, it would be unjust to the Russians to attribute this attitude solely to timidity and submissiveness. On the whole, they accept achievement as the basis of social advancement, and they have a genuine and sincere admiration for the expert. If a member of the top group proves his efficiency, they will readily concede to him the right to a higher standard of living; jealousy has never been a marked trait of the Russians' character.

The same applies to their attitude towards the wholly disproportionate incomes of artists and writers. Respect for the goddess *Kul'túra* is so deeply ingrained in the Russian that he considers it only right that those who serve her well should live in luxury.

There is another reason why these glaring discrepancies in income and living standards are accepted. Descent from the basic social groups of peasants and workers is still plainly discernible in all classes. An awareness of this is sedulously fostered by propaganda and strengthened by the years all classes spend side by side in the same schools.

Finally, it would be unwise to ignore the psychological effect of the official myth which accords first place in the scheme of things to 'the worker'. Thanks to the educational system which theoretically offers unlimited opportunities to all who are gifted, it is a myth accepted by many as reality. But the fact is that the upper class is being recruited more and more among its own kind; the son of a member of the elite has much more chance of joining its ranks than the son of an ordinary workman; this has been shown by the analysis of a post-war questionnaire filled out by nearly 3,000 former Soviet citizens.[9]

But Soviet workers cannot make these investigations and comparisons for themselves. As far as the state is concerned, the main point—regardless of what the truth may be—is that they should believe that the road to success lies open to their children. Khrushchev is doing his utmost to strengthen this belief, and he constantly points to himself as an example.

One of the first novels to appear after Stalin's death was Vera Panova's *Four Seasons*. In her portrayal of provincial life she reverted to the old Russian literary tradition of calling a spade a spade, of taking up the cudgels on behalf of the lowly, and of frankly exposing the weaknesses of the upper class. Sympathy for the poor—and the sinner—is a fundamental Russian trait. It finds characteristic expression in such proverbs as 'Wrestle with sin, but make peace with the sinner'.

Bortashévich, the 'negative' hero in *Four Seasons*, holds a high rank in both industry and the Party. For two-thirds of the story the author portrays him as a most likeable character, a conscientious father and a zealous functionary. Only later is it disclosed that he has for years been a thoroughly evil operator. The reader is taken aback. When an 'old guard' Party man like Bortashevich, a pillar of the regime, turns out to be a swindler, the reader feels bound to ask himself, 'Who among the upper class can I regard as an honest man?' In the same novel Redkovsky, too, is thoroughly selfish and swindles the state. As director of a state building programme, he builds for himself, 'on the side' and at state expense, a villa surrounded by a six-foot wall. As a precaution, he registers it not in his own name but in that of his mother-in-law. Any of his employees inclined to ask awkward questions soon finds himself out of a job.

The author carefully avoids giving the impression that this is purely a question of the older generation, still stigmatized as selfish and egoistical. Her novel contains another 'negative' character, Gennády. This young man, born soon after the revolution of proletarian parents who were fervent Communists, nevertheless turns out to be a thoroughly rapacious and un-principled rogue.

Because of its true portrayal of Soviet life, the novel had an enthusiastic reception in literary circles. Another writer, Mari-etta Shaginyán, commented, 'Nowhere in her novel does Vera Panova moralize'.[10] In other words nowhere does she use these Communist catchwords which till then were regarded as essen-tial to any Soviet literary work. But it was not long before the novel was bitterly attacked; the 'new class' realized with dis-pleasure that it had been portrayed in most unflattering terms. *Pravda*, mouthpiece of the Party, reproached Vera Panova for having taken as her motto 'This is how life is'.[11] (The motto of socialist realism as laid down by the Party is, of course, 'This is what life should be'.) Because she had written a book about ordinary people, her work was denounced as *meshchánskaya lite-ratúra* (bourgeois stuff) 'bearing no relation to the salient char-acteristics of our times'. 'The petty hopes and fears of the man in the street have always gone on from one epoch to another without much change,' *Pravda* wrote. To deal with the eternal truths of human nature is not regarded—by *Pravda*—as the duty of a writer. On the contrary, 'it is the duty of our writers to present in positive and artistic terms the new type of man in all the noble grandeur of his human dignity'. Even though he does not exist!

Similar reproaches have been levelled at Vladimir Dudintsev. One important reason why his novel *Not by Bread Alone* attracted world-wide attention was because it boldly depicted the un-savoury aspects of the elite. Dudintsev, too, follows the classical tradition of championing the oppressed. Instead of extolling the mighty, he exposes them, enlisting the reader's whole-hearted sympathy for his hero, Lopatkin, a free-lance inventor and former schoolteacher who tenaciously holds out against the powers-that-be, is sentenced to eight years' hard labour in Siberia but wins in the end. His opponents, however, all remain unchallenged in their posts, although by suppressing Lopatkin's invention they have caused the state serious damage.

It was not surprising that Dudintsev became the whipping-boy for those who wanted to safeguard their privileges by means of the Party machinery. The dilemma in which Khrushchev finds himself is illustrated by the fact that though he is so fond of proclaiming himself the champion of the little man, he felt constrained to condemn Dudintsev.[12]

The most outspoken attack on the higher bureaucracy was made by Leonid Sorin in his drama *The Guests*, which was per-formed a few times to public acclaim in the winter of 1953-54, during the first swing of the pendulum after Stalin's death.[13] The play's villain is Pyotr Kirpichóv, head of a department in the Ministry of Justice. On the other side are his father, an idealist and an 'old Bolshevik', and his high-minded sister Varvára, both of whom condemn Pyotr's arrogant attitude towards the people.

The old man calls his son a bloated, conceited, anti-social tycoon, a puffed-up careerist, whose soul is eaten up with ambi-tion and choked with ashes. Varvara goes further. She does not confine her remarks to her brother, or even to one section of the people or one generation. From her lips falls the fatal word—'class'.

> Varvara (*to the journalist, Trubin, who, at heart, is on her side*): It seems to me that in a social system in which it is not a man's ability, but his status, not achievement, but possessions, that count—in an enervated society devoid of life-force—there is something alien and repellent. No—it isn't just hate. It may sound absurd, but it is something that reminds me of 'class-consciousness'. Now where has this 'upper class' (*vysshy svet*) in our country come from?

The following quote gives the clue to the real meaning of the play, and to the reason why it was condemned by the Kremlin:

> Trubin: Where did our 'upper class' come from? It is the spawn of meanness and greed, of inordinate ambition,

of their incompetence and our own complacency. When a great deal is given to those from whom little can be expected, no good can ever come of it.

Varvara: In short—from power.

Varvara not only speaks of 'class' and the power that corrupts, but also makes it inescapably clear to whom she refers when, at the end of the first act, Pyotr and the son who takes after him ('Every barman in Moscow knows him') leave the stage, and Varvara, watching them, says: 'How I hate that *burzhúy* type!' It is on these words that the curtain falls, giving them a significance that stays with the audience throughout the intermission—perhaps even longer. The colloquial *burzhuy*, a word in great favour during the revolution to denote a class enemy, is the vulgar form of 'bourgeois', and by using it Varvara brands segments of the Soviet elite as class enemies. The words with which Pyotr's other son parts from his father are a resounding call to class warfare:

I declare war on you! Wherever I meet you, whatever your job and whatever your position—whatever you look like and however you describe yourself—by whatever name you call yourself—I shall know you for what you are, and I shall fight you to the death.

There is just one thing to be added: after a few performances the play was banned and withdrawn.

NOT BY BREAD ALONE . . .

CHAPTER 9

THE PURSUIT OF KNOWLEDGE

A PROVINCIAL TOWN in Siberia. The inscription over the school entrance read 'Ten-Grade School'. I asked if I could see the principal and was shown into the office of a man in his forties, with wise, somewhat tired eyes behind thick spectacles. We talked for a while and he showed interest when I told him where I came from. I was the first visitor he had ever had from the German *Federativnaya Respublika*. Afterwards, he offered to show me around the school.

Because of the long, hard Russian winter, many of the schools have a big recreation room on each floor where the pupils go during the breaks between classes. It was during a break that we began our tour. There was much scurrying about, but the children were quite well-behaved. Most of the girls were dressed alike, in black and dark brown, with white collars and cuffs and a light-coloured pinafore. Only a few of the boys wore the standard grey uniform, like a soldier's, of long trousers, jacket, belt, and cap. They looked very much like the boys of the Tsarist era I had known during my own schooldays in Moscow. Another echo of the past, formerly condemned by the revolutionaries, was the strict discipline. Since the 1920's, when schools were directed to ensure the 'free development of the child', many changes had obviously been made; corporal punishment, however, is still banned; the stigma of being labelled an 'enemy of society', a misfit in the school community, is regarded as sufficient punishment.[1] As far as I could see, the children were none the worse for the re-introduction of strict discipline. Youngsters have no objection to a firm hand, provided the control is just and consistent. What a child most desires is a settled environment.

The walls of the hall were covered with a variety of pictures, some with a political flavour. There was, for example, a large panel on which were pasted the maxims of well-known (mostly Revolutionary) writers dealing with the importance of the Russian language. Portraits of the authors appeared beside some of the quotations. This particular panel had been prepared by the pupils of one class. Another was devoted to the 'Conquest of the Steppes'; it showed pictures of tractors in the vast expanses of Kazakhstan, extracts from speeches by Khrushchev, Party resolutions, and poems.

This enthusiasm for illustrations, posters, and other visual aids to education is reflected in the popularity of art reproductions. In bookshops, particularly in the provinces, a whole section is sometimes devoted to these prints. Some of the popular magazines, notably *Ogonyok*, have special sections illustrated with art reproductions; these are eagerly cut out and collected by children. Very popular, too, in halls and classrooms of schools are hand-painted copies of such contemporary works as S. A. Grigoryev's picture of a teacher and his pupils discussing the bad marks obtained by a lad who stands shame-faced before them, or I. V. Shevandronóv's picture of children reading in a village library.

There are also bulletin boards similar to those in the factories, on which school events are reviewed according to the tenets of 'self-criticism': cartoons of Viktor, who pulled little Lena's hair, or of Natasha, the chatterbox who disrupted her well-behaved classmates. In addition, of course, the bulletin boards show the results of inter-class competition, for it is an integral part of Soviet life that every group—whether a schoolroom, a dairy farm, or an entire province—must compete with others of its kind. Children, I think, enjoy doing things together; resistance to the super-integration demanded by the authorities emerges only in later years when young people begin to discover themselves.

While we were looking around, the children's break ended. It had been their main recess for the day, lasting a half-hour; the others are for only ten minutes. (Each period is forty-five minutes long.) The pupils now returned to their classrooms, where they are not allowed to remain during the breaks. The principal asked me what I would like to see next. On my frequent visits to Soviet schools I have always found that history and literature lessons are particularly interesting. I told him this, and he took me to a class in modern history. It had not yet begun, and when we entered the pupils rose and answered my greeting in unison. I found a seat in the back of the room.

It became apparent that the lesson dealt with citizenship rather than history. The class was studying a speech by Khrushchev. In the previous lesson the teacher had explained Khrushchev's ideas about 'different ways to socialism' and 'co-existence'; now he examined the class to see how much they had learned. These tests were very thorough. One by one, the pupils were called to the blackboard; they had to repeat, as nearly as possible word for word, what they had written down at the teacher's dictation two days before. During the first half-hour only three pupils recited. The marks made by each were then entered in their own record books, which have to be signed by the parents, and in the class records. The teacher devoted the remaining time to dictating outline summaries of other parts of Khrushchev's speech.

The method of instruction was totally dogmatic. The aim was to teach the class exactly what Khrushchev said, not to discuss it. It went: 'What did Comrade Khrushchev say about different ways to socialism?' 'Comrade Khrushchev said first . . . second . . . third . . . ' and so on.

The teacher spoke forcefully and with vivid gestures, throwing back his head and shaking the hair away from his forehead. His authority was obviously great, and he could easily have initiated—and controlled—a discussion.

In the afternoon, when we were together for half an hour, this teacher asked me, 'How would one of your teachers conduct such a history lesson?'

'He would not lecture dogmatically,' I replied. 'He would instead encourage discussion—at least, if he had your ability.'

The teacher was interested. He obviously had never considered the possibility. Why should he? In a totalitarian state those below usually reproduce by rote what is taught by those above, without any attempt to analyse critically.

I asked him, 'How is it that in a history lesson you dealt with a speech made barely two months ago?'

'In the tenth grade,' he replied, 'we study the history of the Soviet Union from the revolution to the present day. The school year is nearly over, and in any case we had reached the present.'

'Plus,' I suggested, 'a directive from the Ministry?'

He nodded.

Afterwards I listened to a fifth-grade history lesson. Instruction in history starts in the fourth grade with a short summary of Russian history from the beginnings of the Kiev State to the present. In the fifth grade world history to the end of the Greek era is taught; the sixth grade continues with Roman history up to the great migrations; the seventh studies the Middle Ages, up to the 'bourgeois revolution in England in 1648'; in the eighth grade modern world history is covered; the ninth and tenth return to Russian history, the former studying the period before 1917, the latter post-revolutionary Russia.

During my visit, the fifth grade was studying the Greeks and had just reached the Age of Pericles, surely an era to fire the imagination of youth and inspire it with a love of the beautiful. But the teacher, a woman, spent the time inveighing against the horrors of slavery. Large, vividly coloured posters, crudely illustrating the sufferings of the slaves, hung on the blackboard. It was painful to listen to her. Of the grandeur of that period she had not a word to say; and on top of that she was dull and unsure of herself. She monotonously repeated the textbook phrases. In the Soviet Union the state requires—indeed demands—that a teacher cram as much as possible into the pupils. The thirst for knowledge among young Russians, their great respect for learning, and their lack of scepticism make them ideal subjects for this type of teaching. But there are indications that a gradual change is taking place, (such as that dealt with in the play *Nikolái Ivánovich* described in the chapter 'A World to Discover').

While the fifth grade was learning about the horrors of slavery in ancient Greece, two and a half million other fifth-graders, from Riga and Lvov in the west to Vladivostok in the east, were looking at the same garish pictures and being taught that Pericles was a militarist and the leader of the slave-owning upper class.

The Soviet Union has no central Ministry of Education. The schools are in the hands of the Education Ministries of the Soviet republics. Only the Ministry of Higher Education has authority throughout the country. But from the beginning of the 1930's until the school reforms introduced by Khrushchev in December 1958, there was one school system for the whole of the U.S.S.R. Whether in a seven-year village school or a ten-year school in a town, the curriculum for each grade remained the same, with certain modifications only for children whose native language was not Russian.

Not only the curriculum is uniform throughout the Soviet Union. The same applies to everything else: school books and visual aids; co-education (re-introduced in 1955—between 1943 and 1955 girls and boys in towns were educated separately); the grading system and examinations (held simultaneously, with identical questions for each grade); and homework (one hour a day in the first grade, increasing to three or four hours a day in the higher grades).

When the lesson on Pericles had ended, the principal was waiting for me at the door to inquire whether I wished to see anything else. 'If you will allow me,' I replied, 'I would very much like to observe a class in Russian literature.'

We went into his study to look at the schedule. An eighth-grade literature lesson was just about to begin. The principal introduced me to the teacher, a grey-haired woman in her middle fifties, neatly dressed and rather plump, with a motherly face. It was obvious from the moment she entered the classroom that the children loved her. They were alert and eager, and they addressed the teacher, Márya Petróvna, in tones of esteem and affection. The subject of the lesson was Gogol's immortal comedy *The Inspector General*.

Whenever I have found myself irritated by the way history is taught in the Soviet Union, I have turned for relief to a class in literature. In the junior grades the emphasis is on language and grammar, but even during the first four years the children are given a taste of such masters as Pushkin and Tolstoy. The eighth and ninth grades study Russian literature from its beginnings to Chekhov; the tenth focuses on Soviet literature from Gorky onwards.

Marya Petrovna handled her subject admirably. For the most part she allowed Gogol to speak for himself, merely explaining in simple terms the quality of irony in his humour and drawing attention to his characterizations. She made the class read a few extracts aloud and added some remarks about the social conditions of the period in which Gogol wrote, but allowed the play to demonstrate for itself its merit as a satire not only on one particular epoch and class, but on human weakness as a whole. She explained that Gogol did not caricature, pointing out that however much he exaggerated, his characters were always living people. And they were, she said, by no means peculiar to his day. Here some of her pupils laughed appreciatively.

The satiric realism of Gogol, the classical grandeur of Pushkin, Tolstoy's devoutness, the romanticism of Lermontov, Nekrasov's sympathy for those who suffer—it would be difficult to imagine a more salutary counterbalance to Bolshevik teaching for the youth of the Soviet Union. Their works, among the greatest in world literature, cannot fail to have a positive effect.

Anyone who imagines that the works of these Russian masters no longer interest Soviet youth is quite mistaken. In the materialistic and utilitarian atmosphere of the U.S.S.R., the young Russian is conscious of the need for something not concerned solely with production, something more than rhymed propaganda. He longs to add to his knowledge of human nature, to satisfy his craving for beauty and romance. These needs are fulfilled by the great Russian writers (and also by the works of a few modern lyric poets).[2]

The study of literature in Soviet schools is approached, of course, as is all teaching of the liberal arts, along Marxist lines. Whenever Pushkin's verse novel *Eugene Onegin* is mentioned, the teacher at once, as is his duty, explains the social conditions under which Pushkin lived and which he describes; everything is explained in the manner laid down by the Communist code. There comes the moment, though, when the teacher finally shuts his mouth and the pupil opens the book for himself. From the very first line, Pushkin speaks directly to the young.

Whatever the comrade teacher may have to say about the class struggle at the beginning of the nineteenth century, or about the exploitation of the Russian serfs by the landowners, pales beside the shining creations of Pushkin's imagination; in the relation of his characters to each other it is not class but common humanity that plays the vital role.

I have sometimes asked young Russians to name their favourite authors. Pushkin is nearly always one of them, especially among the girls. There are countless girls and women in Russia today called Tatyana or Olga, after characters in *Eugene Onegin*—an expression of the profound admiration for Pushkin acquired in school. I am sure that hundreds of thousands of young women know by heart whole passages from his work, especially Tatyana's love letter to Onegin.

And Pushkin's Tatyana is only one of many. His *Captain's*

Daughter, Lermontov's Pechorin and Princess Mary, Tolstoy's Anna Karenina, Turgenev's Liza and Lavretsky, Katerina in Ostrovsky's *Tempest*—these and many others are more alive and vivid in the minds of Russians today than ever before. Of Dostoyevsky I shall have more to say later, since he concerns the older more than the younger generation. Before the revolution a much smaller number of students (30,000 to 40,000 a year) came into contact with these literary treasures. In recent years millions of pupils have graduated from high school; they have all had nearly 3,000 hours of instruction in the Russian language and literature, and they have eagerly absorbed what they have learned.

Why have the Communists allowed their children access to anything so much at variance with Marxist doctrine as the works of the great nineteenth-century Russian writers? One of the reasons, I think, has been the desire to encourage patriotism and a sense of tradition. Another is that all these millions of people in the U.S.S.R. were plunged into one of the bloodiest revolutions in history and hurled from the security of their traditional way of life into a purely materialistic present, devoid of any metaphysical significance. To control these masses, the state has innumerable instruments—the civil administration, the police, trade unions, and so on—whose purpose is to impose order. But this is not enough. The state must also try to educate its subjects in the voluntary acceptance of law and order. How is this to be done?

Religion, with its great moral force, is ridiculed and rejected by the state. As a result of its 'dialectical' interpretation, the much-vaunted Communist morality offers anything but security. It is significant that four decades after the revolution articles should appear in Soviet newspapers calling for 'ethical instruction' in the schools.[3] In this context the humanistic idealism of the Russian classical writers stands the state in good stead. We, of course, find it grotesque that a dictatorship that has left a trail of imprisoned and martyred victims should claim concern with humanity and compassion; but those who reject religion and yet are unwilling to live by terror alone must fall back on humanism if they are to prevent a situation for which the Romans coined the phrase 'Man is man's wolf'.

Gorbatov's story *A Child is Born in Cucumberland*, which appeared during the height of the Stalin era, illustrates this point. On an island called Cucumberland in the northernmost Arctic, a woman is in labour. There are complications beyond the scope of the young doctor on the spot. The nearest gynaecologist lives on another island, more than 500 miles away. The helpless doctor describes the symptoms to the gynaecologist by radio and receives detailed instructions. The ordeal lasts three hours, during which all the Arctic radio posts go off the air to avoid any possibility of interference:

> And the whole Arctic held its breath, waiting for the child to be born, just as though these rugged, brave men— the miners in Nordvik, the scientists at Cape Chelyuskin, the radio operators at Dikson, the workers building the harbour at Tiksi, and those in winter quarters on the island of Bely—were all standing by the mother's bedside, not daring to move or cough, and waiting to greet this tiny new citizen of the world.[4]

It seems a grim paradox to us that in a land ruled by Stalin the birth of one child should arouse so much excitement and sympathy. But Stalin, if he ever read the story, presumably saw no incongruity between this appeal to human kindness and his own brutal regime. As an absolute autocrat he claimed the right to deal with people as he thought fit, for he regarded himself (as have his successors) as the appointed representative and executor of the Marxian law of history designed to govern the evolution of mankind. The more absolute the power he claimed for himself, the more obedient he wished to see his subjects. They were to live moral lives, and multiply; they were to be punctual at their work and carry out faithfully any other tasks he gave them. It was their duty, therefore, to preserve the life of every individual, just as he regarded it as his right to deprive millions of theirs.

So I reflected as I listened to the pleasant Marya Petrovna's discourse on Gogol's *Inspector General*, and I hoped that Russian literature would continue to exert its noble influence on young Russia for years to come. Khrushchev, however, was of a slightly different opinion. In his reform, the time devoted to literature was relatively reduced. As can be seen on the table on page 129 2,856 lesson-hours were devoted to Russian language and literature in the course of ten years of school, while now there are only 2,880 for eleven years.

Next the principal took me through classrooms with 'poly-technical instruction'. For the eighth grade there was a room with carpenters' benches and tools; here for three hours a week the rudiments of handicrafts were taught. In the ninth grade they dismantled, repaired, and rebuilt automobile engines. They worked two additional hours a week as apprentices in one of the town's garages; a truck from there called for them and brought them back to school again. In the tenth grade the sub-ject was electricity, and pupils in this class, too, worked as part-time apprentices. One might perhaps argue that there is nothing particularly socialistic about all this, but it certainly fits our age. It also appeared that the pupils enjoyed it.

For Khrushchev, however, this was not enough. What is called 'polytechnical instruction' reveals the whole problem fac-ing the Soviet educational system. The basic idea behind tech-nical training, on which so much emphasis has been placed since the advent of the Soviet Union, has changed with the years. At first it expressed the instinctive opposition of the old revolution-aries, inspired by the proletarian myth, to any form of education predominantly academic or classical; on ideological grounds they favoured the closest possible link between school and workshop. Under the influence of American ideas, particularly Dewey's 'progressive education', they were anxious to ensure for every child something more than purely intellectual development. Later, this conception of the value of technical training receded into the background because it was found to delay the progress of elementary general education, and above all, because primary importance was attached to the quick creation of first-class techni-cal and managerial cadres for the tasks of economic and national expansion ahead. The main purpose of the high-school grades became the training of candidates for the technical colleges.

This system of education was introduced in the 1930's and until 1958 had undergone little change. Only the number of pupils has steadily increased. As a result these ten-grade schools became obligatory in towns and in the larger settle-ments, while the seven-grade schools still predominated in the country districts. Here and there a few four-grade schools still exist. As the curriculum was uniform throughout the country, a pupil who had completed a four-grade school was automatically eligible for entry into the fifth grade of a seven- or ten-grade school; similarly, a child who had attended a seven-grade school could immediately enter the eighth grade in any ten-grade school.

During the school year 1959-60 about 33,200,000 pupils were educated according to the uniform plan (18,500,000 in the four junior classes, 10,700,000 in the intermediary grades and 4,300,000 in the senior grades).[5] Nowhere else in the world is there a uniform educational system of this magnitude. What is even more noteworthy and new is that most of the urban youth, and much of the rural youth, have a six-year course of instruction in a foreign language; in 1958-59 11,360,000 took this course. The principal languages taught are German and English. In 1958-59 6,800,000 have taken German and 3,500,000 English. French was studied by less than a million.[6] In territories near the Asian frontiers, courses in the languages of the adjoining countries—Arabic, Persian, Urdu, Hindi and Chinese—have recently taken the place of the European languages. These imposing figures indicate that the Soviet Union has wrested the lead from the West in education—at least quantitatively in educational opportunities, and therefore in the potential total of technically qualified citizens.

The Soviet schools, of course, are just as familiar with the problem of the backward pupil as our own—perhaps more so. In some schools, I learned, from 20 to 50 per cent fail to reach the standard required in their grades. But there are no special schools for backward children. The Labour Reserve Schools introduced in 1940[7] were hardly ever mentioned publicly. They trained about a million youngsters a year for purely manual work. Those who attended these schools were obliged for four years to undertake any and every task allotted to them.

In one Soviet discussion of the problem of the backward pupil, the extraordinary suggestion was put forward that if the parents of such children had to pay a fine, they would soon see to it that the children applied themselves more to their school work.[8] And this in a state which calls itself socialist!

Judging by the comments of the Soviet experts, it seemed for a long time that on the whole the educational system was working well. But a few years ago doubts began to arise. It was felt that the system was producing too many 'officers' and not enough

Subject	PRESENT SCHOOL PROGRAMME IN THE U.S.S.R.[29] Periods and grade (small figures refer to pre-reform days)											Periods per week	Periods per 10- (11-) year course
	I	II	III	IV	V	VI	VII	VIII	IX	X	XI		
Russian Language and Literature	12	12	12	10	8	8	5	5	3	3	3	81	2880
	13	13	13	9	9	8	6	5	4	4		84	2856
Mathematics	6	6	6	6	6	6	6	5	4	4 or 5	4	59	2115
	6	6	6	6	6	6	6	6	6	5½		59½	2023
History (including Civics)				2	2	2	2	3	2	3	6	22	796
				2	2	2	2	4	3	4½	1	19½	663
Geography					2	2	2	2		2	2	12	434
				3	2	2	2	2½	3			14½	493
Biology				3	2	2	2	2	3			14	508
				2	2	3	2	2	1			12	408
Physics						2	2	3	4	4	2	17	631
						2	3	3	3½	4		15½	527
Astronomy										1		1	39
										1		1	34
Chemistry							2	2	2	3	2	11	407
							2	2	2	4		10	340
Foreign Languages					4	3	3	3	2	2	3	20	726
					4	4	3	3	3	3		20	680
Sport	2	2	2	2	2	2	2	2	2	2	2	22	792
	2	2	2	2	2	2	3	3	3	3		23	782
Drawing (including Technical Drawing)	1	1	1	1	1	1	2	1	2			11	397
	1	1	1	1	1	1	1	1	1	1		10	340
Singing and Music	1	1	1	1	1	1	1	1				8	283
	1	1	1	1	1	1						6	204
Shop Work and Socially useful work	2	2	4	4	5	5	5	5	12	12	12	68	2491
	1	1	2	2	2	2	2	3	4	4		23	782
Weekly total for each grade	24	24	26	29	33	34	34	34	36	36	36	346	12679
	24	24	25	28	31	33	31	34½	33½	34		298	10132

129

'men of the ranks'. The universities and other centres of higher education began to overflow; many of them stopped accepting new students merely on the basis of their tenth-grade diplomas and held their own entrance examinations, selecting only the best candidates. The number of those who had passed successfully through the ten-grade schools but still failed to gain entry to college rose steadily. In 1956, for example, 263,000 students were admitted to college; but the number who had qualified by the normal standards was nearly five times as great.[9] In 1958 the number of graduates from the ten-grade schools was 1.6 million.[10] Not all of them, of course, wanted to go on to a university, and quite a number had passed their exams by so narrow a margin that they stood no chance of gaining admission. But the vast majority wanted to continue their studies. According to Khrushchev, nearly 3 million pupils who were fully qualified and anxious to enter a university or technical college failed to gain admission from 1953 to 1957.[11]

Such a state of affairs could not fail to have an effect on the schools and on the outlook of the pupils. Typical comments by students were frequently quoted in the newspapers. One girl, reproached because she was making unsatisfactory progress at school, retorted: 'What does it matter? I'll have to go into a factory anyway.' Another said much the same thing: 'I know I'm going into a factory, so what's the use of all this education?'[12] Those who have fulfilled the requirements but fail to gain admission to college constitute a discontented element that fits in nowhere. Further education is barred to them and they have no desire to go into a factory because, with diplomas in their pockets, they consider themselves above mere manual work. Tens of thousands of them hang around at home for a year, drifting and doing nothing, in the hope that somehow or other they will eventually be admitted to a university. The contradictions to which this situation has given rise are obvious. It is true that the schools provide the state with millions of recruits for industry, research, and the professions; but at the same time they encourage ambitions which the state is quite incapable of satisfying.

Merely from the point of view of numbers, the problem has become more acute each year. In the school year 1927-28 there were 169,000 full-time college students.[13] In 1959-60 there were 1,146,000 of them; if students of correspondence and evening courses were to be included, the total would rise to 2,270,000.[14]

The distribution (by professions) of those finishing university or college (excluding correspondence and evening schools) in 1959 was:

Industry, Building, Transport, Communications	108,600
Agriculture	37,500
Education	138,000
Health Services and Sport	29,500
Administration and Law	25,000
Arts	2,400

And to these must be added the graduates of technical schools of all kinds with lesser qualifications, who, in 1959, numbered 528,000 (including correspondence and evening students).[15]

Anyone who belonged to the vast army of nearly 3 million full-time students felt that he was a member of the elite. He had made it. As long as he didn't fail any of the intermediate examinations held during his university career, he would be assured of an upper-class life—of advancing steadily up the ladder of success. For many years the students had been the pride of the regime and the people. The new Moscow University, with its 16,000 students of whom 6,000 live in dormitories, is a symbol of the preferential treatment given to this section of the community. In Novosibirsk a university town is being built. Four-fifths of the Moscow students obtain grants, the more gifted receiving as much as 400 to 500 roubles a month. Their rooms in the Moscow University's dormitory cost not more than 25 roubles a month. Meals are very cheap. Lecture halls, students' quarters, and recreation rooms are luxuriously furnished; the best theatrical companies and orchestras perform in the university theatre, and there is dancing almost every evening. All this has gone to the heads of some of the students; but anyone whose work falls below standard is ruthlessly expelled and directed to some other activity—usually in industry. The majority, I think, are enthralled at the prospects in science and research, and work with enthusiasm and devotion—enthusiasm, however, for science and research, not for politics and the doctrines of Marx and Lenin. The apolitical attitude is nowhere more apparent than among Russia's students.

A further incentive to their studies is the students' exemption from normal military service. They receive elementary military training at the university, and the three senior grades at school devote one of their three weekly sports hours to similar exercises. But practical advantages of this kind are not primarily important. Nor will the proliferation of palatial universities and schools in itself guarantee successful students. The heart of the matter is the intensity of the intellectual drive—an impetus stronger in the Soviet Union today than in the somewhat tired West, and not only among the students.

But a problem of a different sort remains unsolved: the inevitable difficulties of the extension of higher education to all. The first sign that the authorities were modifying their attitude towards education appeared in the press and in books. Initially sharp admonitions were thought to be enough to alter the younger generation's ambitions. *Pravda*, for example, published a cartoon with this caption: 'Some of the young men and women who have passed through the ten-year schools seem to think it would be scandalous to ask them to work in a factory or a *kolkhoz*, and for years they lounge around and live off their parents'. The cartoon depicted a long-haired youth lying flat on his stomach in a field, a cigarette dangling from his lips, gazing at signposts indicating 'To the factory' and 'To the *kolkhoz*', and sighing, 'If only I knew what to do with my life!'[16]

The aversion to manual work does not stem from lack of the required skill; it is the result of propaganda which urged everyone to strive for promotion and success; and, apart from a Party career (not now in favour), these can be reached only through attending a university.

It is hard to say when the idea of a wholesale reform of the educational system was first raised by the Party Executive. Even as late as the Twentieth Party Congress at the beginning of 1956, Khrushchev seemed to believe that sweeping changes would not be necessary. He called for a 'stronger polytechnicalization' of the schools, but still maintained that the compulsory ten-year system, due to be fully implemented by the end of 1960, was the goal toward which Soviet education aimed.[17] A year later, such a leading Soviet educationalist as N. K. Goncharov, vice-president of the Academy of Pedagogic Sciences, believed that the solution of the problem lay in the extension of school attendance to twelve years; this, Goncharov thought, would give the schools a chance to prepare their senior pupils for practical careers.[18] At the same time many of the ten-grade schools tried to increase the time spent on shop work from 782 to 1,160 hours without, for the time being, interfering with the rest of the curriculum.

By the beginning of 1958, Khrushchev must have come to the conclusion that nothing could be achieved by partial reform. Deciding on drastic action, he struck an entirely new note at the Thirteenth Congress of the Komsomol in April 1958, when he reproached students for their contemptuous attitude towards manual work and spoke of the need for a reform of the educational system.[19] A few weeks later the first measures of this reform were announced: in the autumn of 1958, 80 per cent of the available places at the universities were to be reserved for candidates who had already done two years of practical work; only the remaining 20 per cent would go directly to graduates of the ten-year schools. (Actually only 45 per cent went straight from the work bench to university that term.[20]) The automatic admission of those who had graduated with distinction from the ten-grade school was discontinued.[21]

But these were only preliminary measures. Once this dynamic party leader formulated an idea it had to be implemented as quickly as possible. As early as September 1958 he drew up a memorandum on the educational system; it furnished the subject-matter for the 'theses' which the Central Committee of the Party and the Council of Ministers published some months later.[22] After a great deal of public debate, these 'theses' became the basis of the new school law, which the Supreme Soviet passed on 24 December 1958.[23]

The new law made a complete break with the existing system. The ten-year school, until then regarded as the ideal, was to be abandoned. In future, schools would consist of only eight grades. The pupils who passed through these schools would be required initially to take up practical—that is, predominantly manual—work in industry, agriculture, or the administrative services. During this time, in addition to their practical work, they would have the right to take a three-year course leading to a diploma that would entitle them to enter a university. But even during their first years at the university they may attend only evening lectures or take correspondence courses, as they are required to continue their practical work. Only when they have satisfied all these demands are they allowed to devote the last terms exclusively to study.

Because of the recent institution of these reforms, their effects will not be apparent for at least six or seven years.

There are indications that the new regulation will not be as strictly enforced as the law stipulates; not all the ten-year schools have been turned into eight-year schools—quite a few retained the full term, and some even were enlarged to eleven-year schools. Speculation is not within the scope of this book, but we must ask ourselves what light these reforms shed on the Soviet citizen of today, and particularly on the younger generation.

One motive—and, I think, the most important one—has already been mentioned. Khrushchev has realized the political danger inherent in the widening gap between the upper class and the masses, and the possibility of growing demands from the former which the state cannot meet.

The main reason for this innovation is, therefore, not of a practical, but of a sociological and ideological nature. With the help of the new school law, Khrushchev hopes to be able, if not to close, at least to narrow this steadily growing gap. In other words, his new school law is decisive proof that the Soviet state has become a class state. 'For years the percentage of students at the universities and technical colleges who come from the intelligentsia (that is, the upper class) has been on the increase,' Academician A. Kolmogórov admitted.[24] Only by radical measures which demolish the entire educational system—though it has served the state well and has been scholastically successful— can the Kremlin hope to lessen the disparity between the classes.

The actual development did not quite correspond to this blueprint. What had been meant to be a three-year course after practical work in factories, *kolkhozes*, and so on, turned, at least partly, into a three-year high school open to graduates of the eight-year school. Khrushchev's intention to force all the graduates of the eight-grade school, with very few exceptions, into manual work met with opposition. I felt this quite keenly when I visited the U.S.S.R. some months after the reform. It was obvious that none of the principals of the old ten-year schools was willing to give up the two upper grades without a fight. University professors did not like the prospect of getting their young people from the factory instead of from the school.[25] Factory managers, too, were quite displeased with the prospect of obtaining as part-time workers eighth-graders who would simultaneously continue their schooling. 'After all,' one of them told me, 'I need workers, not school kids; my factory is not a kindergarten.' Most unhappy of all were the parents, particularly those of the upper stratum of society, about having their children engaged in manual work after eight years of school rather than going on to the upper grades and the university.

As it turned out, the critics of Khrushchev's reform could be quite satisfied. At the beginning of the 1960-61 school year 75 per cent of the eight-year school graduates in Moscow did not go into factories but instead entered the first grade of the new three-year high school (the ninth grade of an eleven-year course). It is this eleven-year course that has practically taken the place of the pre-reform ten-year school. While Khrushchev's aim had been to confine formal education to eight grades, there are now in Moscow alone 273 three-year high schools, which to all intents and purposes means 273 eleven-year schools.[26] In order to save the upper grades, the schools had to compromise in one respect: they had to add many hours of shop work, mainly in the upper grades. While, as the table on page 129 shows, the ten-year curriculum had carried 782 periods of shop, the new curriculum of the eight-plus-three-year school provides for 2,491 periods. Still, it has remained a *school*, with shop work added to its curriculum; what Khrushchev had demanded was work in a *factory*, with some general education thrown in.[27]

This is probably not yet the end of the story. But it is remarkable that the master of the Kremlin has had to bow to the determined opposition of the intelligentsia and upper class, which, though not organized, have many ways of making their influence felt. The resulting compromise is closer to their wishes than to Khrushchev's.

Khrushchev's reforms are in harmony with his desire to sift and check the rising generation, which he regards as politically unreliable. He is anxious to curtail academic freedom. Since the

Hungarian uprising, accusations such as the following (against the students and professors of Leningrad) have appeared frequently in the Soviet press:

> There are some professors who neither help their students to an understanding of the difficult and changing problems of life confronting them, nor take any steps to refute the many erroneous and demagogic statements made by the students themselves. This is having a deleterious effect on the students' education. . . .
>
> Lectures on social science have been extremely inadequate. Those on the history of the Communist Party of the Soviet Union, on national economy and philosophy are often of a very low ideological and political standard. Pedantry and dogmatism have not been eradicated, with the result that students often learn their work mechanically, parrot-fashion.
>
> Above all, it can no longer be tolerated that some of the professors should seek in a cowardly and pusillanimous manner to avoid explaining complicated events in the political life of the nation, or demonstrating the reasons for certain inadequacies in the process of socialist evolution. . . . In future we must ensure that, of the students admitted to the universities, as many as possible come from industry.[28]

To ensure that there will be no students with 'an unhealthy outlook', paragraph 28 of the new school law stipulates that entry into a university will be granted only to those candidates who can produce satisfactory recommendations from their Party, Komsomol, and trade-union officials—in other words, only those whose political reliability has been more or less confirmed. The 'Pasternak affair' has only increased the Party leaders' mistrust of the intelligentsia.

However, we should not attribute this *volte-face* in school and university policy solely to political considerations. The second industrial revolution, the threshold of which all modern states, including the Soviet Union, have crossed with the beginning of automation, demands a more highly educated industrial worker. The young Soviet citizen of average intelligence who has completed studies in the eight-grade school and spends some years combining factory work with further study will probably be able to satisfy this increasing demand. Whether the man with special aptitude for the higher grades of technology will be helped by an apprenticeship of manual work is another question; some scientists in the Soviet Union expressed grave doubts.

No one knows exactly where this new policy will lead. But one thing is certain. The Soviet people's respect for learning will not decrease; it is far too deeply rooted. Nothing illustrates this more vividly than the immense admiration accorded the surviving pre-revolutionary intelligentsia by the sons of the revolution. Again and again, when I visited schools, I met older teachers like Marya Petrovna who have won the love of their pupils. Every cultural organization has one or more of these white-haired figures with the typical features of the intellectual of bygone days. The word 'academician' (i.e., Member of the Academy of Sciences) has a proud ring in Russia. The art galleries are replete with portraits of these old gentlemen. They have wise and kindly eyes and often wear a goatee and invariably the little skull cap that in Czarist Russia was the mark of the savant.

That the state should tolerate the veneration of the pre-war intelligentsia is understandable. The old gentlemen can no longer be of any danger to the state, but they are useful proofs of the age, dignity, and tradition of Russian learning, and they strengthen confidence in the erudition of the fatherland. The state's attitude towards these old people is not of telling importance; its relations with the younger generation of intellectuals are. But these are passing through a critical phase as, above all, the school reforms have shown. That the authorities have good reason to regard the student generation in general and the members of the *civitas academica sovietica* in particular with some suspicion will emerge in later chapters of this book. For these university students have not been entirely estranged from the proud European tradition that students are the guardians of freedom.

CHAPTER 10

A WORLD TO DISCOVER

A FEW YEARS AGO I spent some months in Moscow working for the West German broadcasting service. Every day, on my way from the Hotel Savoy (now renamed Hotel Berlin) to the censorship bureau in the Central Telegraph Office, I passed a street bookseller. His books were spread out on a rough wooden table and there were always a few people browsing through them. One day I saw, long before I got there, that a large crowd had gathered at the corner where his stall was located. A line of excited people had formed, and there was a surging mob in front of the stall. I pushed my way towards the front just in time to see the last few copies of an eagerly-sought book change hands; fifty or sixty people turned away in disappointment. The bookseller told me he had opened his stall barely a quarter of an hour earlier with a hundred copies of the book, and they had all been snapped up. He could have sold a thousand, if he had had them. The book? A collection of Greek and Roman mythology which had been published in an edition of 100,000 copies.

There was nothing particularly unusual about this incident. Every visitor to the Soviet Union is struck by the crowded bookshops and the huge editions of the classics, both Russian and foreign, that are constantly being published; by the theatrical performances that are sold out to the last seat, particularly if the play is a classic; by the unending discussions on art; by the large audiences attracted to lectures on new books; and by the many eagerly sought-after literary monthlies like *Novy Mir* (a 300-page magazine with a monthly circulation of 150,000), *Oktyábr'*, *Známya*, *Zvezdá*, and many others.

The incident at the Moscow bookstall seems noteworthy for another reason. Could there be clearer proof that the Russian's intellectual curiosity cannot be attributed solely to his urge for professional success? It is true, in a state like the Soviet Union where private ownership of the means of production is prohibited, knowledge is the surest road to success. But the exceptionally keen interest expressed in technical matters by the younger generation transcends such purely material motivations.

I remember the Russian kite and glider fliers of the early 1930's. What enthusiasm they displayed for discovery. I saw young boys launch one kite, then attach a second, a third, and a fourth to it until eventually the pull became so strong that a boy would be lifted fifty feet or more into the air.

Since those days, interest in technology has steadily increased —often at the expense of politics. Books and periodicals dealing with politics have been produced—perhaps even bought—in vast numbers, but comparatively few of them are read voluntarily, though they do contain information that, in view of the constant political pressure, is indispensable. On the other hand, the exclusion of certain kinds of publications has benefited serious reading: the innumerable sex and crime thrillers, the titillating banalities about screen stars and so forth—so prominently displayed in the magazine stands and book stores of the West and the object of billions of wasted reading hours—hardly exist in the Soviet Union.

An atmosphere with little eroticism as is that of the Soviet Union probably explains some of the intensity of intellectual life. In the West the adolescent's interest in sex is constantly stimulated; many of them are more concerned with such 'social' activities as 'dating' and 'petting' than with concentrated study. But the subject of sex is conspicuously absent from Soviet films, plays, newspapers and advertisements. A painting depicting a female nude, shown at an exhibit of contemporary art in Moscow in the winter of 1956-57, created a sensation.

What particularly strikes an observer is the naïve enthusiasm and thirst for knowledge of every kind displayed by these gifted people who have only quite recently learned to read and write. They apply themselves with a discoverer's zest to the tasks confronting them. Until a few decades ago the capacities of the vast majority of the population lay dormant; they lived out their lives uneventfully.

The violence of the subsequent upheaval is explained by the enormous talent and energy latent in the people. In the western world, the path to success has been open to all with sufficient intelligence to follow it ever since the Age of Enlightenment, when rulers and intellectual elite joined hands in a deliberate effort to educate the masses. Our schools have flourished; illiteracy has been virtually unknown for many decades;

and an unceasing process of selection has brought talent to fruition.

It was very different in Tsarist Russia, with its static social system, which began to change only at the end of the last century. Here the mighty reservoir of talent lay almost untapped, until first the industrial revolution and then the Bolshevik revolution released the well-springs from the depths.

Since this happened barely two generations ago, the people still retain their naïve faith in learning and progress; they are now going through that early phase of intellectual enthusiasm which the West has long forgotten and which has been replaced by scepticism and sophistication.

A primitive curiosity is at work in this historically young nation. It manifests itself in a thirst for knowledge, a desire to understand the world—surely one of the most fruitful of human characteristics. Soviet man would, indeed, be fundamentally different from his fellow men if he were not inquisitive and accepted unchallenged everything his rulers set before him. Fortunately he has not lost his desire to get to the bottom of things; on the contrary, he inquires into everything, and he does not stop at national boundaries.

During the difficult years after World War II the people of Europe felt an urgent and long-suppressed desire to travel again, which they satisfied as soon as visas and foreign currency became available. Since 1950, millions of Europeans—in some countries up to a quarter of the total adult population—have made trips to other nations. In the Soviet Union this urge to travel must be even stronger. The present day upper class— with the exception of some diplomats, commercial representatives, technicians, savants, artists, and very few tourists—has not been abroad at all. Since the Bolsheviks assumed power practically no such private travel has been permitted. If the Soviet Government suddenly announced that anyone who wished to travel would be given a passport and a foreign-currency allocation, at least 5 or 10 million Russians would apply. Among them would be some who had no intention of ever returning, but a large number would go simply because of an irrepressible urge to see the world for themselves.

In a book of verse published in 1958 the young poet Yevtushenko wrote:

These frontiers are a nuisance, and it irks me
To know not Buenos Aires or New York.
I'd love to wander freely all round London,
And talk with one and all, and talk and talk.
And jump from bus to bus like any Cockney,
And savour Paris in the early dawn.[1]

These lines are as typical of the feelings of Russian youth as
the philistine reproaches levelled at their author are typical of
the literary bureaucracy. To the ebullient 'Let's see the world!'
spirit of young Yevtushenko, bureaucracy replies with a dry-as-
dust reprimand:

> Mayakovsky [a leading poet who committed suicide in
> 1930] travelled abroad, but not merely for the sake of
> empty amusement. . . . He travelled as a Communist, as the
> ambassador of Soviet proletarian culture, and his behaviour
> was guided by precise ideological precepts.[2]

Realizing the strength of this urge to see the world the Soviet
government has finally begun to permit selected groups of
tourists to travel abroad. But it is trying to counteract their
favourable impressions of foreign countries by frequent negative reports of conditions there.

It is not only the lure of travel that lends fascination to a
foreign country, but everything about it, including its literature.
For a long time, the Soviet people were unable to obtain truly
representative foreign books. They were allowed only those
foreign books written by Communists or fellow-travellers, which
gave such a tendentious and distorted picture of conditions that
they were quite incapable of supplying Russian readers with
reliable information about foreign countries. One of the foreign
authors whose works received wide circulation in Moscow was
the American-fellow traveller Howard Fast; his disillusionment
with Communism and his open break with the Party in 1957—
a painful shock to Moscow—were not revealed to Soviet readers
until almost a year later.

Recently, there has been a slight increase of genuine foreign
publications available in the Soviet Union—enough, perhaps, to
whet the appetite of the intellectual elite, but certainly not
enough to satisfy them. That even this meagre fare became

available was largely due to the efforts of the new magazine *Inostránnaya Literatura* ('Foreign Literature'). Among other works, Hemingway's *The Old Man and the Sea* was translated into Russian and made a deep impression on Russian readers—and writers.

I was talking one day to a Soviet author who, not long before the Russian translation of Hemingway's novel appeared, had himself written a book about the sea—treating it not symbolically as an instrument of fate, but most prosaically as a source of fish. His book provided, in the form of a novel, a complete guide to the fishing industry, with all the necessary information about wind, weather, and currents. I asked him whether he had enjoyed Hemingway's book.

'Hemingway has written a wonderful book,' he replied frankly. 'It's rather like what I had hoped to do with my own book, but in the end mine turned out to be just another "production novel".'

Among other foreign books which have appeared in the Soviet Union in recent years, Graham Greene's *The Quiet American*, A. J. Cronin's novels, and Daphne du Maurier's *Rebecca* have been very popular. Western fashion magazines are in even greater demand than Western books and films. Every time I go to Russia I take a few with me for my friends.

All in all, the Soviet citizen learns little about Western literature, but that little is a great deal more than in Stalin's day; and as he carefully reads everything he can lay hands on, he manages to build up a fair picture of Western cultural trends. Everything from abroad arouses lively interest—orchestras, soloists, the American production of *Porgy and Bess*, exhibitions of paintings. When the treasures of the Dresden Art Gallery were exhibited in Moscow, there was such a rush to see them that people stood in lines all night to gain entrance to the museum the next morning. But the Soviet press has now begun to sound notes of warning because too many contemporary Western plays are being produced in the Soviet Union.[3]

In the spring of 1959 a young workman bombarded me with questions about life in the West. They ranged from Hemingway to hula-hoops to skin-diving equipment (which he was anxious to obtain). When I expressed surprise at the eagerness and range of his questions, he replied, 'Don't you understand? We are discovering the world!'

While I was packing to go to Moscow for the Twentieth Party Congress, I read in a Soviet paper that on the seventy-fifth anniversary of Dostoyevsky's death a new ten-volume edition of his works was to be published. Three hundred thousand copies[4] were to be printed, and they could be obtained by subscription. I was planning to arrive in Moscow three days after that date and I thought I would then still have ample time to order my subscription.

In the centre of Moscow, halfway between the Bolshoi and the Art Theatres, is the bookshop which specializes in subscription orders. It is impossible to miss it, because a large crowd, buying and selling books, is usually gathered in front. The shop is the size of an average schoolroom. On this particular day it was very full. Because of the bitter cold, transactions had been moved from the sidewalk to the inside of the shop. Instead of working my way laboriously through the crowd at the counter where orders could be placed, I asked in a loud voice: 'Where do I order the new edition of Dostoyevsky?' The lively babble of voices ceased. After a second or two there was an outburst of laughter. Taken aback, I glanced rather uncomfortably around the room. What was so funny about what I had said? I soon found out. The first day on which orders could be placed, the shop had sold its entire quota before noon. Quite a few people had stood in line the night before in the cold, taking each other's places at intervals to make sure they would be among the lucky ones. And now, three days later, along comes a fellow who thinks that all he has to do is to put down his money! No wonder they roared with laughter.

It had been the same in cities all over the Soviet Union; within a few hours the whole edition of 300,000 was sold out. If the shops had had them they probably could have disposed of a million or a million and a half copies during the day. (Later I managed to subscribe after all, in a bookshop abroad, which had not yet used up its allotment.)

Of the classical writers of Russia, none irritated the Communists more than Dostoyevsky. They did their utmost to consign him to oblivion. The last time a small edition of his works had been published was in 1926-27, just before the beginning of Stalin's dictatorship. An anthology was published in 1931, but after that, nothing. In the early 1930's all research on Dostoyevsky ceased.[5] Not a single chapter was devoted to him in a three-volume text on Russian literature. It contained merely a brief reference to him as one of a number of writers in the 1860's and 1870's. His name did not appear in the index.[6]

All this is not surprising. Dostoyevsky, the eternal seeker, whose penetrating insight was concentrated on man's soul and his relationship to God, was the personification of a world implacably hostile to Bolshevism. His Pyotr Verkhovensky in *The Possessed* foreshadowed the typical Party functionary in a prophetic and highly unflattering way. Could the authorities succeed in banishing Dostoyevsky from the minds and hearts of the Russian people? It seemed to me a significant test. It should not have been difficult. Nine-tenths of the contemporary intellectual elite—this is my own estimate, since there are, of course, no such statistics—come from families which never possessed the collected works of Dostoyevsky, or even copies of his great novels. Those families which did own them have lived through such troubled times that hardly any has managed to keep its old library intact. One might well have assumed, therefore, that a policy of silence, coupled with an occasional derogatory comment, would have succeeded in obliterating all memory of Dostoyevsky.

This has not been the case. The new intelligentsia has not accepted the way in which the Party has rewritten the nation's intellectual history. Their curiosity and their urge to judge the merits of Dostoyevsky for themselves were so overwhelming that Stalin's successors found it wise to give way.

In 1955 some of Dostoyevsky's novels were re-issued in an edition of 1,300,000 copies.[7] Then came the ten-volume edition of his complete works, including *The Possessed*, of which Gorky, his most bitter critic, had written that it was 'the most talented and at the same time the most vicious of the innumerable attempts to slander the revolutionary movements of the 1870's'. The Bolsheviks, then, have failed to 'liquidate' Dostoyevsky posthumously.

I watched the birth of independent thought at its most impressive—as if in a laboratory—during an exhibition of Polish art in 1959. It was part of a general exhibition of art from the 'socialist countries' held in the huge old Riding School in Moscow. As expected, all the other countries showed examples of 'socialist realism'; only the Poles had sent very modern works, including some abstractions. Every time I visited the Riding School—I must have spent about ten hours at the exhibition—I met with the same situation: comparatively few visitors in the other rooms, but the Polish section mobbed with groups heatedly discussing the exhibit. These groups fell into three kinds:

Those who opposed the new art clustered around the spokesmen for the official 'line' who sat behind little tables, each of which had a sign with the word 'consultant' on it. These official consultants had been put there to demolish the pretensions of the Poles. In doing this they won the approbation of the older people for exposing modernism. Some visitors who used every harsh word they could think up culminated their judgment with 'Éto isdevátel' stvo' (it's an insult!).

The second group consisted of people who could not make up their minds and who were made unsure of themselves by the pictures. One blonde girl with pigtails, who could not have been more than seventeen, suggested in a voice so soft that I could hardly follow what she said: 'But if the Polish comrades send these works to be exhibited here, then they themselves must find them beautiful.' This sentiment was widely echoed. The consultants, who were anxious not to offend the Poles, could find no satisfactory answer. Such questions showed me that many young people, face to face with these paintings, found something disturbing in them and in the fact that another nation quite openly took things seriously which had no place in the reality of Soviet life.

Curiosity, in general, is a major force causing interest in abstract art. 'Silly prohibitions awaken curiosity,' wrote a theatrical producer from Leningrad in a letter to *Komsomolskaya Pravda*. 'Abstract art would not have half as many enthusiastic supporters were it not for the constant efforts to keep them away from it.'[8]

Then there was the third group—to me by far the most interesting; the *avant-garde*, who were full of enthusiasm and were always finding new arguments to strengthen their case. When an opponent of abstract art said 'You can't even tell which is the top and which is the bottom of these pictures', one of the modernists replied promptly: 'It is a mark of the older schools of painting that the object is presented as it appears in nature;

in other words, it is clear that in a drawing of a man the head must be at the top and the feet at the bottom. But abstract artists don't portray things from nature. Therefore one must bring to their work entirely different criteria and methods.'

One young man, a student of aircraft engineering, as I learned later, was asked: 'Tell me one thing: do you really find that these Polish pictures are works of art, or do you say so for the sake of argument?' He replied: 'Whether it is art? That's something it will take years to settle. I myself don't know. All I know is that the kind of art sanctioned in the Soviet Union today bores me to tears; it always deals with things as they are. It offers us representations of our daily lives which we know only too well. They are illustrations. But art? No. For this reason I'm in favour of giving the artist a chance to experiment. And not only the artist, but the public, too. We don't want to be treated like children to whom the grown-ups say: "*This* is beautiful, and *this* is not." We want to develop our own taste. We are an adult people.'

He had spoken calmly, even to his final words, '*My vrósly naród*'—We are an adult people. But these words rang out like a challenge to every kind of spiritual oppression. They were akin to the words of the Marquis Posa in Schiller's *Don Carlos*— 'Sir, grant us freedom of thought!'—which heralded a new epoch in the history of the Western world.

The most surprising thing was that the adherents of the new art should uphold their arguments from so many different viewpoints. These young people were pioneers in a no-man's land, almost devoid of any chance of finding a sympathetic milieu in which to develop their ideas and arguments. Their call for the freedom of the artist was all the more impressive because they were defending a type of art which could not find spontaneous acceptance on a wide scale. This was probably not so much a declaration of sympathy with abstract art as an expression of the drive towards intellectual and creative freedom.

In one of the Polish rooms, a girl in her early twenties was holding forth; a Komsomol badge was pinned to her brown dress. She was talking to a young man who was about a head and a half taller than she. He listened in silence for a while, then he said:

'We all learned in school that fundamentally there are only

two philosophies. One is materialism, according to which matter is primary, and the spirit only secondary; the other is idealism, which holds that the spirit comes first, and matter is secondary. You are a materialist, and this is also the attitude of our state. A materialist will naturally prefer objective art, portrayals of a *kolkhoz* or a steel plant—that I can well understand. But I—I'm an idealist, therefore art means something different to me from what it does to you.'

For a moment the girl was speechless. It was as if somebody in the days of the Inquisition had declared that he did not believe in God. The faces of the other listeners showed interest, but no one took sides.

'What did you say? You're an idealist? Then there is nothing for us to talk about!'

'Of course,' he answered quietly. 'This is not so much a question of art as of philosophy.' The girl with the Komsomol badge seemed to be baffled; then she shrugged her shoulders, turned, and walked away.

I said to the young man: 'What you say about idealism leads, in its logical conclusion, to religion.'

He looked at me unflinchingly and replied with one word: '*Bezuslóvno*' ('Undoubtedly').

'Do you go to church?' I asked.

'No. If I lived in another century, or in another country, I probably would. But here I can't, both for external and personal reasons. So, instead, I look at this type of picture.'

A young man, probably a student, joined in the conversation by asking: 'If other people thought as you do, what would become of the *Kollectiv*?'

In his calm manner, without the slightest suggestion of provocation in his tone, the 'idealist' replied: 'For me humanity is not made up of collectives but of individuals; everyone must work out his fate for himself and must himself struggle to find the answers to the great questions of life.' The other glanced at him, not with hostility but with surprise, quite openly uncertain whether the 'idealist' was speaking in all seriousness or whether he was joking. But it was impossible to find the answer in the young man's expression. The other one walked away, shaking his head.

Then a man in his thirties intervened. 'Can you please explain to me, how does Kandinsky fit into this whole thing? He has been painting pictures of that kind for a long time.'

'I'm not well versed in art history,' the young man said, 'I didn't go beyond the tenth grade. But so far as I know, Kandinsky was experimenting with painting of this kind well before and during World War I. Now what kind of a period was that? It was a time in which men were seeking new truths, a period of transition when the old dogmas, religious and otherwise, were no longer valid, and new ones had not yet been found. We, too, are living in a period like that, and that's why so many people feel that this kind of painting has something to say to them.'

Meanwhile, a new defender of abstract art took the plunge and joined in the arguments with fresh vigour. Soon an old man and a number of other persons in their forties, of unspecified occupations or professions, attached themselves to the group. All were highly critical of abstract painting. The new spokesman for the 'modernists' stood his ground for a little while without producing any new arguments; then I saw him break off suddenly and hurry over to a girl he had spotted. Some of the onlookers laughed at his sudden change of interest.

'Ah!' sighed the old man, 'it's no laughing matter. Our young people worry me. How can they see anything beautiful in such paintings?'

'They don't see anything beautiful in them at all,' said another elderly man. 'They behave like this just to impress everybody.'

'I'm not so sure,' said someone. 'They are true to type, our youngsters. No sooner does something from the West drift our way than they go into ecstasies over it.'

A thin man with the face of a mouse and a tiny moustache then said in measured tones, as if to give his words a special significance: 'You keep on talking about *youth*; but it is really only a question of a very small minority. I come here often and I know all the enthusiasts for abstract art who come here. They don't amount to more than fifty.'

'But those fifty can infect hundreds,' one of the old men said.

And another replied, 'All right, hundreds, but not hundreds of thousands. And above all, the whole thing is only a lot of nonsense. We were all young once.'

Mouse-face was of a different opinion. 'It is something more than youthful folly; more than enthusiasm for a particular fashion in art criticism. It is a question of politics. These young people constitute a *fronde'* (he used the foreign term), 'a political *fronde.'*

There was no comment. I, too, remained silent. The speaker was not wrong; in a dictatorship questions of aesthetics often take on a political significance.

To get this into proper perspective I asked myself: Is the problem of these young art rebels an exceptional phenomenon, involving so few young people that it hardly matters, or is there, in fact, a *fronde* of discontented and angry young men, as there is in the West? It was not only at the art exhibition that I found people ready to think doggedly for themselves; it also happens on the stage. When I arrived in Moscow, *Nikolái Ivánovich,* by the woman playright L. Geráskina, was playing to crowded houses at the Drama and Comedy Theatre. I went to see it because I had heard that it dealt with an intellectual milieu. The principal conflict was between the hero of the title—he is the director of a school—and Márya Ivánovna, who teaches Russian literature in the senior grades. The director is passionately devoted to the highest ideals of education, and his aim is to train youngsters to think for themselves; the woman teacher—unmistakably the 'negative heroine' of the play—is a disciplinarian of the old school. In her eyes the ideal pupil is one who has no thoughts other than those pedantically taught by her. One girl, for example, is sent out of the room because she has had the audacity to question the literary views expressed by the teacher. The teacher says with heavy sarcasm: 'One listens and is amazed. . . . You *think!* Who profits by it? I have given you material to work on, and now it's up to you to give an account of it without interjecting any of your own stupidity.'

In his continual battles with Marya Ivanovna, the director rejects her methods because all her teachings are handed down from above. 'Young people,' he protests, 'are eager to think for themselves, so we must listen to their questions.'

Marya Ivanovna replies: 'And if, in that way, they fall into the devil knows what kind of heresy, do we have to listen patiently too? We know from years of experience that a discussion can lead to dangerous situations. Where are the young people to get their ideas from? Methods such as you suggest encourage

them to criticize and scoff at everything. Our duty is to train
them to be patriots.'

The director replies emphatically: 'Do you really believe that
you are making them patriots?'

The results of Marya Ivanovna's methods can be seen in one
of the pupils, Sergey. This highly gifted youngster poses as a
completely disillusioned cynic who believes in nothing and thinks
only of himself. He writes poems as a release for his bitterness,
as a reaction against the lies and deceit that surround him. He
sees people live without ideals, interested only in their own
well-being. Whose fault is it that Sergey has become like that?
There is nobody to blame but Marya Ivanovna. He complains
bitterly to his schoolfellows: 'She has lied to us constantly that
everything is wonderful for us here in the Soviet Union. She
depicted life in a *kolkhoz* as a paradise on earth! But once, when
we had to dig potatoes in a *kolkhoz* . . . '

Sergey doesn't finish the sentence; but it is obvious that none
of his listeners had found the *kolkhoz* a paradise on earth.

From that time on, the teacher's high-sounding patriotic
phrases ceased to have the desired effect on him. They achieved
just the opposite of what they were supposed to.

Finally Marya Ivanovna leaves the school. The director tries
to instil courage in her timid successor. 'Think, for God's sake,
think!' he says. 'Make mistakes—suffer—but please, *please*,
think!'

People do not want to live indefinitely in the grip of intellectual taboos. Everybody wants to find out for himself and form
his own judgment, also about foreign lands.

Herein lies the significance of the foreign exhibitions. For
almost three million Soviet citizens who flocked to see, for
example, the American exhibition in 1959, this was the widest
available window to the outside world. It is small wonder that
while the exhibition was in progress the Soviet press kept up
an uninterrupted flow of attacks on the United States in an
attempt to counter its influence. But the stream of visitors never
slackened; the people wanted to see for themselves.

Fortunately, the Americans seized the opportunity offered
them, showing not only the latest in washing-machines, but also
providing cultural stimuli. They created an unprecedented and
much appreciated impression of enduring value with the con-

certs given by the New York Philharmonic Orchestra. From an
acquaintance I heard about the effect of one of these concerts.
The great Tchaikovsky Hall was filled to overflowing with
Moscow music-lovers, including many young people. The programme embraced many works not heard for years in the Soviet
Union, such as Stravinsky's 'bourgeois-formalistic' *Sacre du
Printemps* and his concerto for piano and wind instruments. In
his introductory words, the celebrated young conductor of the
orchestra, Leonard Bernstein, said: 'When Stravinsky wrote *Le
Sacre du Printemps* in 1912, he started a musical revolution—
five years before your Revolution.'

The orchestra also earned overwhelming applause for its performance of *The Unanswered Question*, by the modern American
composer Charles Ives. On that evening new musical horizons
were opened for the people of Moscow, who had come to hear
something different from the familiar classics.

It is not only the world outside that the Soviet people are discovering, but they are also making new discoveries about themselves, opening their nation's intellectual treasure-store, which
has been closed to them for many years. In my conversations
with Russians, above all with young people, I kept hearing the
name of Sergey Yesénin; and it is now possible to talk of a
Yesenin revival in the Soviet Union. This richly endowed lyric
poet—perhaps the most gifted Russian poet of our century—
took his own life in 1925. Under Stalin he was the object of
hostile official literary criticism. His work was not published.
But the young people have rediscovered him.

One Sunday in Moscow, I was present at a family gathering
when the talk turned to Yesenin; the young people began to
read his poetry, reciting some of his verses in unison.

On another occasion I was talking to two Russian girls. One
was a technician in a factory, the other a student of physics.
When I asked them what they read, they told me they were
both admirers of Yesenin.

One said to me: 'When I was in Leningrad I got a waiter in
the Hotel Angleterre to show me the room where Yesenin took
his life.' And the other found it highly romantic that the poet
had written a poem in his own blood.

One day, when I was working in the Lenin Library in Moscow, the biggest in the country, I saw an announcement on the

bulletin-board drawing attention to a special Yesenin evening in the lecture hall. After considerable difficulty I managed to get a ticket. The hall was filled to overflowing.

The audience, about half of them young people, listened with deep emotion for two hours. When the narrator finished they were still unsatisfied; he had to go on reciting Yesenin's poems for another half-hour. I glanced around and saw many of the listeners repeating the verses to themselves silently, so well did they know them.

For some Russians, of course, pursuit of knowledge is not the only reason for their avid reading. Some simply like to show off—for example, with the liberal use of quotations. In this respect the Russians do not differ from other people. Not long ago a dictionary of quotations entitled *Krylátiye Slová* (*Winged Words*) appeared in Moscow. Although 165,000 copies were printed, they were snapped up so eagerly that I had great difficulty in obtaining one for myself.

There are, of course, a number of people who show not the least interest in learning. One hears such remarks as 'Why should I bother? The people at the top get the best of everything anyway.' The people at the top (in Russian *oní*, literally 'they', a very popular expression today) are the members of the upper class in general and the officials of the Party and government in particular.

Such an attitude is understandable. But it is startling to discover it as well among those who are industrious and not hostile to the state. A Soviet writer, Lev Kassil, has illustrated this attitude in his account of a conversation he had with a young worker in a Moscow hostel:

> My handsome, broad-shouldered companion was wearing a smartly cut coat, a Russian shirt with a carelessly buttoned collar, and boots over the tops of which his trousers were neatly rolled. Scarcely had we begun to talk in general terms about books, art, and scientific discoveries when he waved the subjects aside and spat expertly into the far corner of the room. 'No, you must forgive me,' he said. 'I'm fed up with that sort of thing. I've got enough to live on, and that's that. I mean, what's the point? I've completed my training in a trade, I've got my job, and that's

all that matters. At the moment we are in great demand. Without our know-how they'd get nowhere. Building— above all, housing construction—is at the top of the list today. Right?'

'But I'm told you are regarded as a first-class foreman,' I interrupted. 'You're certainly not lazy, you seem to be efficient, and you could go far. . . . Doesn't the prospect interest you?'

'I don't see anything particularly interesting in it. I'll soon be able to buy a motor bike. That will suit me fine. I'm earning over a thousand a month, and the great thing is that every day when I finish work I'm free. If I start going in for higher education I'll find myself sitting around with a grant of, at best, three hundred roubles—and that only if I pass the exams. If eventually I become an engineer, they'll make me a *nachal'nik*. I'll be earning little more than now—and I'll be saddled with responsibility for the rest of my life. What would I get out of it? It doesn't make sense! As things are, I can well afford to pour one down the hatch whenever I like. . . . '

And his colleagues said of him: 'He's the best man on the job, and naturally he thinks of himself first.'[9]

Another writer indicates that this attitude is not confined to men. Galina has been studying medicine in Moscow, but has given up her studies to marry an engineer. A few years later she runs into her former teacher. Here are some of the comments she makes to him:

'Quietly and gradually the urge had taken root and ripened in me to order my affairs in such a way that while I put into my life what was its due, I should get in return the chance to enjoy all its pleasures to the full. So on the one hand I applauded all the splendid and high-minded sentiments expressed in films, and on the other I yearned rather enviously for glamour—even though that might mean the life of an aristocrat. In my heart I rejected utterly the self-sacrifice of which so much is written in our Soviet books. Nor was that all. I began to "philosophize" with my friend Rimma—you remember her, of course—on the question of how much longer self-sacrifice will continue to be demanded

of us. Even when Communism triumphs, won't it still be
the same? Won't the hero still be asked to sacrifice himself unquestioningly, or, to be more accurate, to sacrifice
his comfort, his well-being, his time, his health, and his
peace of mind? At Rimma's parents' house a small group
of engineers and managers used to meet regularly. Sitting
around the table, and ignoring our presence, they, too, used
to say the same thing. I remember thinking at the time:
It's all very well for teachers to preach that sort of thing;
they only try to convince us because they feel it is their
duty, because the school curriculum demands it. But these
engineers, who are extremely well-informed, are under no
obligation to convince anybody, so they can speak freely
and frankly. All this stuff offered to us in the cinema, in
books and lectures, is nothing but propaganda. . . .

Nor am I willing to sacrifice myself today. When great
men willingly sacrifice themselves, that's a different thing.
Their attitude is both understandable and justifiable. But
my sacrifice won't enrich anybody's life. Don't misunder-
stand me. I have no intention of taking everything life has
to offer and giving nothing in return. For example, I don't
agree with Rimma that there is no need to work. But in
return I do expect to be allowed to enjoy my own life to
the full and without restrictions. Surely it should be possible to reconcile the two? Why should a desire to enjoy
life be regarded as something reprehensible?

When I hear people talking about 'true happiness' in an
ice-cold shack in the virgin lands, or out there in the *taygá*
at the world's end, I can't help thinking: well, obviously,
it takes very little to make these people happy'.[10]

Those Russians who prefer the 'easy life' seek their relaxation,
when the day's work is done, in the lighter forms of entertainment provided by foreign films. They like these films because
they are free of all problems and politics. Those not too frequent
films from the Western countries, in which important questions
are treated seriously, are generally banned. Although they do
not present an alluring image of non-Communist life, they inspire self-criticism and contradict the propaganda line of 'a degenerate West stupidly reeling to its downfall'. The trashier

foreign films are regarded by the Kremlin with equanimity; indeed they are favoured, because they fit in conveniently with the Party's anti-Western propaganda. In recent years Russian films and books have also shown a tendency to be less ponderous. Nevertheless, an intense effort towards intellectual self-improvement still governs the pattern and rhythm of life. And, unless I misread the signs, it will continue to do so for many years to come. It is therefore a factor we must take into consideration in our assessment of international affairs.

But the Kremlin, too, should bear it in mind. This natural thirst for knowledge, which the regime is exploiting, will inevitably stimulate the critical faculties. If the processes of human thought are to develop at all, they must develop as a whole; to exclude certain intellectual needs is not, in the long run, possible.

For years the state, through newspapers, magazines, films, books, radio, television, and Party gatherings, has hammered one slogan into the minds of its citizens: We must produce more goods more quickly! Evolve swifter production techniques, build faster planes! And each one of these appeals is, in fact, an appeal to the critical faculty. For what must you do if you want to design a better machine or a faster plane? The first thing you must do is to examine the existing type critically, studying in detail every part of it, and ask yourself in what respect it is unsatisfactory and in need of improvement.

It is quite impossible to foster the critical faculty and expect it to confine itself to machines—and not concern itself with forms of government and human relations. When you teach a man to think, you teach him at the same time—whether you intend to or not—to criticize. Therein lies our chief hope—a hope we cherish as we watch the Russians follow their difficult road.

CHAPTER 11

FREEDOM OF THOUGHT

ONCE, on a two-day train trip in Siberia, I met a man who proved to be the embodiment of the perplexities confronting the intellectual Russian. I travelled in a coach that was enlivened by the presence of two very vivacious women conductors. One of them, Tamára, was strikingly attractive, and, whenever she was off duty, all the would-be lady-killers on the train gathered around her in the two girls' compartment. Occasionally I joined them and we were all very happy together, joking and singing —until the chief conductor found out and put an end to this unauthorized gaiety by driving us back to our own compartments. It was then that I invited one of Tamara's admirers to join me in my compartment and continue the conversation we had begun earlier. He had told me that he was a writer, and he was carrying a bulky typewritten manuscript which he showed to all and sundry.

'Tell me,' I said, 'what are you doing in the wilds of Siberia?'

'Looking for ideas,' he replied emphatically. 'Looking for a theme for a novel.'

Then he settled down to tell me all about it. He had sketched out the plot of a novel and had had it accepted by one of the state publishing houses. He delivered it chapter by chapter to the publisher and received the advance payments agreed upon. Finally, with great pride, he had delivered the last chapter. But the publisher had bad news for him. 'I'm sorry,' he said, 'but we won't publish your book after all. And I'm afraid I must ask you to repay the advance or submit an alternative, acceptable manuscript.'

The reason? A change in the Party line. Stalin had just been exposed at the Twentieth Party Congress—and Stalin was the hero of his novel. I did my best to console him. 'Couldn't you cut Stalin out of the book?' I asked. 'Why not alter the plot a bit and make it acceptable?'

'That's the tragedy,' he replied, with a dejected gesture, 'Stalin runs like a golden thread through the whole book. I was particularly proud of the way I had succeeded in weaving him in so that plot and hero became indivisible. . . . If I cut Stalin out, the whole book will fall to pieces!'

I expressed my sympathy, but it was hardly any consolation to him. He was furious and did not hesitate to show it, even to a stranger from abroad. When he left me, I said, 'You take my tip. Wait three years. By that time Stalin will have been sufficiently rehabilitated, and your book will be taken without alterations.' He snorted, and his expression showed that he was in no mood for joking. However, rather than joking, I was really making a prediction. As it happened, I was a poor prophet; Stalin's partial rehabilitation came much sooner. Within a year my companion could have had his book published. For all I know, perhaps he did.

This encounter showed that in a way anti-Stalin pressure was having an effect on Soviet intellectuals similar to that created by pro-Stalin pressure earlier. But while a few years earlier, when the old dictator was still alive, young Soviet authors would have regarded such treatment as a matter of course, they now dared to voice their displeasure. Under Stalin the people had lived in one huge barracks. No leave was granted, and the daily routine from morning till night was carefully outlined for every one of them. The people had never known anything different, and they plodded on without any undue grumbling among the ranks. Evidently men find it easier to put up with constant coercion to which they have become accustomed than to endure it once they have had a taste of freedom. Things formerly accepted without complaint then begin to irritate them. The question is: Will the living spirit of Russia eventually become accustomed to the narrow channels the state has prescribed, or will it one day feel the urge to overflow unchecked?

Stalin's dictatorship lay on the intellectual life of the people like the heavy iron lid on a pot. No one really knew what was inside the pot, or whether there was anything inside it at all— except the turgid broth, made from the official recipe, which for a quarter of a century had been dished out as Soviet cultural life. During the years since Stalin's death, nothing has aroused my curiosity so much as the contents of that pot. I waited eagerly to see what would emerge, for no form of culture is more characteristic, more readily accessible, or more illuminating than the world of literature.

Scarcely was Stalin dead and the lid lifted than the pot began unmistakably to boil; with relief the world realized that it contained, after all, something other than the familiar and detested stew. The first signs came in the form of lively criticism of the political control of literature. A scant six weeks after Stalin's death the lyric poet Olga Berggolts wrote:

> Our poets devote themselves to important themes, but the librarians tell us that many of the new volumes remain untouched on their shelves. At any literary soirées when a lyric poet is present notes are frequently passed up from the audience: 'Please read us something lyrical.' There you have it! What we had already read to them obviously was not regarded as lyrical, and the reason, I think, is that so much of our verse lacks the most important element of all —the human element, man himself.
>
> Equally to blame for the way in which artificial emotions have been substituted for human feelings are those sanctimonious critics who raise a cry of 'pessimism and decadence' at the slightest sign in any poem of misgivings or grief on the part of the poet (for example, over the loss of a loved one), particularly if this moment of melancholy is not instantly banished and the situation restored by some joyful event, such as the success of the bereaved lover in exceeding his quota in the production of cattle fodder. . . . The deadly balancing out of fake emotions means that the reader finds in poetry no reflection of the many burning and vital problems, passions, and experiences that fill his own life. Love has all but disappeared from our lyrics.[1]

Ilya Ehrenburg once declared roundly that in controlled literature it is not human beings, but pieces of machinery, not human emotions, but production processes that are described. Even the most brazen of publishers in Tsarist days, he wrote, would not have dared to dictate their plots to a Chekhov, a Tolstoy, or a Gorky; but in the U.S.S.R., where this is the normal practice, innumerable books owe their creation not to their authors' ideas but to the instructions of editors. As a result of constant interference, authors are not inclined to write anything derogatory about the present—even if it is only about the weather. Writers, Ehrenburg said in conclusion, have been relegated to the status of army clerks.[2]

The critic V. Pomerantsev goes a step further. He brings up the whole question of writing as a profession. The insistence of the political authorities that everything should be seen through rose-coloured glasses results, he asserts, in a flood of stereotyped and quite unreadable books.

> These things are not novels—they are mass-produced goods. If you've read one, you've read them all. . . . You could well believe that they were not created by men, but rolled off the assembly line. . . . When an author speaks to me of 'my book', I always retort, 'What do you mean, *your* book? What's in it that's yours?'[3]

Pomerantsev is indignant over the cowardice of authors, their constant concern to 'cover their rear' (*perestrakhóvka*); he pours bitter scorn on all who laboriously adopt the prevailing—and so variable—politico-literary line as the model for their work.

When the Party line, which had long demanded only positive heroes, suddenly veered and called for both positive and negative characters in opposition to one another, one writer, Pomerantsev tells us, cried out despairingly at a meeting of the Soviet Writers' Association: 'Comrades, what am I to do? I've just finished a book in which all the characters are positive!' Pomerantsev agrees that writers have good reason to be apprehensive. They have been delivered into the hands of the state publishing monopoly. They have been confronted, he says, with critics who are professional slanderers and snoopers, and who produce 'not reviews, but court judgments'. He implores Soviet writers:

> You must know what you are fighting for. Don't bother your heads about the state prosecutors. Do not write a single line that you do not feel. Be independent. . . . The honest writer must not bother about the expression on the reader's face, whoever the reader may be.

But even more convincing than these theoretical effusions is the new spirit that has emerged in the works of the writers themselves. The first book to arouse comment because of its freedom from ideological slogans and its concentration on the human factor was Vera Panova's novel *The Four Seasons*. Where she has allowed politics to creep in, it has obviously been done as an afterthought and as a sop to the censors.

It is interesting, for example, to compare the first and last entries of a diary incorporated in the book. The keeper of the diary is a schoolboy named Seryozha who suffers from tuberculosis.

> January 12. The unknown girl was at the skating rink again. The young men all clustered around her, but she took no notice of any of them.
>
> January 13. Went to the skating rink. The unknown girl flashed by and looked at me. Our eyes met. I deliberately stayed where I was until she came around again. Once more she looked at me. I thought to myself that in theory, anyway, a woman can learn to love a man who has a physical disability. But the question is: can she love him without indulging in that feeling of pity which is so wounding to a man? If she can't, then all is over between us. She was wearing a white fur cap, with long ear-flaps.
>
> January 18. Went to the rink of the Inland Waterways Trade Union. A miserable rink. They're professional watermen, and they can't get themselves a decent skating rink! . . .
>
> February 5. Oh, these women! Today I went to the cinema. Just as the lights were going down, she appeared in her white cap, arm in arm with some lout. . . . The usherette showed them to their seats, and they rushed down the aisle hand-in-hand. After the show I didn't see her again, and I was glad.
>
> A truce to tears, enough of pain!
> A curse upon thee, treacherous one
> Who caused my heart to bleed in vain!
>
> A good lesson for all idiots who hang around skating rinks and damned near catch pneumonia! I cast you from my heart forever.

And then, out of context but ideologically 'correct', comes the next entry:

> February 15. Night. There has just been an announcement on the radio—an event of historical importance; the

U.S.S.R. and the Chinese People's Republic have just concluded a treaty.

A novel better known in the West than Vera Panova's is *The Thaw* by Ilya Ehrenburg. Ehrenburg, who has a particularly sharp nose for any changes in the political climate, published this novel shortly after Stalin's death. The Russian title, *Óttepel'*, was soon adopted throughout the world to describe the first post-Stalin period. But while the word 'thaw' is closely connected for us with slush and mud, the Russian word, derived from *tepló* (warm), evokes the end of winter's icy grip and the first promise of spring.

Ehrenburg, too, dispensed with political jargon. 'Ideas don't pay,' says one of his characters, a young painter, 'but they can certainly break your neck!' As often happens in contemporary Soviet novels, the 'old idealists' find themselves face to face with the sober, at times even cynical, younger generation. The most positive character in the book is an old teacher who had played a part in the victory of the Revolution. He is depressed because he feels that he speaks with the voice of a past the young no longer understand. Young people say of him:

> It's laughable. . . . Father idealizes everybody. He's probably still thinking about the girls who 'joined the people' [a favourite phrase of the nineteenth-century revolutionaries] or who fought for the Revolution and ended in a prison. Nowadays girls marry film producers or factory managers.[4]

But the thaw did not last long. By the beginning of 1954, less than a year after Stalin's death, an icy wind was blowing again, although the counter-offensive was conducted with less disastrous results for writers. By the time of the Second Congress of the Writers' Association at the end of 1954, the writers were once again marching together in step, in good order, and under military discipline.

When I compare it with the first Writers' Congress of 1934, which I attended, I realize how low the standard has sunk. Then, Maxim Gorky was the chief speaker. He was, of course, long past his peak as a writer; at sixty-six he was already a very old man, bowed under the burdens of a hard life, the most bitter part of which had been the few years when he had had to pay for Stalin's grace and favour with a series of compromises that weighed heavily on his conscience. The Kremlin cherished him; he had been won back with difficulty from residence in Italy to enhance Soviet prestige at home and abroad. But his once-prolific pen had now run dry. His speech, with its superficial review of pro-Bolshevik world literature (in which he cited Till Eulenspiegel and Sherlock Holmes as the great heroes), was unworthy of him. Even so, the humanity of the man, those features so eloquent of suffering and pity, endowed the Congress with an air of reverence which even Zhdanov's inflammatory utterances could not destroy.

But the highlight of the 1934 Congress was the statement by Bukharin. He was then the leading Party theoretician and had been one of the most famous of Lenin's comrades-in-arms. He inveighed in his theses on lyrical poetry against the prevailing tendency to make literature a tool of politics. He appealed for the restoration of the standards which had been lost in the general tendency to hail every line written even by a completely unknown author as literature if only the writer was a 'proletarian'. With courage he used a Latin quotation that is the direct antithesis of the Stalinist doctrine: *Nascuntur poetae* (i.e., poets are born, not made). To his audience—mostly writers engaged in the mass-production of heroes of cast-iron and concrete—he held up Goethe's *Faust* as an example which none could hope to equal, but to which all should aspire; and he asserted that Demyán Bédny, the much-praised laureate of the Kremlin, and men like him, did no more than string together political slogans in metre. On the other hand Boris Pasternak, then known to only a few of the connoisseurs, was, he declared, a true poet. It was no wonder that Bukharin did not bask for long in the sunshine of Stalin's favour. Four years later, after a scandalous public trial, his life ended in a GPU cellar.

Nevertheless, under an apparently conformist surface, the pot continued to simmer. The revolt of the literary conscience after Stalin's death recurred after his 'second death' at the Twentieth Party Congress of 1956, when the late dictator was morally liquidated. It is true that Khrushchev was not addressing writers when he spoke of the reappraisal by historians of the Stalin era, but the writers were anxious not to lag behind the historians.

A number of courageous works appeared at once; Dudintsev's biblically titled *Not by Bread Alone* was only one, although the best known, of many. In much the same vein, and published at about the same time, was Daniel Granin's *Mind of His Own*, which depicts the struggle of an idealistic young inventor against the forces of bureaucracy.[5] In his pessimism (for which he has been sharply criticized) Granin goes much further than Dudintsev. The bureaucrat who stands in the way of the young inventor had himself once been young and idealistic; thus Granin implied that the hero, too, will one day become older, more cautious, and more selfish, and will no longer judge things on their merits, but from the viewpoint of expediency.

Even the carefully muted Soviet press could not conceal the fact that books like these had a profound effect on the younger generation. In May 1957 the Party writer Leoníd Sóbolev compared the effect of Dudintsev's novel to an atomic explosion.[6] But while Dudintsev's and Granin's heroes were described as isolated cases, their creators discovered a host of like-minded people. Many names—some new, some already well known— thrust themselves before the public during the winter of 1956-57.

Judging by Khrushchev's own words,[7] the second volume of *Literatúrnaya Moskvá*[8] (published in an edition of 75,000 copies at the end of 1956) was regarded by the Party as particularly dangerous. Its 800 pages are full of encouragement to heretical thoughts about the Soviet state; it contains poems by writers considered undesirable by the Party, such as Ivan Katáyev, who ended his life in exile, and Marína Tsvetáyeva, who returned to the Soviet Union from abroad and committed suicide in 1941. Equally illuminating is the issue of *Den' Poézii*[9], containing Pasternak's ambiguous words about long-lost friends in his epilogue to *Doctor Zhivago* (which, along with a few other poems from the novel is about all the Soviet public has been allowed to see of Pasternak's masterpiece).[10] The works of the late emigré Búnin, defamed for decades by the Soviet authorities, and winner of the Nobel Prize for literature, were published in five volumes in 1956. Among new novels, particular interest was shown in Anna Váltseva's *Apartment 13*, which boldly portrays the social layers of Soviet society as exemplified by a number of people living under the same roof ranging from a retired officer of the state security forces to a political undesirable who has been pardoned and has just returned from a Siberian camp.[11]

The publication of these works in the very months when the whole of the Soviet empire was being shaken by the events in Hungary and Poland was a bitter pill for the Party to swallow. There was almost an element of desperation in the way it tried to bring these undisciplined writers to heel. It strongly resisted their demand for freedom of the mind. *Pravda* assailed all who, 'in the guise of taking up arms for freedom of thought, were in reality fighting against direction and control of the arts by the Party'.[12] The artist was to be no more than a pedantic clerk whose task was to illustrate faithfully the Party line. In its campaign, the Party made use of the Writers' Association's journal, *Literaturnaya Gazeta*. Here are a few significant extracts:

> Never before has anyone screamed so loudly about freedom and democracy as the murderers of Egyptian children [at Suez] and the instigators of the counter-revolutionary rising in Hungary are screaming today. . . . The bourgeois reactionaries never cease trying to exploit such slogans as 'Creative art must have absolute freedom'; 'Literature must be completely independent of politics'; 'Art is above class distinctions'—all of them fallacies long since exposed by Marxism-Leninism.[13]
>
> When class war is in progress, there can be no real freedom for the arts without the guidance and support of the people's government.[14]
>
> We are no friends of freedom as a thing in itself. We are opposed to that kind of literary freedom which strikes at the fundamental principles of loyalty to a cause. The only freedom of thought we support is freedom within the framework of Marxist-Leninist doctrine.[15]

From the beginning of 1957, the independent-minded writers were subjected to a veritable bombardment of admonitions and threats. But for the first time in many years they stood firm, with Dudintsev in the forefront. That spring, in a meeting of the Moscow branch of the Writers' Association (by far the most important branch in the country) at which he was violently attacked by the Association's bureaucrats, Dudintsev had the courage to stand up and demand freedom for writers. In his speech he quoted a personal experience during the catastrophic defeats of 1941:

> I well remember the first days of the war in defence of our fatherland. I was in a fox-hole, and there was an air battle raging over our heads. The Messerschmitts were shooting down all our planes, even though we were numerically superior. At that moment something snapped inside me, because I had always been told that our fighters were better and faster than anybody else's. I have been accused of gloomy, pessimistic tendencies. It is not true. All I ask is that we shall never see a repetition of what we saw then. And I have the right to ask it.

Dudintsev's critics dubbed him 'panic-monger'. He retaliated by accusing them of avoiding genuine and constructive discussion:

> Surely it should be possible to let go of us, as one does with beginners in the water, and to let us swim on our own. We wouldn't drown. But, alas, I am conscious all the time of the safety line with which they hold up little children, and it prevents me from swimming.[16]

In May there was a plenary session of the Writers' Association; those most bitterly attacked were either absent or refused to speak, so their behaviour was described as a 'conspiracy of silence'. Sobolev, a staunch Party man, rose in great excitement and pleaded with the rebellious writers to break silence. He said:

> This silence of yours is dangerous. It confuses your readers. Don't you realize that those among you who should have come forward today and have not done so will be hypocritically encouraged by the Western press? That the 'hand of friendship' held out to you will be steeped in poison? That if you entrust yourselves to the arms waiting to welcome you, they will crush the life out of you? That the lasso has already been thrown over you to drag you still farther from your own people? Don't you realize that you are giving our enemies a pretext to talk about the 'heroism of silence'? Heroism of silence, indeed! What a foul and poisonous perversion of the truth! Very well—stay silent.

History will pass the final judgment on your 'heroism of silence'.[17]

Khrushchev himself was obliged to intervene. He made three speeches to the writers, full of threats and specific instructions about their future work. Here is a sample:

> People who lose touch with the solid ground beneath their feet, and stray from the right path . . . have a false and distorted conception of the task of literature. They seem to think it is their duty to look only for defects, and to speak primarily about the negative aspects of life. . . . They are the disseminators of false and injurious ideas and opinions. . . . Dudintsev's book is a conglomeration of false and negative assertions that makes tendentious attacks on us from a hostile standpoint. . . . He deliberately uses glaring colours and takes a malicious pleasure in exposing such weaknesses as exist. . . . It is an attempt to present reality through a distorting mirror. . . . A libellous book like Dudintsev's . . . is an attempt through literature and art to inject foreign and bourgeois ideas into the minds of the Soviet people.[18]

Such massive and concentrated pressure could not fail eventually to subdue all opposition. At a meeting of the Prose Section of the Moscow branch of the Association Dudintsev said he now realized that 'by and large, the criticisms levelled at my book have been fair and just'.[19] Vera Panova's next novel, *A Sentimental Story*, set in the 1920's (practically ancient history), was completely colourless[20]; and Granin, in *After the Wedding*, sang a hymn of praise in honour of Khrushchev's agrarian policy.[21]

But there was more that could be done by anyone who wanted to please the Party bosses. He could, for example, make a direct attack on his recalcitrant colleagues in a novel. Vsévolod Kóchetov produced, in *The Brothers Yershov*, a thorough-going anti-Dudintsev novel.[22] One of his principal characters is an inventor, though of a different stamp from Dudintsev's Lopatkin. Lopatkin is an ascetic, fanatical technician, while Kochetov's Krutilich is an unprincipled man who chases women; Lopatkin fights in a good cause, while Krutilich thinks only of himself; Lopatkin is a genuine inventor, while Krutilich only plays the part, and if by chance something good comes from his drawing-board it is sure to be a plagiarism. Kochetov follows this simple formula all through the book. He attacks the tendencies that have irritated the Party in recent years by the simple process of portraying as scoundrels those who display them.

The *cause célèbre* of the campaign against the freedom of writers was, of course, the 'Pasternak affair'. During the 'thaw' Pasternak optimistically submitted his more or less autobiographical *Doctor Zhivago* to the literary journal *Novy Mir*. After some time, the book was rejected in a long letter whose contents were not divulged until two years later.[23] The rejection was made on the grounds that the book was contrary to the spirit of the times. In the meantime, however, a draft had found its way into the hands of the Italian publisher Feltrinelli. When it became known in Moscow that Feltrinelli proposed to publish an Italian translation, the Soviet Embassy in Rome did its utmost to dissuade him; so did Alexey Surkov, the trusted First Secretary of the Writers' Association. It was this intervention by Moscow that first thrust the book and its author into world headlines, a whole year before the award of the Nobel Prize. Although Feltrinelli was a member of the Italian Communist Party, he stood firm against pressure from Moscow and published the book in the autumn of 1957. On 23 October 1958 the Swedish Royal Academy awarded the Nobel Prize for literature to Pasternak, who acknowledged the honour in a memorable telegram: 'Immensely grateful, moved, proud, astonished, humble.'

Two days later the storm broke. *Literatúrnaya Gazéta* branded the author as a 'traitor' and a 'Judas'. On 26 October, *Pravda* called him a 'weed', a 'miserable snob', a 'useless man', and a 'vicious philistine'. At a hastily summoned meeting of three managing committees of the Writers' Association, held in Moscow on 27 October, Pasternak was expelled from the Association; the vote was, of course, 'unanimous'.[24] There were demonstrations staged against Pasternak in the village near Moscow where he lived. The newspapers printed indignant letters from people who had never even seen the book. Pasternak decided to refuse the Nobel Prize.

At a meeting attended by Khrushchev on 29 October, S. Semichástny, First Secretary of the Komsomol, described Pasternak as worse than a pig, since a pig at least refrained from fouling its own trough; it would be better, Semichastny suggested, if Pasternak left the country and ceased to pollute the atmosphere with his presence.[25] Because of the implied threat, Pasternak wrote to Khrushchev on 31 October:

> Whatever faults and mistakes I may have committed, I had no idea that I should find myself in the centre of a political campaign launched by the Western press around my name. . . . For me, to be forced to leave my country would be death, and I beg you, therefore, not to take this extreme measure against me.[26]

Why did the Kremlin pounce with such fury on a man who had remained aloof from politics and regarded his book as an unpolitical work of art? Strange as it may seem, it was precisely the absence of political content in the novel that goaded the authorities into behaviour unworthy of a great power. I have attempted an explanation of this apparent paradox in a later chapter, 'Retreat from Politics'.

Since then the Party and the literary bureaucrats have been keeping a particularly wary eye on the more prominent of the recalcitrant writers. But it is not easy to hold clever intellectuals in line. Dudintsev proved this with his symbolic *New Year's Tale*.[27] I shall not join the guessing game as to whether or not the land of darkness, that object of his two heroes' concern, represents the U.S.S.R. One thing is certain, though: The type of recent enigmatic Soviet literature, of which Dudintsev's story is only one example,[28] certainly does not represent what the Kremlin calls socialist realism.

The important thing, of course, is not the behaviour of the established writers but the fact that hitherto unknown authors are constantly slipping through the net of censorship. The first and second creative waves of 1953 and 1956 have been followed by a third one, originating among the younger generation in 1957 and continuing through the following years. One of the most noteworthy figures in this group was young Yevgeny Yevtushénko. Everything he wrote was exciting and new; he looked around with the eyes of one who had only just awakened. It is not coincidence that the title of one of his books is *Poems of Morning*.[29]

It is significant—and, for the Communists, discouraging—that the Maxim Gorky Institute, founded in 1932 by the Writers' Association for the encouragement of young authors of proven loyalty, became the main breeding ground of heresy. In a poetry seminar a young student, Bella Akhmadúllina, declared:

> They say poetry should be joyful and say 'yes' to life. In my opinion art is not called upon to give pleasure to people but to bring them sorrow.[30]

To emphasize their opposition to drab socialist realism, the students of the Gorky Institute have been devoting their attention to—pink horses! One of them said:

> I think I have described quite clearly the kind of horse that appears to me in my dreams. A pink horse, the like of which has never been, is not now, and never will be, and, above all, which no one in the world wants. Do you follow me? Only that which is completely useless is really beautiful.[31]

That was in the summer of 1957, and one might have thought it would be the end of coloured horses. But at the beginning of 1959 reports came from Kharkov about a group of enthusiastic young artists who called themselves 'The Light-Blue Horses', after a story by one of their number, Yevgeny Grebenyúk[32] and in the summer of 1960 there appeared verses about a boy painting blue dogs.[33]

In the literature of the last few years we find, particularly among the young writers, a very strong tendency towards humanism. 'Please permit me to leave, Comrade Captain,' says a young, heart-sick soldier to his superior who—the setting is World War II—wishes to drink with him to celebrate the young soldier's feat of strangling a German with his own hands.[34]

The age-old quest for morally right conduct (right by the eternal laws of conscience, not by the ever-changing Party line) is back in force. Take the moving conversation between a man amnestied after long exile in Siberia, and Boris, his friend's son. Boris is tortured by the suspicion that his father might have been somehow responsible for the friend's fate. When he wants to know the truth, the older man calms him down: 'Your father never said a single bad word about me.' But Boris persists: 'Did he say a *good* word?'

The old man tries to explain: with the conditions prevailing under Stalin, no good word could have helped him anyway. Seeing how disturbed the boy is by this answer, he says in surprise: 'Would you really have preferred your father to say in vain a good word for me even if, as a result, he and your whole family would have had to suffer?'

Boris answers ('passionately, in grief and despair'): 'Yes, yes, yes, yes.'[35]

The young writers dare to show compassion for those who have erred, even if the wrong done by them was directed against the fatherland; in several stories sympathy is extended to returned prisoners of war who had served with the Germans.[36] The most frequently expressed desire of the young writers is for the freedom to search for truth. Time and again, sentences such as these can be found: 'We demand the right to search.'[37] Or, in answer to a stuffy request not to overstep the established boundaries: 'The new things we are searching for almost always lie outside the boundaries.'[38] Of those who do not think by themselves but let others make the decisions, it is said: 'Sheep live like this.'[39]

For many years the role and characterization of the hero has been the focal point of Soviet literary controversy. The problem of 'the hero of our time' goes back to Lermontov's novel of that name, which was first published in 1840 and immediately won the hearts of the Russians. Lermontov's Pechórin has played an important part in Russian cultural history. Not only was he the personification of Lermontov's era, but he also captured the imagination of Russian readers—as he still does today—and, by influencing their outlook, contributed to what became known as the typical Russian. Other 'heroes of our time' who have also made contributions are Pushkin's Onegin or Turgenev's Bazárov (in *Fathers and Sons*).

The Communists are anxious for their writers to produce a contemporary 'Communist hero', a model who will help them to mould—that is, Bolshevize—Soviet man. But by demanding the portrayal of a type that does not exist, and could therefore never seem anything but unreal, they are setting their writers an impossible task.

During World War II the Soviet rulers tried desperately to make their writers produce the ideal hero, and many books were written in which the authors spared neither colour nor imagination. But the Soviet critics themselves had to admit that their writers had not yet been able to conjure up a true 'hero of our time'.

There are good reasons why this controversy should have raged during and after the war. Until then the Communists had imagined that the 'red hero' was firmly established in Soviet writing. The Bolshevik novels and plays of the 1920's and 1930's teemed with 'new types'—Civil War leaders, commissars, Party men in their leather jackets, and so on. All these types, brought vividly to life in the excellent Moscow theatres and in films, appeared to be 'new men', but it became obvious that it was not the men who were new but the conditions under which they lived. The 'new man' soon became a conventional figure, and—worse—a bore.

Only after the violent impact of a new, almost forgotten reality —the war—did the people become aware of the lack of vitality in Soviet literature. It forced the Russian people to look at things from a new angle. There were more shocks to follow— disillusionment in finding at the end of the war that, after all, things did not become any better; disappointment when the possibilities that seemed to open with the death of Stalin failed to materialize; the revolt against the Soviet regime in countries long claimed as 'loyal people's democracies'.

The Soviet leaders realized that the ideological crisis went too deep to be solved by courses of Marxist-Leninist indoctrination. They turned, therefore, to the writers. It was the writers' job, they felt, to conjure up before the eyes of the people a compelling figure who would capture their imagination and fire them with the urge to march onwards in the direction dictated by the Kremlin. Many Soviet writers tried to do this. They did not succeed. Then there suddenly appeared in a Soviet novel a 'hero of our time' who went straight to young people's hearts— Lopatkin, the individualist, the lone wolf, who spends his life fighting against the bureaucratic state.

In the past Russia's great writers have often stirred the people profoundly. Tentative efforts made recently seem to indicate that this would happen again today if the Kremlin gave the writers a free hand. The characters they create have an infinitely greater effect on the people than the arid ideological tracts turned out by the Party hacks—at least where writers have had the courage to describe honestly the problems that confront the people.

What has been said about writers is also more or less true of other artists. Except for the pure propagandists, most of them try to serve art, even though they live in a harshly materialistic and propaganda-ridden atmosphere. Among painters, for example, the effort to escape from politics has resulted in a marked increase in the painting of genre pictures. Scientists are trying to preserve some measure of freedom of research in spite of all government pressure; this is more difficult in the humanities than in natural science. Countless physicians follow the dictates of their conscience rather than those of the state when, for example, they disregard the strict rules which govern the issuing of sickness certificates.

I believe that the growing needs of the new intelligentsia, their urgent insistence on greater creative freedom, on a revival of the liberal tradition, as well as their increasing material demands, are constant factors in the evolution of the Soviet Union. I believe that their intellectual needs and material demands are growing faster than the willingness of the regime to satisfy them. Here, as in other aspects of Soviet life, the graphs of supply and demand do not run parallel, and this discrepancy is still another example of the tensions in Soviet life.

The fight for a measure of religious freedom is an important aspect of the struggle for freedom of thought. But it is difficult to arrive at any firm conclusions. Only one thing can be stated with certainty: a large percentage of the present Soviet population, particularly the younger generation, simply has no precise knowledge about Christianity.

The house in which I grew up was not far from the Kremlin, on the other side of the Moskva River. My old Russian *nyánya* (nurse) was fond of taking me for a walk through the Kremlin grounds, which were open to the public except when the Tsar was staying there on one of his visits from St. Petersburg. My *nyanya* was very pious and never forgot to pray in the Kremlin churches, among which the Blagovéshchenskaya, built in the fifteenth century, was her favourite. I followed her there only with trepidation because of the large fresco on one of its inner walls showing Jonah being swallowed by a whale. The fish seemed to me gigantic and horrifying, and it haunted my dreams.

During Chancellor Adenauer's visit to Moscow in 1955, when I visited the Kremlin again for the first time since my childhood (under Stalin it had not been open to visitors), I went straight to Jonah, the prophet. I hardly recognised the fresco. The mighty whale of my early memories was in reality the size of a mackerel.

While I looked at the fresco, thinking of my dear old *nyanya*, a group of girls passed on a tour through the Kremlin. 'Look, Anna Ivánovna,' said one of the girls to the young teacher as she pointed to the fresco, 'what does this mean?'

The teacher glanced at the picture. Obviously she was not familiar with the subject, but as a teacher she felt obliged to know all the answers; so she said matter-of-factly and as if she were in a zoology class: 'Can't you see? A man is eaten by a fish.' The girls continued on their way. Very likely none of them had ever seen a copy of the Old Testament.

On the other hand, every visitor to the Soviet Union who spends a Sunday morning in a church is impressed by the deep religious fervour that surrounds him. Religious indifference and ignorance (the results of atheistic education) *and* profound immersion in religious feelings exist in the Soviet Union today side by side. It is impossible for the foreigner and perhaps even for the Soviet citizen to assess the relative weight to be accorded to either of these two attitudes. Who can speak with certainty about this most intimate question, man's belief in God?

That a question like this is still discussed after more than four decades of Bolshevism has led to the mistaken notion in some quarters that the Russian Communists have become essentially tolerant toward religion. If professed materialists, absolute rulers of a totalitarian state, still allow the Church to exist—even making use of it as an instrument of their foreign policy—then perhaps their materialism and atheism should not be taken too seriously.

Those who say this have never understood the Communists. Their attitude toward religion is one thing, their treatment of the existing Church at any given time quite another. The position of the Soviet leaders regarding religion has remained practically unchanged since the turn of the century; for them, religion is not a question of metaphysics, but one of sociology and history—a barrier to progress, or, as Karl Marx put it, the opium of the masses. They believe that matter is primary, spirit is secondary. This thesis is not just an embellishment of their doctrine; it is its very core. To be sure, the Communists have been forced to dilute the meaning of matter on the philosophical and scientific level, but as yet this has not caused them to change the eminently important practical consequences of their thesis about the primacy of matter, consequences such as: the dogma that mankind develops according to causal-mechanical laws and that history is nothing but a chain of class struggles; the assumption that human existence can be planned; the denial of an autonomous morality (whatever aids what the Communists call progress is 'moral', no matter how immoral it may be); the conviction that the final victory of Communism is as inevitable as the downfall of all opposing forces, including religion, since they are merely symptoms of class relations that have been overcome, and are doomed to wither away.

Whoever believes in the autonomy of the spirit, denies the philosophical basis of Communism and thereby its justification; whoever believes in God is, in the eyes of the Communists, a traitor serving a foreign king. But this does not mean that the Church must be destroyed by a frontal attack; this has been tried under Lenin and Stalin, and it did not work. There are other methods. If an enemy cannot be annihilated at once without too great a risk, the Communists proclaim a state of co-existence, assuming that he will degenerate and eventually collapse by himself. (At the same time of course, they do whatever they can to accelerate this process.) Such tactics determine the Soviet leaders' policy towards the free world as well as their treatment of the Church at home.

During recent years many complaints about the strength and even the growth of religious sentiments have appeared in the Soviet press.[40] Whoever has occasion to check, for professional reasons, *Noviye Knigi*, the weekly list of new Soviet publications, has found that the number of atheistic books and pamphlets is increasing rather than decreasing; in October 1959 a new atheistic review appeared, *Naúka i religiya* (*Science and Religion*).

It seems that various religious sects (particularly the Baptists) are gaining numerous new followers—a phenomenon well known from other periods of stress in Russian history. Having found that many people prefer the colourful religious ceremonies for family events to the drab customs prevailing in the Soviet state, the government is trying to provide the non-religious celebrations with some secular glamour—for example by building Palaces of Happiness where marriages can be contracted among marble pillars and rubber plants.

With all due caution one may perhaps say this much: the older generation, except for the militant Communists, have preserved a good deal of their religious attachment, and with some of them it has even grown. The middle generation, who have been in the thick of economic and political struggles, are far less concerned with religion, being largely agnostic. Among the younger people there is much metaphysical searching but according to my observations this does not generally lead to anything as concrete as the Orthodox Church; whether it will grow and where it will lead, nobody can yet say.

INDIVIDUAL AND STATE

CHAPTER 12

THE KOLLEKTÍV

PERSONAL IMPRESSIONS of a country and its people can be gathered most easily on journeys. That is why trains so often provide the setting for incidents recounted here.

On one occasion I was passing through the immediate vicinity of Moscow. A woman in my compartment had got a speck of dust in her eye and couldn't remove it. Such a mishap could occur anywhere—on any train in any country—and usually, if all efforts with a handkerchief failed, the sufferer would ask whether there was a doctor on the train. But that did not happen this time. Another woman in the compartment, obviously a stranger, came to the rescue. She gently held the victim still, pressed her open mouth to the affected eye, and removed the foreign body with her tongue.

The human warmth which found expression in this spontaneous little action is perhaps rather primitive; such behaviour is, at any rate, seldom encountered in Western countries. This particular quality in the relationships between Russians seems to be a fundamental trait in their character and has survived all the vicissitudes of recent years.

In personal—though not in political—matters the Russian has far fewer inhibitions than we have; the desire to keep his distance from people is foreign to his nature. I had been used to this kind of behaviour ever since my childhood in Russia, but my wife, much more reserved than I, found that it got on her nerves during the years we spent in Moscow. When we were among Russians she always felt rather ill at ease, because they seemed to expect her to demonstrate openly and enthusiastically the same good fellowship that came naturally to them. If she sat somewhat bewildered and unintentionally stiff in her chair, her host or one of the guests would rush up to her at once, saying, 'Why don't you like us?' and entreat her to have a glass of vodka or wine, on the assumption that perhaps it was only the lack of a drink that made the foreigner so shy. Moreover, the sight of men embracing and kissing each other, which is so embarrassing to Englishmen and Americans, is commonplace in

Russia, particularly when friends or relatives are meeting or seeing each other off at railway stations.

In fact, in comparison with the Russians, the rest of us are rather taciturn and self-contained. It is only on political issues that experience has taught the Russian reserve, unless the person to whom he is talking is either a close friend or a chance acquaintance whom he is not likely to meet again. When, after the war, the Americans interrogated displaced persons there were often surprising revelations: some of the DP's, old acquaintances who had considered each other loyal Soviet citizens, did not find out until they met on foreign soil that they shared anti-Bolshevik opinions.[1]

But the more carefully politics is avoided as a topic of conversation, the more eagerly and frankly are private affairs discussed. Western civilization has bred in us an aversion to being conspicuous in public, a horror of being involved in 'scenes'; such reluctance is not—or perhaps I should say, not yet—found among Russians.

I once witnessed a woman shoplifter arrested in Germany. The detective whispered the customary 'Please follow me quietly', and the woman took great pains to do what she was told as unobtrusively as possible. On the other hand, a couple of years ago I saw the Moscow police arrest a woman who had been selling something illegally at a street corner. This incident was far from being unobtrusive. The woman screamed like one possessed and fought tooth and nail until the police finally threw her bodily into an open truck. And all this took place, not on a side street, but barely a hundred yards from the imposing Foreign Ministry building in Smolensk Square.

Nor is there ever any question of the Russian public turning discreetly aside from such distressing misadventures; even in their amusement at other people's misfortunes the Russians often show a quite primitive lack of restraint. I once went by steamer along the coast of the Kola peninsula in the Arctic. When we left Murmansk, the asthmatic old tub was already overloaded with passengers. At each of the twelve fishing villages where we docked, the same wild scenes were repeated. No sooner was the first wail of the ship's siren heard than a half-dozen rowboats and launches sped towards us from the shore. Before the anchor was down a torrent of passionate appeals broke out.

Every single person in the boats frantically waved a slip of paper—a transfer order, a leave pass, something—and shouted at the top of his voice that, whatever happened to the rest, he must be allowed to get on board.

At one of the villages three passengers disembarked. The gangway was lowered for them, and although we already had more passengers than was allowed, the boatswain shouted that three new passengers could come aboard. But which three? There was a bitter struggle at the foot of the gangway—the next steamer was not due for a fortnight. The sea was running high, and the boats kept crashing against the steamer's side and began to fill with water. The men cursed furiously, the women wailed and beseechingly held their babies aloft to the boatswain, while children whimpered and clung to their mothers skirts. In the boats fights broke out, and the strongest battled their way to the best positions. One boy of about fourteen actually had his hand on the railing of the gangway when a man pushed him aside. Convulsed with fury, the boy aimed a vicious blow at him. At that moment the boat plunged into the trough between two waves, the man lost his balance and fell headlong into the sea, along with his trunk.

All this time the passengers aboard the steamer had watched from the deck rails, shouting with unmistakable glee. Now there was a great roar of laughter, and when the man rose to the surface, drenched and minus his luggage, they could hardly contain themselves. 'Hey! Where's your trunk?' shouted one of the passengers. 'He's checked it already!' cried another. In the meantime, while the boatswain's attention was distracted, eight people had clambered up the gangway. The boatswain rushed down as though he had gone berserk, pushed them back into the boats with his foot, and ordered the gangway to be raised.

While all this was going on, the people in two of the boats, not seeing much hope of getting aboard legitimately, had rowed around to the other side of the ship. With the agility of monkeys some of them grabbed a rope hanging over the side to climb aboard. In this way a girl reached the deck near where I was standing, and then she turned and leaned over the side to retrieve a bundle which someone in the boat was holding aloft on the end of an oar. Fearing that she might lose her balance, I held on to her tightly as she leaned over and managed to grab it. But we were unlucky. The captain, who had watched the illegal boarding from the bridge, now ran toward us, storming and cursing; he seized the girl's bundle and flung it back into the boat below. Like the man with the trunk, the girl had lost every shred of her pitiful possessions, for the steamer was already under way. The anguished howls of those left behind were answered with roars of laughter from those who had got aboard and now seemed to find the whole spectacle riotously funny, forgetting that a few minutes earlier they themselves had been in the same predicament. Or perhaps they had not forgotten, and their laughter was a slightly hysterical expression of relief.

On the other hand, Russian life abounds in sympathy and eagerness to lend a helping hand, particularly among the peasants who have little or nothing to spare. German prisoners-of-war, who, in the earliest days of their captivity at least, were among the poorest of the poor, tell countless tales of how the Russians, undernourished themselves, helped them. A young Polish woman, deported from Lvov to the Soviet Union shortly after the beginning of the war, told me how kind people had been to her, and without asking anything in return. The natural human feeling—'After all, you're only another poor devil like myself'—is widespread, and it goes a long way towards making a tough life tolerable.

Further, the strain of living in hard times under a ruthless regime has taught people the value of friendliness. Under a reign of terror, or in the face of natural catastrophe, it is a lesson easily learned by people all over the world. In Russia there is not and never has been much need for the spur of such special circumstances. The Russians have lived for centuries in close human relationship; the joys and sorrows of the individual are shared by his community, into which even the stranger is readily accepted. A few years ago I went to the funeral of a young girl. I arrived rather late, and the coffin, which (according to the Russian custom) had been carried open to the cemetery, had by then already been closed and lowered into the grave. But when the girl's mother caught sight of me, she had the coffin raised again and re-opened, so that I might take a last look at her daughter's face.

One of my most vivid childhood memories is of the death of

a peasant woman in the village where we used to spend our holidays. Her sickness must have been painful, for the poor woman cried and groaned unceasingly. She lay in the main room of her hut, and the villagers filed past her bed in a long, orderly and constant stream to watch her die. In childish awe and curiosity I joined them two or three times, and I remember the strange feeling that gripped me each time I stepped over the threshold into the darkened room where, with candles burning before the ikon in the corner, the peasant woman lay in her death throes and the long-haired priest intoned his prayers, while the villagers shuffled by with undisguised curiosity.

The average Russian undoubtedly derives a special pleasure from being in the company of his fellow men—even without the help of alcohol. This gregariousness makes him readier to accept a certain amount of collectivism, a readiness that is all the more understandable when it is recalled that for centuries Russians lived under a village communal system, the *mir*. Until the agrarian reforms of 1907, the peasants' lives were controlled by the *mir*, which was responsible for the taxes and the charges which the peasants had to pay the landowners for the right to cultivate their holdings. Life under the *mir* probably contributed a great deal to that sense of equality common to all Russians. In a *mir* the land belonging to the community as a whole was divided among the individual families according to the number of 'souls'; no other factors, such as efficiency or industriousness, were taken into consideration.

The Bolshevik state exploits this predilection for group life by claiming to see in it a readiness to accept the state-sponsored group life that attracts the Russian as not something organized and subject to external supervision, but something which has developed naturally and spontaneously. Groups of this kind, however, hardly exist now, and such rare examples as come to light from time to time are at once denounced as 'unhealthy manifestations' and cliques. In the eyes of the Soviet state every type of spontaneous solidarity that does not come under the state's direct control is evil. What the Communists want is the *kollektív*, organized and controlled by them.

Most people belong to more than one collective, since there are collectives covering every branch of their activities—work, sport, hobbies, and so on. Realizing that it cannot maintain its iron grip on every one of its 200 million subjects individually, the state seeks to incorporate them in collectives, which are easier to control. The state is as interested in the psychological aspect as in the organizational. In the future, as the Communists envisage it, the collective will become the only possible way of life, and no one will be able to do anything outside its framework. For that reason the collective concerns itself not only with public issues, such as school or factory problems, but also with the private lives of its members. To this end the collectives have adopted the practices of some religious communities. The sceptic risks being 'excommunicated', as it were, and the loneliness of his guilt makes him long for the day when he will be admitted once more to the community of the faithful. The following significant piece of advice was given in an educational journal: 'Let the young man who has gone astray have time to think things over and to worry for himself how he should behave; but eventually, if there is no other solution, he must be told that for him there is only one path—the path of duty.'[2] It seems clear from the context that this path is intended to lead to an unconditional confession before his teachers and fellow students, so that he may win forgiveness and re-admission into the community.

The issues on which the individual is required to obey the collective may be political, but they can also be purely personal. In Y. Trifonov's novel *Students*, a whole chapter is devoted to the deliberations of a Komsomol committee on the private life of young Sergey Palavin. One of the novel's principal characters and (though this is not apparent in the first part of the book) a negative hero, Sergey has seduced a girl and then deserted her. The case is examined in great detail at the Komsomol meeting. In the end Sergey is severely reprimanded for having 'violated the principles of Communist morality'. In his final speech, Sergey, 'sad, and forming his words with difficulty', confesses that he is despicable, mean, and selfish.

Nauseating though this kind of thing may seem to us, the Russian, who is far less self-conscious in public, finds it easier to swallow. Nor is it, I think, the collective as such that worries him primarily, or even the coercion inherent in it, but rather the feeling that in a collective he must be perpetually on his guard and suspicious of everyone else. The atmosphere of spying and conspiracy in the collective is quite out of keeping with his spontaneous nature.

For years people in the Soviet Union have been schizophrenic; they have thought one thing and said another. But they are now beginning to rebel. Once when I was talking to a student, he voiced some very strong criticisms of the Soviet Union.

I asked him, 'Aren't you afraid to speak so openly to a foreigner?'

His features were set in an expression of firm decision. 'I've had enough of being afraid,' he said. 'My whole life has been spent in being afraid about something—afraid that somebody should rebuke me publicly; afraid that somebody should cut my scholarship; afraid that somebody might order me to leave school and go to work in Siberia . . . afraid, afraid, afraid! I'm not going to be afraid any more; for once I must say what is in my heart.'

That this is not an isolated incident was confirmed when I saw the play *The Factory Girl* by Alexander Volódin in the Red Army Theatre.[3] The characters are almost all young people, the workers, and above all the women workers of a textile factory. The heroine—the factory girl of the title—is a bright young thing, something of an *enfant terrible,* who will not be submerged in a collective and protests vigorously against any kind of regimentation.

'I find it boring to be in the best work crew,' she says. 'I would rather be in the worst!' And she adds: 'What can I do? I just have a critical mind.'

In another scene the girls are supposed to show a factory inspector from the Ministry how happy and well-behaved they are during their 'break'. They are seated, neatly dressed, in the recreation room; one of them is reading aloud, to impress the inspector with the high level of their activities during their break. Finally the great man actually arrives, finding everything spotless and in order. But just as he is turning to leave, and the Komsomol official responsible for the whole comedy is ready to give a great sigh of relief, the 'factory girl' speaks up.

This idyllic scene, she confides to the distinguished guest, was staged solely for his benefit; the pretty aprons will be put away again carefully as soon as he has gone. No sooner has she broken the ice in this way than the other girls also begin to unburden themselves. It becomes apparent that the spotless appearance of the workshop was only for the visitor. 'For a whole week we've been busy with nothing but cleaning up, instead of fulfilling our work quota; tomorrow we start catching up with our quota, and everything will be dirty again.' The visitor leaves in considerable embarrassment; the Komsomol official cries out in despair, 'Everything was so beautiful! Only one had to open her mouth, and everybody started gabbing away.'

In the end, the factory girl is fired. She loses her room and is left all alone in the street. 'I know how all this has happened,' she says. 'I have one fatal fault; I can't pretend. In our country, people say one thing and do another. And if anyone dares to say anything against it—he's had it!'

And this girl was the heroine—in the eyes of the playwright, the producer, and the public—and one of the most popular figures on the Moscow stage. The fact that the censors have not banned it probably means that the present Soviet leaders wish to leave a few legitimate outlets to pent-up feelings.

Some of the methods used to make people accept collectivism and conformity are indirect; there is the constant, and on the whole successful, use of the word *kul'turno*, for instance. Just as we in the West say to our children 'A well-brought up boy would never behave like that!' the Russians are incessantly reminded that some things are *kul'turno* (worthy of a civilized being) and other things are not. *Kul'turno* has become one of the most commonly used words in the language. '*Kul'turno*', said a man next to me in an expensive Moscow restaurant when he noticed with satisfaction that the sugar cubes were wrapped individually. Once when I arrived in Warsaw on a Russian train some of the passengers began to stroll down the platform in their pyjamas as they are accustomed to doing in their country. '*Ne kul'turno*', said the conductress reproachfully. And I once even heard a student tell his friends that it was *ne kul'turno* to fasten the lower button of a single-breasted jacket.

This systematic education has had some success. It is true that people's thoughts and feelings have not really been affected by the persistence with which collectivism has been thrust upon them; but the policy has certainly conditioned their outward behaviour. The man who is part of a *kollektiv* is more conventional in his behaviour than the man who leads a life of his own. But this does not apply to the Soviet Union alone; in the West, too, the more closely a man's life is bound up with the community in which he lives, the greater the effect on him of communal influence. The people of an isolated village or the members of a military unit or student fraternity are more likely to be conformists than the inhabitants of a big city, who hardly know their neighbours' names. But when I compare my recent observations with those I made in the early 1930's, I am inclined to think that today Soviet man is less collective-minded than thirty years ago, and that both individualism and the number of individualists have increased. I would go so far as to say that open protests against the pressure of collectivism are now beginning to be heard.

The first signs of protest appeared in the years after Stalin's death. Scarcely had a little more freedom been granted to writers than novels like Dudintsev's appeared, in which the hero was a decided, often an extreme, individualist, and the part played by the collective was anything but glorious. One of the sharpest attacks levelled at the power and despotism of the collective—and the one most vigorously repudiated by the Party —is contained in a poem by the Armenian writer Paruir Sevak entitled 'A Difficult Conversation'. The poet describes the thoughts of a man on the way home from a meeting of a collective (probably his Party cell) at which he has been morally censured for his relations with a married woman. Full of bitterness, he thinks back over the five hours of humiliation he has endured and the arguments he put forward in his own defence. 'There is no single key that fits all human hearts,' he cries, clenching his teeth in rage at the thought of his questioners' petty-mindedness and the repeated, futile advice that he should 'be sensible, be wise'. He recalls the meeting itself, the green baize table, the doltish, hostile faces, the peevish arguments, the clouds of tobacco smoke. In his mind's eye he sees himself again standing there, tongue-tied and with halting speech, confessing and promising to improve.

> I love you as I never loved before,
> And yet I gave my word to love no more . . .

And he sees again the smug, triumphant faces, and castigates the hypocrisy which condemned him, not for what he had done, but for the frankness with which he had done it.[4]

The poem was published in *Novy Mir*, and four issues later the magazine printed a number of responses to it. In one of them the poem is condemned because it casts doubt on the wisdom of the collective and disregards the fact that 'in reality, in the vast majority of cases, the collective has been proved right, and those who have been reprimanded have been forced to admit —sooner or later, and however difficult such an admission may have been for them—that the reprimands they had received were well deserved'. The writer of the letter is greatly agitated because 'the poet and his hero raise their voices against the right of the public to deal, through the collective, with questions affecting the sanctity of the family'.

But the Armenian poet also had his defenders. One woman wrote to the editor: 'While it is generally recognized that it is the duty of the collective to intervene in the private affairs of its members, it is equally its duty to give due consideration to the particular circumstances of each individual case. How true it is that "there is no single key to fit all human hearts". The problem of people's private lives must not be approached with the mind of a public prosecutor.'[5]

Stress begets counter-stress; this is an axiom older than those formulated by Marx, and one of the 'dialectics' of life. But these dialectics the Communists are prepared to admit only when they believe them to work to their advantage. And yet the whole history of the Soviet Union, surely, is proof that the true laws of evolution and dialectic prevail regardless of the nature of the political system.

CHAPTER 13

DO 'THEY' KNOW BEST?

Nature and history have combined to implant and develop in the character of the Russians certain traits that have helped their rulers to establish a dictatorship over them. Nothing is more astonishing to the outsider than the Russian's capacity to endure hardship and his readiness to bow to the inevitable—traits that Tolstoy never tired of praising.

On my journeys through Russia I have come across many instances of this readiness to accept as a matter of course every decree of fate or state. Once I had to wait between trains for most of the night at a small railroad station in the Urals. The tiny waiting room was filled to overflowing, there were not enough benches, people were squatting on the floor, and there was such a stench that I preferred to walk up and down outside in the snow. Hour after hour went by. Finally I was so tired that I went into the waiting room and sat on my knapsack. After a few minutes I dozed off. But not for long. Someone shook me vigorously. Befuddled with sleep, I dimly made out the face of the station attendant.

'You can't sleep in here, citizen', he said, and went off to wake all the others.

'Of all the damn silly things!' I said to the man next to me. 'What does the idiot mean by waking us like that?'

'Well,' he replied calmly, 'he's quite right, you know. Sleeping isn't allowed in the waiting room. If it were, every Tom, Dick, and Harry would come in and bed down for the night. I had to wait at a station once for two days and two nights, and I didn't sleep a wink the whole time.' He said this not without a trace of pride in his achievement.

Another time, I was on a Soviet ship on the White Sea. There were about 150 deck passengers. A strong, icy wind was blowing, and only the bridge offered some shelter. Close to the funnel and in the warmth beside the engine-room hatches about forty people were huddled. They had been the first aboard and had managed to secure these desirable places, where they remained, rooted to the spot, for fear someone else would move in if they stirred. Nearby there was a boiler, from which the passengers could get hot water for their tea at any time of day or night. Under the boiler a woman had made herself comfortable, except that every time anyone came there, hot water was splashed over her legs. 'Aren't you being scalded?' I asked. She shrugged. 'It doesn't matter', she said. 'In two days I'll be home, and then I can smear my legs with grease,' and with that she dozed off again.

The Russian capacity for getting used to circumstances has been one of the main props of the regime. The foreign observer seldom meets with any enthusiastic advocacy of Communism, but he finds everywhere signs that the nation has got used to it and that the people have resigned themselves to their fate. Most of them, indeed, are incapable of imagining any alternative.

Once I was walking with a Russian friend along Gorky Street, Moscow's showplace. He wanted to buy some butter. As we pushed our way into one of the state-owned food stores he turned to me and said: 'In the West shops like this are privately owned, aren't they? You know, I can't imagine what it must be like to go into a shop that isn't owned by the state.' He made it sound as though he had said: 'I can't imagine how anyone could prefer to ride in an ox-wagon rather than an automobile.'

Before I had time to reply we had joined a long line shuffling towards the counter. When it was our turn to be served, my friend's polite request was met with a terse 'No butter' from a shopgirl in a grimy apron. He shrugged, and we went out again.

'How do you like your state-run economy?' I asked. 'In a country as rich in natural resources as the Soviet Union, one of the leading shops in the capital has no butter. Still, I suppose that could happen anywhere. But they might at least give you a civil answer. One of these days you must visit me in my country. We'll go into any shop you like, and you'll soon see the difference between our system and yours. The elimination of competition in your country has led to intolerable bureaucracy. And the salespeople apparently are not even under the slightest obligation to be polite to their customers.'

He muttered something to himself. Obviously I hadn't convinced him. Then he said, 'A few years ago this shop didn't even exist, and now here it is. Don't you call that a remarkable bit of progress?' There you are, I thought to myself, just another Soviet citizen who is impressed because he has never known anything else.

Readiness to submit to authority, then, must be considered one of the Russian traits; the people are by nature not inclined to be critical. Whenever a decision is taken in the West, whether by a schoolteacher or by the government, we are ready to scrutinize it and find some fault. In the Soviet Union, when a teacher makes a suggestion, he can usually be sure that his class will agree with him without much reflection. This alone can explain how the authority of the teacher, deliberately undermined by state propaganda after the Revolution, was so swiftly and completely restored in the change of policy at the beginning of the 1930's. I also believe that if the Russians were told that they had to tighten their belts and renounce the good things of life, they would accept it more readily than we in the West would tolerate such a sudden lowering of our standard of living.

Strict and often barbaric family discipline, the discipline of life in the *mir*, conditioned the masses to subordinate themselves to the will of others, even when they felt that the demands made on them were unjust. To these influences has been added the unceasing insistence on the virtue of obeying those in authority. The Communists have intensified this insistence; it begins in kindergarten, goes throughout school, and particular emphasis is laid on it during military training. But it is also at work in civil life, with its strong military flavour of ranks and uniforms and its emphasis on the giving and obeying of orders. Then again, the individual is usually allowed little freedom in the shaping of his own professional life; each move is imposed on him from above. The transfer of skilled labour from one place to another was, for a long time, carried out in a manner which, in other countries, is applied only to the movement of troops. Respect for one's elders and betters, for one's teachers, and, above all, for the Party and its leaders is preached incessantly. Familiarity between the people and their leaders is considered undesirable. Typical of this attitude is *Pravda*'s criticism of a passage in Katayev's war novel *For the Power of the Soviet*. The hero is an exemplary Party man, a famed partisan leader named Gavriil, whom his followers address by the affectionate nickname Gavrik. *Pravda* takes strong exception to this: 'The age of nicknames ended long ago, and we find it very difficult to believe that anyone would address a respected man and an important Party official as Gavrik.'[1]

But the authority of the state in Russia is nourished by roots that go far deeper than police tyranny, externally conditioned habit patterns, and the influence of education and propaganda. The Byzantine theocratic tradition, in which state and church were united, has helped to create the psychological climate for the present leaders' claim to be the embodiment of truth. Even the mystical concept of Moscow as the Third Rome—the city that after the fall of the first Rome through heresy and the destruction of the 'Second Rome' (Constantinople) by the Turks, claimed to be the last and only centre of true Christianity—found an echo in the Third International. For that, too, had its seat in Moscow, and as heir to the First International (founded by Marx) and the Second (Socialist) International, claimed to be the sole repository of pure socialist doctrine.

Changes at the topmost level of the Soviet hierarchy almost always occur with great suddenness and are announced to the people in general terms. This invests the leaders with an aura of mystery, of something incomprehensible to the ordinary citizen which must be accepted with deference and awe. While the correct interpretation of the laws of dialectical materialism remains the private preserve of the innermost circle, the masses have no choice but to submit to their leaders' superior wisdom, much as the people used to be taught that their only access to God was through the mediation of the priesthood. In the eyes of the peasants the village priest was often greasy, slothful, uneducated, and rapacious; and yet, because he was believed to be a link with the divine, he possessed the halo of authority.

Today the people look on the petty Party official as someone who pesters them and keeps them busy, but who, as the representative of the Party machine, embodies Communist power and wisdom. Both priest and Party functionary have in turn been credited with possession of the sole, absolute, and indivisible truth—the former through the revelations of God, the latter through the no less infallible medium of 'scientific' knowledge.

This attitude is fostered by the Communists. While we in the West have learned, and our young people are taught, that there is always a choice among various possibilities, the Soviet people are directed towards the one and only truth discovered by their leaders. This form of education considerably simplifies government. When only *one* truth exists, all that the leaders in the Kremlin need to do is convince their people that they alone hold the key to it, thus creating for themselves a sacrosanct position of authority, not unlike that wielded formerly by the Tsars and the religious leaders. With this authority, the government can sit enthroned behind the red walls of the Kremlin, as though endowed with supernatural powers. The people, just as they formerly believed that their priests were in direct communion with God, will become convinced that the Party leaders possess clear insight into the ways of the world, exact knowledge of the laws of human, economic, and political evolution, and the ability to act in accordance with these laws. Portraits of those temporarily at the helm of the ship of state will be hung on the walls, like the ikons of former days, and carried in procession through the streets.

During many conversations in Russia I have had the opportunity of assessing how far these two factors—the authority of the state based on a secularized version of religious sanctity, and the old messianic beliefs—have helped the government to deal with the simple Russian who has not been absorbed in and organized by the Party. I remember particularly a visit to a *stolóvaya*, one of those relatively inexpensive restaurants which are always crowded. When everybody sits close together it is easy to enter into a conversation with the person next to you. On this particular summer evening I was sitting next to a man in his late forties who had lost his left arm in the war. He told me he worked in a large factory on the outskirts of Moscow and had spent the afternoon shopping in the city. First he grumbled about the poor service in the *stolovaya*. Then, patting his empty sleeve with his right hand, he said: 'It was a bad business, the war with you Germans. We should have been fighting side by side instead of against each other. We have great respect for the Germans. They're a *printsipial'ny naród* (a people with principles), like the Russians, not a sloppy lot of compromisers like the British and the French.'

'I'm not sure your judgment of us is correct,' I answered. 'The time when we were, in principle, against all compromise is now past, and as the result of our experiences of the past twenty or thirty years we have switched from the all-too-simple "either-or" to a complicated pattern of "on the one hand, and on the other". One of these days you people will realize that the world can't be divided neatly into black and white.'

'But there is only *one* truth,' he protested.

'That may well be,' I admitted. 'But we ordinary human beings don't know what it is, and we must therefore seek ways and means of getting closer to it. The most likely way of finding the truth, surely, is by frank discussion between people of opposing viewpoints.'

'We don't care much for that,' he said. 'Two plus two is four, and it's always four, because that's the truth, not because it's a compromise between three and five.'

'I'm not talking about that kind of truth,' I said. 'Those are simple facts of mathematics or natural science, and neither we nor anyone else would contest them. But there is an endless array of questions to which the answer can't be found in one inevitable truth. For example—should a *stolovaya* like this belong to the state or to a private person? Should tractors belong to the state's tractor stations or to the *kolkhozes*? [At that time this was a live issue; Khrushchev has since sided with the *kolkhozes*.] Or take some of the problems that face my own country. Should we re-introduce conscription or build up a professional army? Should we admit all parties to our parliament, or only those which receive at least 5 per cent of the total votes? To all such questions there is more than one answer, and we think the chances of finding the best one are greatest if we thrash out every possible aspect of the problem.'

'No, no!' the Russian retorted. 'There can be only *one* right answer, and all your new-fangled methods of compromise are no damn good. In any argument the one who's wrong must give way to the one who's right.'

'What you are saying is that the Party has the right to enforce its decision even on those who disagree—and I think the latter quite often represent a majority of the people. What about what happened during the compulsory collectivization of agriculture? Do you really refuse all protection to those who do their own thinking?'

'Without discipline and obedience there can be nothing but chaos,' he replied.

'But why,' I persisted, 'do you believe the Party leaders will find the correct answer?'

'Because they understand and apply the laws of historical evolution.'

'And why do you think they have a greater claim to such understanding than other people?'

'*Im vidnéye*,' he replied, using a common Russian phrase that means roughly 'because they see things more clearly.'

I asked him if he was a Party member, and he replied that he was not.

'Tell me,' I went on, 'how do you reconcile your theory that these people are in a better position than you to judge things, with the erratic course they have been steering during the past thirty years? If there *is* only one correct answer to any question, surely it can't be one thing today and another tomorrow—"Yes" under Stalin and "No" under Khrushchev, and vice versa.'

'Conditions change, and methods must change with them.'

'Of course conditions change, but surely you don't think that's the whole answer. Take Stalin. At first he was little short of a god, he was Stalin the infallible, the man who had the right answer to every question. Then, a few years after his death, he was exposed—by his old colleagues and his successors—as a tyrant guilty of the most horrible atrocities. I expect you know all about the speech Khrushchev made in private session at the Twentieth Party Congress?' He nodded. [The speech had been read at the time to Party members in factories, and its contents passed on by them to the others.] 'And now we are given another portrait of Stalin, which shows him as neither an infallible superman nor a monster, but a mixture of the two. Well, where does the truth lie now? You tell me!'

For a time he toyed with the food on his plate without replying. Finally he said, 'You know, sometimes one honestly doesn't know what to say . . . '

If I have succeeded in describing, however briefly, the psychological climate in which, more than forty years ago, the Bolsheviks inherited the centuries-old empire of the Tsars, the reader may understand why the people have largely adjusted themselves to the Bolshevik ideology. But we should not overestimate the significance of the ideological element. In the innumerable conversations I have had with friends and acquaintances about their private lives, their plans, and the personal decisions that have affected their lives, I can hardly recall a single case in which ideology played a decisive role.

But there is an important exception. One ideological precept is firmly rooted in their minds, and, incidentally, signifies quite a success for the Bolsheviks. Marx enunciated one doctrine that responded to the people's desire for simple explanations—the thesis that the evolution of society is governed by specific laws, exactly as is the development of all forms of natural growth. According to this Marxist theory, humanity is progressing in-evitably from its primitive origins—by way of the slave-owning society, feudalism, capitalism, and socialism—to Communism. This has been widely accepted by the Russians, with the result that in the eyes of many even a badly functioning socialism, with all its subsidiary irritations, appears 'higher' than smooth-running capitalism.

A Moscow history student once explained his own viewpoint to me by means of a historical comparison. 'On the eve of the French Revolution,' he said, 'there was a marked difference be-tween the standard of living of the aristocracy and that of the young *bourgeoisie*. In the ducal châteaux of the Loire everything was more gracious, more luxurious than in the overcrowded houses of Paris and Lyons. The difference then was as great as that which now exists between your capitalists and our workers. However, that had no effect on the course of history; feudalism was inevitably followed by the era of the bourgeois and the capitalist. And yet, even while life was at its gracious zenith in these châteaux, their owners were, as a class, already a spent force, doomed to destruction. The new class, the *bourgeoisie*, at that time primitive and uncouth compared with the aristocracy, was already standing poised, ready to assume the role of victor in the days to come. Today, it in turn is old and tired, ripe to be replaced by the vigorous young class of the proletariat.'

This is not the place to discuss in detail the Marxist theory of social evolution, the fallacy of which is being daily made clearer by the steady advance of the Soviet upper class in the opposite direction; it is enough to state that this theory has been widely disseminated throughout the Soviet Union.

There are, of course, millions of people in Russia who are unhappy under the present system, and there are some who hate it. But since they have accepted that mankind must inevitably pass through a period of socialism, they tend also to accept the inevitability of the conditions under which they live. This attitude is invaluable to the Soviet authorities; for who can fight, with any prospect of success, against the absolutely inevitable? And who, indeed, would waste time complaining about it? Man finds it easiest to accept the things that seem immutable, and that is one of the reasons why there has been nothing in the Soviet Union comparable to the anti-Hitler plot of 20 July 1944, no uprisings such as the outbreak in the Soviet zone of Germany in 1953 or the Hungarian fight for freedom in 1956.

Until recently it was difficult to get a definite opinion from the average Russian on what Communism really is, and what form it will take once it is established. The first reaction to questions like this was one of surprise; it was something the Russians did not appear to discuss among themselves. Surprise was usually followed by vague and evasive answers. A friend of mine (not a Russian) put this very question to a Soviet teacher, who, after some hesitation, replied, 'You will find the answer to that in the *Great Soviet Encyclopaedia*'. But if you persisted in asking, you were generally given the conventional formula that Marx coined in his *Critique of the Gotha Programme*: 'Communism is a system based on the principle "From each according to his ability; to each according to his needs".'

That was the reply I received from two Moscow students with whom I was sitting one sunny day on a bench in the Alexander Park, not far from Moscow University. 'I've heard the formula before, of course,' I said, 'but I can't make head or tail of it. Tell me, how would it work in practice?'

They thought for a while, and then one of them said: 'The Communism envisaged in the Marxist definition can be achieved only when we succeed in producing in the Soviet Union more of everything than we need, in place of the general shortage that exists now. So long as there's a shortage of consumer necessities like shoes, clothes, food, and housing, we will have to remain in that phase which, as distinct from Communism, we call Socialism. During the socialist phase men are rewarded "according to labour performed" but not provided for "according to their needs"—that is, regardless of how much they have earned. Our first task, therefore, must be to create this super-abundance of goods. This we are gradually doing by following the principle that such goods as are available must go primarily to the people who deserve them most because of their efforts to increase production. This will go on until the required abundance is created; then, and only then, will we be able to implement the second half of the formula and give "to each according to his needs". And when that happens we will have reached the era of true Communism.'

'All that sounds very fine in theory,' I said. 'But who is to decide what are the needs of each individual? Suppose you feel the need to travel across Africa, or to buy a car. To whom do you make your need known? Who decides whether your needs should or should not be satisfied?'

'Well—only reasonable needs would be considered, that's obvious,' one of the students replied.

'But that doesn't answer my question. Who is to decide which of your needs are reasonable?'

After a longish pause, the other student replied, 'I'm afraid we haven't thought this thing through in such detail.'

'Then may I give you my opinion?' I asked. 'In every country in the world, including your own, men are paid according to the work they do, and there are definite scales of remuneration. One man makes ninety articles in an hour, another makes a hundred, and a third makes a hundred and twenty; these are all definite, easily established facts, and the pay can be reckoned accordingly. But there are no mechanical measures for establishing whether a man's needs are reasonable and justifiable or not. The decision on that question will, I suspect, be in the hands of the ruling bureaucracy. This means that under Communism men will still be subject to the whims of bureaucrats—more so even than to-day, when a man's work can be measured in tangible terms. I once read somewhere that the Soviet Union employs more than two million accountants in the operation of its state economy. That's staggering enough, but under your Communist system you'll need at least a couple of million more bureaucrats to examine the validity of the claims put forward. The very idea of a situation in which a man will have to convince some official that new shoes for his children, a new dress for his wife, a garden hose, a typewriter, or the collected works of

Dostoyevsky are "reasonable needs" fills me with dismay.'

For some time my young companions remained silent. Eventually one of them said: 'People themselves will change, and somehow or other an answer will be found to these questions. At present we're all selfish and greedy; if anything is to be had free, everybody rushes in to grab as much as possible, regardless of whether he really needs it or not.'

'As a matter of fact,' his friend interrupted, 'we've always thought that one of these days a start would be made with free distribution of specific goods which have become plentiful. After all, there's plenty of air, so everyone can breathe as much of it as he likes without paying a cent for it. In a few years, with new methods and the opening up of new arable land in Kazakhstan and Siberia, we'll probably have more bread than we need.'

'So you think,' I cut in, 'that one day we'll read on the front page of *Pravda* an official decree of the Central Committee and Council of Ministers stating "Effective 1 January everyone may obtain as much bread as he wants free of charge"?'

'Why not? I grant you that at first people probably will abuse the new privilege a bit, since they won't yet have shed the selfish impulses of the past. But after a few weeks, when they find mountains of stale or mouldy bread in their cupboards, they'll soon realize their folly, and afterwards they'll take only as much bread as they can use, or, as Marx puts it, "according to their needs". And if some remain incorrigible, a sharp rap over the knuckles will teach them to behave decently. Entry into the phase of perfect Communism presupposes, of course, that men will bring to it a full measure of good will and readiness to adjust to the higher order of life that has been created.'

As he spoke the young man became enraptured with his own vision, and when he finished he looked at me expectantly.

'Hm!' I murmured. 'It would be most interesting to be present during such an experiment. I would apply at once for a visa so that I could come to the Soviet Union to watch developments with my own eyes. But I see some serious snags. Bread doesn't fall ready-baked from heaven. Millions of people and machines will be needed to grow the crops, and all these workers and machines will have to be paid and maintained. Let's take a figure at random. Suppose the state so far pays the peasants 50 billion roubles for all the grain produced in the Soviet Union.

This money (and more) it gets back from the people buying the bread. If the government decides to give away the bread for nothing, it will have to have the money with which to pay the peasants (or—after money has been 'abolished'—the goods necessary for the peasants) from some other source, either through additional taxation or by increasing the prices of other goods such as shoes or clothes. So what people save on free bread will be taken from them in some other form. The free issue of bread you envisage wouldn't be a further step towards Communism; it would simply be a stunt, which even in a state with totalitarian propaganda would be exposed sooner or later. For nothing you get—exactly nothing. That applies not only to the Western economy but also to every other economic system in the world. And to realize this you don't need to have studied economics at a university; ordinary common sense is enough. Am I right, or not?'

The two young men had lit cigarettes and were puffing away vigorously. 'My friend is a history student, and I'm learning Chinese,' one of them said at length. 'Neither of us, therefore, is an expert on economics. But we do think that your great fellow countryman Karl Marx must have worked things out when he evolved that formula, and our leaders will know best what to do when the time comes.'

This conversation took place before Khrushchev's declaration about 'transition to Communism' at the Twenty-first Party Congress. Since 1960 the U.S.S.R. has been flooded by statements, articles, pamphlets and books describing what life will be like once Communism has been established completely, and this has culminated in the publication of the draft of the new party Programme in the summer of 1961.[2] Whatever the reasons prompting the Kremlin (one of them was probably the challenge of the Chinese, who claimed that their 'people's communes' were a short cut to Communism), some features of this promised land of joy and happiness do not seem very attractive to the Russians. They learn from these blueprints, for example, that under Communism they will have to live in huge collective housing units with little privacy and still less private property.[3] This hardly fits in with their idea of happiness, least of all while they are beginning to enjoy—after years of enforced collective living in overcrowded houses—their newly-built modest apartments. Their present state of mind is aptly described by Granin in the opening paragraphs of his recent novel *After the Wedding*, in which the newly-weds, moving into their one-room flat, rejoice over their just acquired privacy: 'Neither the dazzlingly white ceiling with the plaster rosette in the centre, nor the shining yellow parquet, caused as much joy as those four thick and soundproof walls that, like ramparts, ensured their privacy.'[4]

CHAPTER 14

THE FATHERLAND

OF ALL THE PILLARS that support the Soviet regime, the strongest, I think, is the patriotism of the Russian people. It is a kind of love for the mother country peculiar to the Russians, a natural phenomenon that existed ages before the Bolsheviks were ever heard of, and which their long years of attack have failed to shake. It is the love of little mother Russia—her vast expanse, her language, her songs, and her proverbs—and although in bygone days Tsar and Church were also important elements in it, Russian patriotism has survived both the extinction of the monarchy and the state's bitter war against the church.

I still remember the first time I came across this particular form of patriotism. It was in the summer of 1930, when I spent two months in Russia. Among the people I met was a Russian girl of my own age. She came from a middle-class family, had lost her parents in the upheavals of the revolution and civil war, had herself experienced much suffering and injustice, and was now just barely managing to eke out an existence. At first our conversations were confined to generalities, but later we began to talk politics. 'We talked' is perhaps not quite accurate, for she did all the talking, and she complained bitterly against the Bolshevik regime, its cruelty and malevolence, its complete disregard for happiness and human dignity. It was obviously a great relief to her to be able to pour out her woes to a foreigner who could have no possible reason for denouncing her later. It was only after she had unburdened her heart that I was able to get a word in.

I had no difficulty in sympathizing with her complaints or, for that matter, in pointing out further abuses which she had not mentioned and which seemed to me particularly evil. But then a complete change came over her. She began to contradict me sharply, explaining the necessity of the Party measures I had criticized. The more I said, the more heated she became, and she ended by defending Bolshevism. Later I often came across similar, though perhaps not quite so violent, examples of sudden shifts from criticism of the regime to vindication of it—switches inspired purely by patriotism.

The significance of Russian patriotism first became clear to the outside world during World War II. In the beginning, the Red Army was fighting for the Soviet state and Stalinism. But was the whole of the Red Army really fighting? Hundreds of thousands laid down their arms at the first opportunity. Stalin had reduced a patriotic people to such a condition that their love of the homeland was overshadowed by their hatred of the regime, by the hope of a change for the better with the help of the Germans. Then Stalin himself changed course; the slogan of an anti-fascist war for the advancement of socialism was transformed into an appeal for the 'great patriotic war', the 'great war for the defence of the fatherland'. And it was this that in the end led the Red armies from Stalingrad to the Brandenburg Gate.

In the eyes of Soviet citizens the fact that the Soviet state survived the onslaught of the German divisions which had swept without much apparent effort across the rest of Europe, and that the Red Army eventually surged forward from the Volga to the Elbe, provided the most convincing proof of the might of the Soviet Union. Not everybody will agree with Soviet propaganda claims about the manner in which victory was achieved, the part played by Russia's allies, and the causes that led to the final collapse of Germany; but that does not alter the salient fact that victory was won.

The senseless and appalling atrocities committed, on Hitler's orders, against Russian prisoners-of-war and civilians in occupied territories made it easier for Stalin to push this change of line. But it had started long before. As early as spring, 1934, Stalin had issued a decree about the teaching of history, which was no longer to be approached from the international viewpoint but primarily on a national basis; as a result Russian history was rewritten for the second time in a single generation. After the Revolution Soviet historians had spent years denigrating the Russia of the Tsars as one vast and bloody prison, painting a sombre, terrible background against which the Bolshevik state would shine all the brighter. But with the change introduced in 1934, the Soviet historian was to portray Russian history from its very beginnings to the present day as a single and logical entity.

I have described in detail elsewhere this reversal of policy and its development since 1934.[1] Here we are concerned not with Stalin's decrees but with the reaction of the people. Their patriotism, affronted first by Stalin and then by Hitler, rallied again to Stalin the moment he presented himself as the symbol of Russia and of resistance to the foreign invader. I think the Bolsheviks have succeeded in representing the Soviet state as the heir to Russia's past, and in drawing to it that love of the homeland innate in all Russians. Throne and church, music and literature, the conquests of Siberia and of the Caucasus—all have been blended harmoniously like the elements of a great propaganda film.

One day I joined a group of Russian sightseers touring the Kremlin. The guide spoke of the treasures of the imperial armouries and of the churches converted into museums as normal features of the Russo-Soviet historical picture. As we were being conducted through the Uspenskaya, the Cathedral of the Assumption, he said: 'And over there in the corner, comrades, you see the tomb of a great Russian patriot.' We all turned our heads towards the tomb, and I wondered to whom he was referring. I already knew that Tsarist generals had been transformed into heroes of the Soviet Union. But neither Kutuzov nor Suvorov was buried there.

'There lie the remains of the patriarch Hermogen', the guide went on, 'who was murdered after gallantly resisting the Polish invaders.' He did not mention that this prince of the church had played a prominent part in suppressing the peasant revolt of 1606.

There was certainly a ludicrous side to the official encouragement of patriotism in Stalin's day, when everything from aircraft to the electric bulb was claimed as a Soviet invention. It was only after Stalin's death that this mania subsided; but the tendency is beginning to appear again—for example, it is now asserted that colour television is based on an invention of a Russian, Mikhaíl Lomonósov (1711-1765).[2] The successes of Soviet science are presented as results both of Russian genius and Communist leadership; thus not only Gagarin was decorated after he orbited the earth but also—Khrushchev!

During the de-Stalinization phase of 1956 I had an interesting conversation. The woman I talked to was in her late thirties, simply dressed, and a professional of some kind, probably a teacher. We had met in a bookshop, where my attention was first drawn to her by her look of disappointment when, in response to her request for four or five books, she received the same reply 'No'. I invited her to have tea with me in one of Moscow's few cafés.

The general excitement over the sudden denunciation of Stalin had loosened her tongue, and it had, indeed, loosened the tongues of a great many of her compatriots; during this period Soviet citizens were able to speak more frankly, perhaps, than ever before. One thing she said remains vividly in my memory:

'Do you know what I particularly hate about the whole business? I never liked Stalin—I knew too much about him, and some of my own family were unjustly condemned; but after all he was the regime, and you can't spend all your life hating the regime you have to live under. You can't go on forever bemoaning your fate day in and day out. So you try to convince yourself that things are not so bad after all. I don't know if you see what I mean. But there is such a thing as a feeling of being at peace with your fate, even when your life is bitter and joyless. You can either rebel against fate—but who does?—or you can come to terms with it, and the best way of doing that is to touch up all the drab pictures of the daily round with a little bright colour.'

She put into words the things which, I felt, others were also thinking, but which I had never before heard so clearly expressed. There are, apparently, opponents of Bolshevism who create their own picture of the world they live in, because it makes life easier. The daily lot is hard enough as it is. If, in addition, you feel compelled to say to yourself that everything you have been through is pointless anyway or, even worse, that it has perhaps served only evil ends, then life becomes intolerable. Soldiers who believe in what they are fighting for will endure the hardships of war better than those who feel they are battling and suffering in an unworthy cause.

Knowing that many Soviet citizens give themselves up to wishful thinking of this sort, I sometimes found it difficult, in conversation with them, to attack and expose the weakness of their positions. But whenever I talk to Party officials or representatives of the Soviet state, I never pull my punches, and I never hesitate to tell them bluntly about the antipathy I feel towards the system they represent. With the ordinary citizen it is a different matter. Who, from the safe haven of immunity, would wish to rob people of the consolation that makes life bearable—even when one knows that it is mere illusion?

An episode that occurred in 1955 comes to mind. I went for a drive in the country near Moscow with a group of Russians I had met quite casually. The conversation was lively and dealt mainly with contemporary literature, in which we were all interested. Then we reached the moment that comes in any conversation with Soviet citizens, and which I knew so well—the moment when their outward self-confidence and their inner uncertainty clash and when this produces a compulsion in them to elicit from the foreigner an assurance that all is well in the Soviet Union. As we drove past long blocks of new buildings I heard nothing but exaggerated expressions of self-congratulation—'A year ago there wasn't a sign of that huge block!' and so on, with pauses to give me an opportunity to exclaim 'How wonderful! The world has never seen anything like it before!' But I said nothing. And eventually came the question, in a rather obviously casual tone: 'Have you built any houses in Germany since the war?'

'Oh yes,' I replied, in an equally off-hand tone, 'we've been building about half a million apartments a year.'

There was a moment of silent consternation. Then one of the women in the group broke the silence. 'With American money!' she said scornfully.

'Immediately after the war,' I replied, 'we had the good fortune to receive brotherly help from the Americans.' I used the word 'brotherly' deliberately, because it is one the Soviets themselves are so fond of using when speaking of their aid to other countries. 'But for many years we've needed no help from anybody.'

This reply spoilt the friendly atmosphere of the outing, and soon afterwards my Russian companions took leave of me with some formality. Instead of bolstering their self-assurance, I had shattered it. I felt sorry for them.

The Communists have not forgotten the lessons of World War II, and they have encouraged patriotism ever since. Apart from the family, patriotism and devotion to the regime are the only loyalties they tolerate. They can go on doing this only so long as they can point to successes which support their claim to be the rightful custodians of the Russian heritage. But a series of national failures could make things very dangerous for them. From what we have seen so far, it is not very likely that the Soviet people will rebel if things go badly for them personally; but they might well rebel if they were convinced as Russian patriots that they could no longer support a Bolshevik policy that was proving catastrophic. We must, however, be clear on one point; the situation would have to be unmistakably disastrous, not merely a run of setbacks.

Another great asset of the regime is the dynamic energy of the Soviet people, which every visitor becomes aware of as soon as he enters the country. This drive is by no means self-explanatory, for the Soviet citizen himself derives only limited personal benefit from it. The modest improvement in living standards bears little relation to the demands which have been made on the people decade after decade. New factories, mines, dams, and canals are being built all the time, but they seem to have a life of their own, to be beneficial only to each other, rather than improving the living standards of the public. Where, then, did the Russians' enthusiasm for work stem from, since for a long time it did not lead to any appreciable improvement in their living conditions?

The goad of the 'plan' and the production norm; the draconian discipline imposed on the workers; the severe penalties for failing in a given task; the absence of any logical relation between wages and prices, which compels people to work extremely hard in order to raise their living standards even a little—all these things offer only a partial explanation of the dynamic force that undoubtedly exists. The impressive reconstruction and expansion of the Soviet Union could not have been brought about by these factors alone; the pressure imposed from above must be reciprocated by a drive from below. What, then, are the reasons for this drive? As I have shown elsewhere, the great discrepancy between the poverty of the population and the vast riches of the country must have inspired a powerful urge to overcome this poverty by exploiting the natural wealth that lies dormant.[3]

The determination of the Soviet people, and particularly of

the younger generation, is very different from that which existed during the First Five-Year Plan or during the Revolution itself. It is not political or ideological, but is like the drive shown by other nations at times of great economic expansion— by the Americans, for example, in the pioneer spirit that drove them irresistibly onward to conquer and open up the American West.

Closely linked with the urge for economic expansion is the belief that technology is a panacea. The mystic light in which the Russians are inclined to see something which the rest of us have come to regard with unemotional sobriety can be understood only when their psychology is taken into account. A deeply religious people whose emotional fervour has been deprived of its expression within the framework of its church is now seeking new forms and objects of faith. People who have laboriously plodded, step by step, through the process of technical development regard technology with a far more sceptical eye than the Russians, who, in the beginning, simply adopted its formulas and achievements. The suddenness of their leap into complex modern technology—the construction, for example, of a modern steelmill or even an atomic energy plant—blinds them to everything but the positive aspects. The reserve with which automation is regarded in the West, where its drawbacks as well as its advantages are recognized, is something as yet unknown in the Soviet Union.

But there is a limit to all things. The unceasing torrent of invariably optimistic Soviet propaganda is fraying the nerves not only of foreign visitors but also of the Soviet people themselves. No note of pessimism is allowed to creep into anything concerning the Soviet Union or its officially sanctioned interpretation of history.

On one of the main boulevards of Moscow there stood for many years a statue of Gogol. When I was a child I never passed it without stopping to gaze at it. Gogol, who died insane, was shown seated in an armchair, brooding, melancholy, his chin sunk on his chest. During the 1930's it was still there. But on my first post-war visit in 1955 I found that it had been replaced by a new Gogol, standing with head erect, gazing into the future, and radiating optimism.

Even Chekhov, that master of tender melancholy, has been remodelled as an optimist by Soviet literary historians. No one has been praised more for his faith in the future or been held up more frequently as an example of a good Communist than Mayakovsky, the young poet of the Revolution, who committed suicide in 1930 in despair at the direction the Soviet regime was taking.

However the people may react to official optimism, it seems to me that on the whole they now regard the future with more confidence than they did in the 1930's. Although reconstruction and expansion have brought only minor benefits to the people as a whole, the national advance has given rise to a feeling that things are progressing, that eventually the man in the street will also reap the benefit.

One final thought on this subject. The imperial mission— the urge to expand and the desire for power that have existed in the Russian people for centuries—is now proving of great value to the Bolsheviks. The dynamic force which extended the boundaries of the once insignificant state of Moscow to the shores of the Pacific is still an active and potent factor. The incorporation of half of Europe, the swift spread of Communism to some 600 million Chinese, its thrust into Korea and Vietnam, the influence exerted by Moscow on the former colonial world —all these things have increased the self-assurance and the sense of mission that received their first great impetus from the winning of World War II.

The dynamic urge of this imperial mission is to be found primarily, of course, among those in the Soviet Union who feel themselves to be masters in their own home—the Great Russians. It is much less prevalent among the many non-Russian elements in the U.S.S.R., and even less so in the East European states that have fallen under the domination of Moscow. The drive there, as the events of the autumn of 1956 proved, is not towards Bolshevism but away from it.

CHAPTER 15

THE CONTENTED AND THE DISCONTENTED

SOVIET MAN possesses some characteristics that make it easier for the authorities to fit him into the Bolshevik regime, and others that make it more difficult. How, then, does he stand in relation to the realities of the world he lives in? Is he contented with them or not? Let us first look at the surroundings in which he works, for in a totalitarian state his reaction to his immediate environment is also a political factor.

A Harvard study has shown that of the former Soviet workers and peasants who were driven westwards by the war and did not return to their homes, two-thirds had been discontented with their lives in the Soviet Union.[1] It is not possible to conduct a survey of this kind within the Soviet Union, but it is obvious that discontent is far greater among the industrial workers and peasants than among the 'new class'. From what I have seen, I would say that it is considerably greater among the peasants than among the industrial workers.

Not only is the peasant poorest, but he is also forced to work and live in conditions that daily offend his peasant instinct for personal ownership. He does not feel that the Soviet state belongs to him. It was primarily the peasants who welcomed German troops with bread and salt in 1941. And it was primarily the sons of these peasants who laid down their arms in their hundreds of thousands, preferring German captivity to continuing to fight for Bolshevism. However, it is precisely this—the most discontented—section of the community that is least inclined and least able, to formulate any political ideas or demands. The peasants' one great desire is to free themselves from the coercion of the *kolkhozes* and the whole system of collective agriculture; beyond that, as far as I have been able to judge, they have practically no views at all on the future political structure of the Soviet Union. They are less interested than any other section of the community in political freedom beyond the confines of their villages. The Harvard study came to the conclusion that the desire for civil freedom was weakest by far among the lower social groups.[2]

210

I think it can be said that for a long time to come the Soviet regime has less to fear from the middle and lower classes than from any other group. They live far too miserably, are far too poverty-stricken and too deeply immersed in the struggle to achieve their allotted production quota and earn their daily bread to be capable of taking political initiative without adequate leadership. Furthermore, some of the more capable and active members of the lower social strata, their potential leaders, drop out from the ranks of the opposition; the chance of climbing into the upper class is so alluring that they prefer—at least for the moment—to accept it.

If the need arises, the regime can always increase the supply of consumer goods, and thus cut the ground from under the feet of any potential opposition. Stalin's successors employed these measures to considerable effect while they felt their position was insecure. They paid the peasants more for their products and offered the population as a whole a wider variety of goods. Soviet man is certainly far from being pampered and is still grateful for even the most modest improvement to his lot. The regime, therefore, does not need to go to any great expense to give the people the feeling that things are getting better.

In spite of his discontent, the industrial worker is in a very different position, psychologically, from the peasant. He is courted by the regime as the keystone of the state, and although he knows that this is not really true he enjoys his prestige. The power of propaganda in such matters in a totalitarian state must not be underestimated. The rapid expansion of industry has also increased the worker's self-assurance. He has the confidence of a man who is good at his job and who knows that the smooth working of the whole structure depends on his skill. The feeling that he is indispensable is clearly discernible in the skilled Soviet worker's awareness of his status. Any direct and practical attempt to exploit the strength of his position is, however, prevented by the fact that since the ascent of Stalin, the Soviet trade unions have been obedient instruments in the hands of the Party and the state. Their prime function is not the protection of their members' interests, but the fulfilment of the state plan by their members.

Barely thirty years ago it was possible to mobilize ignorant peasants and thrust them into the primitive workshops and factories of the First Five-Year Plan. It was a policy that even at the time was very costly, and the path of breakneck progress was littered with the wrecks of tens of thousands of machines rendered unserviceable by the peasants' ineptitude. At the present technical level, with automation already casting its shadow, such a procedure would be impossible. Modern industry needs an ever-increasing number of skilled and responsible men to serve it. Almost anyone can wield a hammer, but it takes an expert to handle and use precision tools if they are not to be ruined; so the regime, whether it likes it or not, is obliged to show more consideration to the highly specialized craftsmen than it gave to the army of workers who toiled in the first blast furnaces of Magnitogorsk.

There is a very good reason why the problem of productivity is being so intensively discussed by Soviet leaders. The time when it was easy to recruit millions of extra workers from the villages has passed. Reserves of manpower are dwindling and are almost exhausted. An increase in production can therefore be attained only by an increase in the productivity of each worker. But an increase in individual productivity above the level considered acceptable during the early years of industrial expansion becomes possible only if the individual worker, above all the skilled worker, is prepared to put his heart into his work—and he will do that only if he is more or less content with his job and working conditions.

The measure of a man's contentment with his occupation does not necessarily tell us anything about his attitude towards the regime. A large number of Soviet citizens like their work, but not the state which benefits from it. In a population made up mainly of state employees, where occupation and state are so closely linked, it is to be expected that the individual's attitude towards each will bear some relationship. It is to the regime's advantage that its potentially most powerful antagonist—the upper class—is relatively satisfied. The Harvard study reported that four-fifths of the members of the intelligentsia questioned, and three-fourths of the senior employees, were content with their occupations in the Soviet Union.[3]

From my own observations, I do not believe that the Harvard figures apply to these social groups within the Soviet Union itself; for it must be remembered that the *émigré* often sees things in a much more favourable light when he turns his yearning eyes back to his own country. But I am fully prepared to accept the fact that the majority within the 'new class' are content with their jobs. It is inconceivable that a group, a large percentage of which likes its work, should want to overthrow the regime— at least so long as it is in a position to satisfy part of its aspirations.

The growing desire for material well-being, therefore, is also of political significance. An example may help to make this clearer. When I left the Soviet Union in 1936 the great department store GUM, in Red Square, did not exist in its present form. If it had, it would have been an object of tremendous admiration. People would have thronged its counters in wide-eyed astonishment. Today they can buy things at GUM which they never even dreamed of in 1936. But if you mingle with the customers now, you will hear quite a lot of criticism—prices are too high, quality is poor, service is not all it should be, and so on. In other words, the people are becoming more discriminating and exacting. This may well be followed by a desire—particularly among the upper class—to make their criticisms heard. But once the upper class begins voicing its criticism, this will not be confined to prices and the quality of goods. For it is in this group's interest that the Party should not make detached and isolated decisions influencing its income and security, but should be attentive to its desires and needs.

It is, above all, the younger generation of the elite that makes increasing demands as a matter of course, and these demands increase more quickly than they can be satisfied. When the older generation of Bolsheviks passed judgment on the actions of the Party leaders, they used to ask themselves whether the measures taken were in harmony with the spirit of the Revolution. But the criterion applied by their children is 'To what extent does the regime satisfy our personal desires?'

The fact that every person in the Soviet Union is more or less a state employee, an official, as it were, must, in the nature of things, stifle the development of independent political thinking. The outlook of a government official must, because of his position and function, differ from that of people who earn their living independently. His attitude is conditioned by the habit of obedience and pension expectations. This is particularly true in the

Soviet Union, where the government servant has even less chance than his Western counterpart of being able to 'retire with dignity to his country estate' to continue his life in comfort and peace. Even when he has retired on a pension, he is not a free man, but has to carry out certain political tasks—not the least of which is the disagreeable duty of keeping a watchful eye on the doings of his neighbours.[4]

Among high-ranking civil servants there are, of course, some who are in a position to put forward their own requests; but this group's primary concern is to maintain and strengthen for themselves and their children the positions they have won by great effort, and often enough by methods that weigh heavily on their conscience.

Louis Fischer, a Western journalist who lived in the Soviet Union for a long time during the 1920's and 1930's, has since had two conversations in Moscow with people of this kind. He was dining with a celebrated Soviet writer who knew Europe well and spoke several Western languages fluently. The two men were alone, and the Russian spoke frankly and critically about the prevailing conditions. But when Fischer suggested that the only real remedy was greater personal freedom, he raised his hands in horror. 'For heaven's sake!' he cried. 'Anything you like—but not freedom!' On another occasion a professor used practically the same words. Both took the view that if the peasants gained their freedom they would at once abandon collective agriculture; the towns would be without food; and the workers would demand the right to strike and a say in the direction of the factories. Both writer and professor saw the future of their country in terms of black and white, with no intermediate possibility—either Communism or chaos. They disliked Communism, but they feared chaos even more. As far as they were concerned, the years of Communist domination had obliterated all possible alternatives, just as they had obliterated the men who had had the courage to fight for these alternatives.[5]

How much easier this makes it for the regime to maintain its hold is obvious. I did not get the impression that the new elite was in any way rebellious. Such an attitude would run contrary to historical precedent; for the first few generations at least, *parvenus* have always shown themselves politically docile and conservative.

The interest of the Soviet upper class—apart from the Party itself—is concentrated more on material than on political issues. This the Party leaders realize. They bribe the elite with relative prosperity and are confident of being able to go on doing so successfully. If the regime is prepared to give its upper class high incomes, good professional opportunities, promotion, and prestige in state and society; if it is prepared to guarantee them a certain measure of personal security and refrain from interfering intolerably—and if at the same time it holds in check the masses who were mobilized in the name of equality during the Revolution—then most of the 'new class' will remain content, for as long, at least, as the Soviet state continues to appear powerful and stable.

The least contented among the intelligentsia are, roughly speaking, the oldest and the youngest. Among the pre-war intellectuals the only exceptions are those who have risen to the highest positions under the Bolshevik regime and have nevertheless survived the bloody purges unscathed. One such exception is the physicist Pyotr Kapitsa, who returned to the Soviet Union in the middle of the 1930's and has received highly preferential treatment in recognition of his outstanding abilities. But, as a rule, the regime has never fully relented in its suspicion of the old intelligentsia. Most of them have suffered too much and have been too deeply humiliated ever to become convinced adherents of Bolshevism.

On the other hand, an intellectual proletariat has appeared, composed of those secondary-school students who have been prevented from continuing their studies. Since the state is the sole employer, it is against the state that any occupational discontent will inevitably be directed. Many young people have been disappointed in their high hopes of successful professional careers. This cannot fail to have some effect on their political outlook; a regime that first offers great prospects of advancement and then side-tracks millions of its senior students to the assembly line and village is bound to arouse considerable resentment.

When the future of Bolshevism is discussed in the West, it is sometimes said that there is an irreconcilable contradiction between a technology that needs free research in order to expand and a totalitarian state, and thus between technicians and Party functionaries. But as I have already mentioned, it can be assumed that the spirit of critical thinking once awakened will not allow itself to be blocked indefinitely by political taboos. True, neither under Hitler nor under Soviet dictators did technology deteriorate, as the V-2 rockets and the Sputniks clearly show. But this is far from justifying any claim that modern technology thrives best in a totalitarian state, for it was the free people of the United States—to confine ourselves to military progress— who produced the first operational atomic bombs. The weakness of a totalitarian state lies in the limitations it imposes, and indeed in the paralysing influence it sometimes exercises, on individual initiative; its strength, compared with a democratic state, lies in its almost unlimited capacity to concentrate its resources on a given objective.

Interest in the preservation of its privileges is probably also one of the strongest motives governing the thoughts and actions of the officers' corps. There is not much likelihood at present of political opposition from the Soviet Army. Such internal opposition as existed was swept away with the army's most able leader, Marshal Tukhachevsky, and thousands of other officers in the savage Stalinist purges of the 1930's. For a long time now the great majority of officers have been members of the Communist Party. The proportion of Party and Komsomol members among the officers was put at 86 per cent by Marshal Vassilevsky in 1952 and by Marshal Malinovsky at the beginning of 1958.[6] Innumerable political commissars are firmly entrenched in the army. Their official duties vary, admittedly, according to the political climate, but they are always there to serve as the eyes and ears of the Party. For many years the state security forces, too, had their own agents in the army ranks.

If further proof of the complete subordination of the armed forces to the Party was needed, it was furnished in October 1957 when Marshal Zhukov passively allowed himself to be degraded and banished by Khrushchev. To the Russian people Zhukhov was not only the greatest military hero of the last hundred years; he was also the most popular figure in the whole of the Soviet Union. 'As long as Zhukov is there,' Russians used to tell me, 'nothing very terrible can happen, either at home or abroad.' Then suddenly he was put out to pasture like an old carthorse, and not a soul in the length and breadth of Russia raised a voice, let alone a hand, in protest. That the Soviet Marshals, his closest colleagues, should have nothing but abuse for him, and that Marshal Konyev should devote twelve columns in *Pravda* to stripping him of all his greatness as a soldier and a man—this was only to be expected.[7] The weight carried by military leaders is cancelled out by their rivalries; most of the Marshals have been corrupted by the luxury and glamour with which the Party has surrounded them, and they follow whoever happens at the moment to be in control of the Party machine. But the most significant feature of the whole affair is the fact that even in the somewhat relaxed atmosphere of the post-Stalin era nobody—not a single officer of any rank—dared to protest against the denigration of a great and revered military leader. When a Communist Party leader can do this to the army, he may say to himself that there is nothing he cannot do.

When the Hungarian revolt broke out, exactly a year before Zhukov's fall, many people in the West wondered whether the Soviet Army would carry out its orders, whether it really would advance with armour and artillery against the men, women, and children of a nation fighting for its freedom with bare hands. A few Soviet soldiers did, indeed, baulk at the idea and deserted, but that made little difference. The juggernaut rolled on until its bloody task had been accomplished. Tito's words on 11 November 1956—'It is with heavy hearts and against their will that the Soviet soldiers are marching into Hungary'—were probably true; but willing or unwilling, the Soviet troops marched on.

The Soviet army—and here is the lesson to be learned from Hungary and the smooth elimination of Zhukov—is an obedient tool in the hands of the Party leaders. I think it will remain obedient as long as the control of power within the Party remains clearly defined. The Soviet armed forces could become an independent political factor only if the Party leadership were involved in a crisis and the Kremlin were thrown into confusion. The recognition of this possibility is undoubtedly one of the reasons why the Party leaders are always anxious to settle any internal disagreements as quickly as possible, and thus prevent the initiative from passing into the hands of the army.

The non-Russian, or, more precisely, the non-Great Russian, nationalities must be considered separately. Twenty-five years after the Revolution, the widespread hostility shown by them against the Soviet regime in World War II astonished the whole world. Since then, they have been condemned to political silence. But it seems to me that they look forward to a loosening of the bonds of dictatorship more eagerly than the Russians themselves, for they hope thereby to become more independent of the 'foreigners' wielding power from Moscow.

The urge for independence is strongest among the Ukrainians, and it was manifested in both world wars when German troops marched into the Ukraine. Hitler, however, was interested in the Ukrainians only as a reservoir of forced labour. The Ukrainians' disillusionment, coupled with the reprisals taken by the Soviet Army when it regained its strength, dealt a severe, perhaps fatal, blow to their determination to assert their independence. Many thousands of them were deported to eastern Siberia, and large numbers were compelled to remain there after the war. But in the hearts of many Ukrainians—whether they live in the Ukraine or elsewhere in the Soviet Union, or are emigrants—a flame of resentment against the Russians still burns side by side with their hatred of Bolshevism. During a crisis, this might become a significant factor; on the other hand, it might well compel the Great Russians to show more consideration towards a government of which they would normally disapprove but which keeps the Ukrainians in check. Not very different from the attitude of the Ukrainians is that of the Baltic nations within the U.S.S.R.

Next to the Ukrainians, the Georgians have resisted incorporation in the Bolshevik state for the longest time. The fact that it was one of their own countrymen, Josef Djugashvili, alias Stalin, who ruled over the Soviet empire made it easier for them to reconcile themselves to their lot; and the Georgians, though they could hardly have had much love for him, have never forgiven the men in Moscow for their treatment of Stalin after his death. According to the published reports, the only disorders that followed de-Stalinization took place in Tbilisi, the capital of Georgia. A Moscow railway porter told me at the time that he had seen a train come in from Tbilisi with practically all its windows smashed.

The Turkic peoples living in Russia were subjugated by the Tsars in the second half of the nineteenth century, but retained their national identity and their religion, Islam. During the Revolution large areas freed themselves from Russian domination under the banner of a pan-Turkic movement and were then subjugated for the second time with ruthless and bloody force. The levelling process, the campaign Moscow has waged relentlessly for many years against all independent movements, has not been without effect. But the ultimate result is still in the balance.

The Bolsheviks have persecuted, incarcerated, and liquidated the adherents of the pan-Turkic movement. But this has given a powerful impetus to the nationalist feelings of the splinter states that they themselves created: Uzbekistan, Turkmenistan, Tadjikistan, Kirghizia, and Kazakhstan. It is possible that the new-born nationalism of Uzbekistan, Turkmenistan, and the rest —firmly based as it is in history, language, and folklore—may in the long run prove more of a thorn in the side of Bolshevism than the vague and nebulous pan-Turkic concept of the past. For it is only since the Soviet authorities, aiming at closer political control, compelled the nomad tribes to settle permanently in one area that this new nationalism has been able to base itself on a specific region. The equally violent economic penetration of the Central Asian territories, which has raised their economic standards and thus enhanced their self-assurance, has also strengthened their feeling of independence.

It is true that the Soviet authorities have deposed, liquidated, or exiled the nationalist intelligentsia of these peoples. But they are teaching the native population to read and write and training them for the technical professions. The new native intelligentsia which emerges from these schools may prove more amenable in many ways than the old; but they are already becoming more ambitious in their claims than their elders ever were, and they will undoubtedly cause the Russians considerable headaches in the future.

The Russification that has inevitably accompanied the economic revolution in Central Asia has increased anti-Russian feeling. In Tsarist days this hostility was confined to a relatively small section of society, since most of the local population had no contact at all with Russians. Today there is no Uzbek, no Kazakh who has not had personal experience of the Russian, and not all these experiences have been happy. During the second half of the Stalin era the Russian Bolsheviks were encouraged to regard themselves as superior to the non-Russians, and this policy has now borne bitter fruit. While in Tashkent, I observed the arrogance with which Russian *nachal'niki* ordered their Uzbek subordinates about.

The Russian has a marked aptitude for the assimilation of modern technical knowledge; in addition he has by far the best educational facilities in the Soviet Union. Since the acquisition of technical knowledge is being encouraged by every available means, the Russian rises more quickly to the top than the non-Russian citizens of the U.S.S.R. In very many cases a Russian is the top man not because he is a Russian, but because he is the most suitable man—if only from the point of view of language. But for the local population it amounts to the same thing. They say, 'All the plums go to the Russians', or at least, 'The Russians are given a much better chance'. The persistence of these anti-Russian forces in Soviet Central Asia came to light during World War II, when hundreds of thousands of men of these races were ready to fight under Hitler against the Soviet Union.

It is difficult to estimate how strong these forces are today. People forget more quickly than the historically minded are inclined to think. When I visited Kazakhstan in the autumn of 1935—that is, immediately after the nomads had been forcibly settled, with a million lives lost in the process—I was astonished to find how little there was in the people's attitude to remind one of those events. When I walked through the broad fields where rice was being harvested, when I photographed a group of flat-nosed, giggling Kazakh girls beside a tractor-driven threshing machine, when I saw them dancing and singing in the evening, I could never have guessed that two or three years earlier an appalling upheaval had occurred in the lives of every one of them, claiming innumerable victims.

The chances that the non-Russian nationalities will have any effect on Bolshevism must not be over-estimated. The reaction of a Ukrainian or Georgian lawyer or doctor is closer to that of a Russian lawyer or doctor than to the reactions of a Ukrainian or Georgian peasant.[8]

In concluding this brief study of the attitude of the various groups and classes of the Soviet population towards the regime, it is essential to turn our attention again to the young, for in the final analysis it is the 'yes' or 'no' of the rising generation that will decide the fate of this regime.

Children are not aware of social problems, and Soviet children absorb as a matter of course the political phrases on which they are brought up, in the same way that they absorb all the other impressions and fragments of knowledge presented to them. That one has parents or else is reared in an orphanage; that two times two is four; that the Soviet state has the best constitution and the most benevolent government in the world; that everyone must go to school; that there are automobiles and airplanes —Soviet children learn all this automatically. Like the children of all nations throughout the ages, they grow imperceptibly into their environment.

Russia's young people emerge into the harsh realities of the world under the surveillance of teachers in whom the liberal heritage of the nineteenth-century Russian intelligentsia is still a living force. They try to remain loyal to it by idealizing and beautifying, for their own benefit and for their pupils', the state they serve and the conditions in which Soviet man lives, giving it a liberal and friendly appearance. This is bound to lead to disillusionment as it is expressed in a letter by two adolescent daughters of an army officer:

> 'In school they teach us one thing, and in the newspapers and books we read the same thing. But in life everything is quite different. Then is everything a lie? Do the newspapers lie, the teachers lie, the writers tell untruth? . . . Is everything that we believed in, that we were told, nothing but lies?'[9]

There is a great difference between the world of school and university and the world in which young people find themselves afterwards. It is this, I think, that accounts for the tenacity with which Soviet citizens in their thirties and forties cling to the memories of their schooldays; they are fond of using the word *svétly* (bright) in speaking of them. Those were the shining days—bright indeed compared with the sombre workaday world that now surrounds them, and bright, too, because in those days they basked in the warm glow of ideals and ideas to which subsequent realities offer so depressing and so disappointing a contrast. What they learned about Communist ideology as children sounded far more alluring than the reality they encountered later. And it is because the Soviet leaders consistently blow the trumpet of propaganda too loudly that the Russian later in his life is so conscious of the discrepancy between promise and reality. Every day he hears—and indeed joins in singing—the song that proudly proclaims, 'There is no land in which a man breathes so freely as in the Soviet Union'; yet he lives in greater fear of the state than any of his contemporaries in Western countries. The recognition of this contrast leads inevitably to indifference to politics, and ultimately to cynicism.

It might be said that a young man brought up in the West in a devout Christian home and school must be similarly disillusioned when he sees the way many people who call themselves Christians behave. But the comparison is not valid because the Christian is not taught that man is innately good, and he is prepared for the discrepancy between ideal and reality. Bolshevism, on the other hand, starts with the assumption that to be *good* all one needs is an insight into the laws of dialectical materialism; it is a concept that allows no room for evil in the world except in the wholly inadequate fringe occupied by such figures as 'foreign spies', 'agents of bloodthirsty imperialism', and 'remnants of the capitalist past'.

I can best summarize this study of segments of the Soviet population by saying that there are some who support the state and others who are dissatisfied; side by side with the factors working towards consolidation are the forces tending towards disintegration. If one tries to strike a balance it seems that Soviet man is far less favourably disposed towards Bolshevism than has been generally assumed. In any event, he certainly does not regard the Soviet state as *his* state, as Moscow propaganda would have us believe. On the contrary, I find, having lived for many years in both the United States and the Soviet Union, that the average American identifies himself more closely with his state and its government than the average Russian with his.

CHAPTER 16

RETREAT FROM POLITICS

When I walked into the lobby of my hotel in Moscow one day in March, some of the male guests were shaking hands with the pleasant woman at the reception desk and offering her their congratulations. Then I noticed that the woman at the news-stand and one of the cleaning-women were receiving similar attentions. It seemed rather coincidental that all of them should have birthdays on the same day. But when I offered my own good wishes to the receptionist I discovered that it was not a birthday but International Women's Day.

Originally 8 March had been purely a revolutionary campaign day marked by demonstrations in favour of women's rights and other political aims. The unrest that led to the February Revolution of 1917 followed a demonstration organized on Women's Day of that year. (It was actually on 8 March, but according to the old calendar then in use in Russia, the day fell in February.) However, nowadays 8 March has as little political significance in the minds of the Russian people as Mothers' Day does in the Western world.

The front pages of the newspapers, of course, carry leading articles on feminine problems, but on the back pages are advertisements such as 'Buy your 8 March presents from a member of the Jewellers' Trust'. The shops are more crowded than usual, and men go shopping as eagerly as they do on Christmas Eve in the West. Children buy presents for their woman teachers; women and girls put on their best clothes, and many wear flowers. The evening is festive, with dancing, singing, and drinking.

I remember from my childhood in Moscow the devotion with which the Russians used to celebrate name-days—in fact, with far more enthusiasm than they observed birthdays. On Tatyana Day or Olga Day there was always great excitement in the families which included a Tatyana or an Olga. For men the custom had the advantage that they only had to remember the names of their women friends, without worrying about birthday dates. Today in Russia things are simpler still; you don't even have to remember the names. On 8 March you can confidently offer your good wishes to anyone of the female sex.

It is rather comforting that the Russians have not lost the capacity to transform the political into the personal. For a very large number of Soviet citizens, particularly the younger ones who know the Revolution only from their history books, the two revolutionary days—7 November and 1 May—have hardly any significance as days of political struggle; to them they differ from ordinary days chiefly because nobody goes to work.

This process of stripping the revolutionary anniversaries of their political significance is part of the general decline of interest in politics. When I was in the Soviet Union around 1930 every conversation sooner or later turned into a political discussion. Today that seldom happens unless a foreigner deliberately turns the conversation in that direction.

This change is most obvious among the younger generation. The message reported to have been sent by the apolitical Yugoslav youth to the Party—'For us the knowledge, for you the state'—might well serve as a motto for many young people in the Soviet Union. In restaurants I have heard young people discussing every subject under the sun, except politics. They talk about their schools and universities, their teachers, their friends, their ambitions, their work, and how much money they earn—but of affairs of state, not a word. If by any chance a political issue is raised, it invariably turns out that the youngsters who raise it are, as it were, 'professional' politicians—officials of the Komsomol or some such organization.

Nevertheless, it would be a mistake to regard this apathy or even hostility towards politics as a disadvantage to the regime; it strengthens the already great interest in higher education, in the professions, and in technology. The urge to enter one of the technical professions may be described as a kind of 'inner emigration'. Millions wish to make the grade, not only in the hope of rapid promotion, but also because these professions offer the prospect of a life that is relatively uncomplicated by politics; in this sense medicine and teaching are regarded as technical professions.

Pro-Stalin, anti-Stalin, pro-Khrushchev, anti-Khrushchev—these are no longer matters of universal concern. Too much has already gone by the board, including many illusions. Just as people who could not bear witness to the tyranny of the Musco-vite princes migrated as settlers to the forests of the far north, so millions today hurry as fast as they can into the technical professions, as far away as possible from the strains and tensions of politics. There is no doubt that the men who designed and built the Sputniks are all enthusiastic inventors and technicians. But how many of them, I wonder, are enthusiastic Communists? Major Gagárin, we were informed by Moscow, had only joined the Party in 1960, that is shortly before his epoch-making flight through space.

Neither apathy nor active hostility towards politics need re-strict Soviet man's efficiency or zest for work. The greatest achievement of the younger generation since the war has been in Siberia. The number of young men and women who have gone beyond the Urals to work must be close to a million. During my tours in Siberia and the newly opened territories in Kazakhstan, I have come across a great number of them. They lead an arduous and exacting life; but the Russians, as World War II showed, stand up well to hardship. Return, particularly from such remote projects as the new dam at Bratsk, north of Irkutsk, is made very difficult for them. Of the burning eager-ness of the First Five-Year Plan I have found no trace. Every-thing now is much more prosaic. The Party is making vain efforts to re-kindle the spirit of those days. But whether the young people undertake their hard tasks out of enthusiasm, as Soviet propaganda would have us believe, or for other motives, the fact remains that their achievements are impressive.

The tendency to turn their backs on politics and their obvious indifference to the political slogans hurled at them are, to my mind, the most striking features of the Soviet people of today. They are fed up with politics and the indoctrination to which they are incessantly subjected. They are beginning to show resistance. In particular the educated younger generation has demonstrated clearly that it is not prepared to take the torrent of propaganda and slogans seriously. The young poetess Bella Akhmadullina spoke for many of her generation when she said: 'I am apolitical.'[1]

A foreign girl who recently spent some months in the Soviet Union, mostly among young people, described a cabaret show she attended that was organized by a Moscow college. One of the sketches dealt with the possibility of a trip to Mars. The general revulsion at Marxism was well brought out in the punch line: 'Now, of course, we will be given another required subject to study—*Marsism*.'[2] It was a Soviet intellectual who told me the joke in which someone asks: 'What is the difference between Capitalism and Communism?' The answer: 'Under Capitalism man exploits man, under Communism it's just the other way round.'

In the turbulent autumn of 1956 the students of the Bauman Technical College in Moscow demanded a referendum on the question 'Is it really worth while adhering to the curriculum?'[3] In reality this was a diplomatically phrased criticism of the Marxist-Leninist course of indoctrination. Once I observed some students memorizing Marx's theory of surplus value; they were doing it mechanically, like schoolboys repeating the parts of a French irregular verb. The words themselves obviously conveyed nothing to them.

The Revolution and the First Five-Year Plan had a romantic aura about them; young people particularly were inspired, even intoxicated. Now they are suffering from a hangover. One of the best-known contemporary writers, Valentin Ovéchkin, wrote recently:

> Today the Komsomol members spend their time in purely childish activities—the appointment of a sponsor for a calf, the collecting of scrap metal. Compare that with what they did during the civil war, in the initial years of Soviet might, during the first days of collectivization! At the age of sixteen Arkady Gaidar commanded a regiment; twenty-four-year-old Shors commanded a division. Lads of twenty and twenty-two were organizing revolutionary committees, *kolkhozes*, and the like.[4]

It was not entirely by chance that Ovechkin chose the Komsomol as his theme. This youth organization, which has a membership of about 18 million,[5] has lost much of its former *élan* and is now not much more than an ancillary service in the educational system and a recruiting centre for any special activities the Party wishes to initiate. The Komsomol secretaries, depicted in books for teenagers as superb leaders, in reality enjoy only very modest prestige and are regarded much more as agitators, political careerists, and denunciators, whom one cannot trust. This is the result partly of young people's lack of interest in politics and partly of the measures introduced in Stalin's day to mould the youth of the country into willing tools of Party and state. This process reached its peak in the resolution passed by the Komsomol in 1944, which imposed on the organization the obligation to 'support the teachers and to pay due attention to the opinions they express'.[6] Since then the director of a school has been given the right 'to veto the implementation of erroneous resolutions carried by the Komsomol organization in his school'. A few years ago I heard of a student meeting called by the Komsomol in Moscow to reprimand a student who made uncomplimentary remarks about one of the professors. Twenty years ago this would have been unthinkable. Teachers were regarded as contemptible, practically insufferable reactionaries, while the younger generation itself was considered to be the true leader to a better future.

As a result of Komsomol's official character, whenever the younger generation becomes really concerned with any political question—as, for example, with the Hungarian uprising—they do not look to the Komsomol for clarification. The Komsomol itself has been trying to counteract this significant development, but has succeeded only in exposing its own impotence. In Moscow at the beginning of 1957, for example, the Komsomol ordered the mobilization of 500 student brigades of at least 100 members each, to give a hand in the town's rebuilding programme. It was hoped in this way to provide a physical outlet for the unrest into which the students had been plunged by events in Poland and Hungary. But authority over men's minds cannot be achieved by such means. There were highly undesirable repercussions; a political black market came into existence. All kinds of student leaflets were spontaneously produced and surreptitiously distributed, one of which bore the significant title *Heresy*.[7] Cynicism and destructive criticism became rife among the students. A favourite joke among them was: 'Have you heard about the man who had to fill in a questionnaire on whether he was a loyal Marxist-Leninist? He wrote, "I have loyally followed every twist and turn of the Party line".' In some cases there was even overt and direct rejection of the regime and its policy. There is emerging in the Soviet Union a type of youth described by Lev Kassil as 'primitive nihilists, who leap eagerly into any discussion in order to play the part of the opposition'. This is how Kassil describes a Komsomol meeting:

> The young men and women mount the rostrum, encourage each other, speak to the best of their ability, and indulge in spirited clashes with other speakers. Suddenly, in reply to the impassioned words of one of the speakers, words obviously springing from the heart, there comes a shout from a distant, dark corner of the hall:
> 'Got it, boys? Patriotism!'
> [An obvious gibe at the patriotic hyperboles of both the speaker and official propaganda.]
> Then someone else, anonymous in the crowd, shouts: 'Loud applause! The meeting springs to its feet!' [A reference to the stock phrases used by the Soviet press in reporting speeches by the leaders.]
> The local *Nibonicho* [abbreviation of *ni boga ni chorta*—neither God nor the devil, the new name given to youthful opponents of the regime] has gone into action.[8]

Herein, I think, lies the real reason for the condemnation of *Doctor Zhivago*. The Kremlin leaders and their literary deputies reacted violently, not because the novel is anti-revolutionary (it is not), but because it is wholly apolitical. Its main message is that it is the human soul that counts, rather than political events. The characters look down from a lofty height on the feverish turmoil of history; they are not against the Revolution, but they refuse to identify themselves with it; it is something outside their lives—like a storm. Pasternak might easily have described in the same way the fate of a handful of men in an open boat on raging seas; between them and the storm there is no causal link. Towards the end of the book, Lara, Zhivago's beloved, says over his coffin:

> The riddle of life, the riddle of death, the enchantment of genius, the enchantment of unadorned beauty—yes, these things were ours. But the small worries of practical life—things like the reshaping of the planet—these things, no thank you, they are not for us.[9]

If Pasternak had been merely an eccentric and solitary voice, Khrushchev and company would perhaps have dismissed the book with an angry shrug. But because they knew that Russian youth was more and more inclined to consider human life first and to regard the reshaping of the world as a 'small worry', they did their utmost to brand the author by using the favourite argument of dictators that he was a traitor to his country and the ally of a foreign enemy.

This thought I developed in a review of *Doctor Zhivago*,[10] which I sent to Pasternak. A few weeks later a letter in German arrived, postmarked 25 December 1958 at midnight in Moscow, and bearing characteristic signs of caution: the envelope did not carry the sender's name, the letter itself was unsigned. But the handwriting was unmistakable. The key sentence was: 'I am very happy about the kinship of your understanding. All your reflections are very close to me.' This meant that Pasternak agreed with my analysis of his book and with the reasons I had given for the government's rage. This he confirmed when I visited him at his home about a year before his death.

The younger generation in the Soviet Union has also other nonconformist tendencies that have nothing to do with politics. The Soviet *jeunesse dorée*, the children of upper class families, provides a good example. Soviet writers sometimes use *zolotáya molodyózh'*, a literal translation of the French phrase, when referring to them; but these young people are more often referred to as *belorúchki* (little white hands), or *barchukí* (little masters). In *Krokodil* the 'little white hands' are a regular target.

To try to ensure that their children have an easier life than they themselves had is an instinct common to parents the world over; but the hardships and privation suffered in their youth by today's Russian parents were of such exceptional severity that they constantly promise themselves, 'I'm going to make sure my children won't have to suffer as I and my forebears were forced to'. As a result, they are inclined to pamper them.

From time to time one reads reports of the wild behaviour of these young people. One of the most notorious cases was that of the country-house orgies in which the participants included the sons of two Ministers, Kabanov (Foreign Trade) and Petukhov (Heavy Machinery), and the daughters of a major-general, a colonel of the State Security Service, and a lieutenant-colonel of the air force.

Another way in which young people express their reaction to the regime's over-insistence on politics is to become a *stilyága*. The young *stilyaga* conforms to his own interpretation of what is *stil'no* (stylish); he lets his hair grow long, wears coats with thickly padded shoulders, is a devotee of jazz, and peppers his conversation with a few American words—cents, for example, instead of *kopeks*. At the cinema he prefers 'westerns'; he collects the latest recordings of modern music and knows all the American 'jazz kings' by their first names. I have seldom seen any genuine *stilyagy*; perhaps they follow their cult only among their own kind—in their parents' country houses. But a great number of young people are semi-*stilyagy*, imitating the genuine article without going to extremes

In a totalitarian state, any deviation from the official line—even in clothes—has political implications, particularly when, as in this case, the new fashions emanate from the other side of the political fence. The anti-Western demagogues and the authorities never weary of pointing to the Soviet jazz fans and bearded existentialists as typical of capitalist decadence. Youngsters who are determined to show how intractable they are can do it, to spite the regime, by adopting everything they consider to be American and exaggerating it. There is, perhaps, a hint of the old anarchist in these *stilyagi*, and certainly that urge towards the romantic which is common to all youth but finds little outlet in the sternly rational Soviet Union.

The regime is doing its utmost to win over the younger people by providing ornate and sumptuously furnished clubs. Originally these were meant to serve as training grounds in ideology, but they would be empty today if they hadn't changed their character. To make them more attractive, various activities have been organized—stamp-collecting, photography, handicrafts, model aircraft construction, chess, dancing, hiking, and so on.

Sports are increasingly popular and entirely free of political implications. In the Soviet Union, as elsewhere, there are far more spectators than players. Hundreds of thousands cram the stadiums every Sunday to watch the leading football teams.

These are not private clubs, but teams from various industries and departments. The best known are Shakhtyór (mining), Metallurg (the metal industries), Lokomotiv (the railways), Sparták (light industry), Torpedo (tractor and machinery industry), and Burevéstnik (colleges). The exceptionally strong Dynamo team is recruited from the sports clubs of the state police. The rivalry among the teams and the commercialization of the sport have assumed vast proportions. The Russian football fan is called a *bolél'shchik* (from the verb *bolet'*, to suffer or to feel passionately). I read with some surprise in a short story how the trainer of a football team tried with highly 'capitalistic' methods to lure another team's best player to his own club.[11]

In the theatre and cinema there has lately been a tendency towards pure entertainment, devoid of political significance. The trend would be even stronger if the Soviet playwrights had any flair for writing light and entertaining plays. The ferocious earnestness with which they have been inoculated for decades has got into their blood and bones, and the despairing cry of the Party press for Soviet satirists has found little response so far. This appeal really amounts to asking for a fusion of irreconcilables. The satirist must be permitted to deride the shortcomings of the system—if he is allowed to poke fun only at trivialities, he might as well remain silent.

Last, but by no means least, the younger generation, particularly the less sophisticated among them, seek fun and entertainment in dancing. One evening I went into one of the Parks of Culture in Moscow—not the celebrated Gorky Park, the showplace on the banks of the Moskva, but a smaller one, of which there are several in the capital. These consist of gardens, a cinema, sometimes a small summer theatre, a volley-ball court, refreshment stands, and a fenced-in dance floor. Entry to the dance floor costs five roubles. Forty or fifty couples were dancing to the melody of a Dunayevsky waltz. About the same number were watching through the fence. They were the Soviet Russian counterparts of that class of society which the founders and leaders of Bolshevism so often scorned and ridiculed—the petty bourgeois. Most of them were minor employees and working people. They had come from the overcrowded apartment houses surrounding the park to seek relaxation from their hard and exacting daily lives. The dances were just what these young people needed for their distraction—light melodies, with a little sugar and a little romance, even a few jazz tunes which were becoming increasingly popular. There was nothing these youngsters could do about the shaping of the world and the Soviet Union, but they could at least taste the joy of life, untrammelled by politics, in a public park.

Others seek recreation in the countryside. In old Russia, well-to-do families possessed *dáchas*, wooden country bungalows, in which they spent the summer, the mothers and young children staying for several months, the fathers coming out for their holidays and week-ends and acting as the family carrier for purchases needed from town.

These *dachas* and *dacha*-dwellers still exist, and it is the new privileged class that spends the summer in them. The masses have found a substitute. When I was in Prokópyevsk, in remote Siberia, I asked the mayor how many town families had little gardens in the country. His secretary looked up the files and told me there were 'about 60,000'. Prokopyevsk is a town of 250,000 inhabitants. Hence nearly every family has its small plot of land. At this rate the Soviet Union, with an urban population of nearly 90 million, should have some 20 million of these gardens; and in fact, according to statistics published in 1953, there were then 18 million, averaging 500 to 600 square yards each.

If you take a bus or a trolley out to the suburbs of Moscow on a summer evening, you will find it crowded with garden and *dacha* owners. As soon as they leave their factories and offices they hurry to the outskirts of the town where, on their own little strip of land, *bábushka* and the goat and hens are waiting for them, and life really begins.

Of course, Khrushchev did not like this picture. During the last few years there have been an increasing number of attacks against 'private ownership tendencies' which, it was said, find their expression in *dachas* and private gardens. The payment of government loans for the construction of private homes and *dachas* has been stopped; the private gardens of city dwellers have been declared undesirable though they are not yet prohibited. Sweepingly it is said: 'Real estate obviously prevents the normal education of the young citizen of the future Communist society.' The use of private cars has been criticized.[12]

For our analysis of Soviet man it is, of course, less important to reflect on what Mr Khrushchev does than to consider the attitude of the population that forces him to act as he does. Eighteen million private gardens for the town dwellers, in a country where there were none before the Revolution! Could there be more striking proof of the longing of Soviet man for a little corner of his own, where he can be himself, and where politics cannot penetrate?

CHAPTER 17

DESIRE FOR PERSONAL SAFETY

ONE DAY in the spring of 1956 I read the following notice in the *Moscow Evening News*:

FACULTY OF LAW

On 8 March 1956, at 3 p.m., M. P. Shalámov will read his thesis for the degree of Doctor of Jurisprudence in Lecture Hall No. 47, Lomonosov University. Subject: The Soviet theory of circumstantial proof and its application to criminal procedure.

This was something I didn't want to miss. In the large lecture hall I found the audience divided into three groups. The 'Learned Council' of the Department of Law, consisting of twelve professors in ordinary business suits, were seated at a table in the centre of the hall; on their left were three chairs for the 'official opponents' appointed by the Council, consisting also of professors of law; and finally, in the auditorium sat Shalamov's colleagues and relations and the general public.

The proceedings, which lasted about three and a half hours, were typical of the Russian love of the ceremonial and were in full accord with the old Russian tradition of public examination. In building up professional cadres, a matter of vital importance today to the Soviet state, the regime has refrained from developing any procedure of its own. But far more interesting than all that was the thesis itself.

Those who remember the show trials staged in the 1930's know that the courts worked almost exclusively on confessions alleged to have been made by the accused; even the wildest admissions were not investigated—admissions, for example, of conspiratorial meetings in hotels abroad which, in fact were said to have taken place long after the hotels in question had ceased to exist. Under the Criminal Code verdicts based solely on confessions were, and still are, admissible.

Naturally, therefore, I pricked up my ears when the candidate began to question the value of confessions. A man should not be convicted solely on his own admissions, he declared. In the first place he might have various reasons for confessing to a crime. He might be anxious to shield somebody else; he might fear his accomplices; he might be hoping to conceal a more serious offence by pleading guilty to a lesser one. Second, the candidate said, 'We are all aware of the methods by which confessions have been manufactured, and we all know of cases in which the court has taken no steps to verify a confession, but has convicted the accused on the strength of it'. Shalamov's thesis also contained an urgent warning against a too-ready acceptance of circumstantial evidence of guilt. Among other things, he recommended that the word *veroyátno* (probably) should not in future be permitted in criminal procedure, and that it should be clearly stated whether a fact had been established or whether it had not.

All these statements met with the approval of the audience; one member of the Learned Council went so far as to assert that the use of circumstantial evidence in criminal procedure was a relic of the feudal and bourgeois eras, and was out of place in the Criminal Code of the Soviet Union. The entire discussion was carried on quietly and objectively, but to me it was extremely exciting. For what I had just witnessed was an undeniable step towards the restoration of justice in the Soviet Union. The people sitting in the lecture room and discussing the problems of Soviet criminal law were members of the 'new class' and some of the members of the Learned Council belonged even to the old upper class, as was obvious from their age. A group like this is, of course, keenly interested in seeing that justice is put on an orderly footing, so that they, who have worked their way to the top, may enjoy the fruits of their labours in security guaranteed by law.

What the members of this new elite may have thought about justice while they were fighting to gain supremacy is beside the point. Now that they are at the top, their main concern (as always with people who have risen by their own efforts) is to see that the advantages they have won are not endangered. The way Stalin was attacked, after twenty years of adulation, may well have been painful to some of them, but the criticism levelled at the distortion of justice during the Stalin era was music to their ears.

Nevertheless, I should like to warn anyone who, on the basis of this, may be tempted to conclude that all is now well and that the Soviet Union is heading toward the rule of law. If it had depended on the Russian people, or rather on the Russian legal profession, the Soviet Union would have become a constitutional state in the 1930's. That it did not do so was not their fault, but, as the present regime has admitted, the fault of the regime of that time. Like all dictatorships, it had little difficulty in finding a minority of lawyers of the Vyshinsky type who were prepared to be the ruthless tools of their masters.

No developments since Stalin's death have been of greater benefit to the Soviet people than those in the field of justice. Some of these recent improvements are undeniably steps towards the creation of a state in which law has some meaning. I don't want to exaggerate, and I am not suggesting that they are more than the first steps along a path that is long indeed. All this, however, should not deter us from sharing the satisfaction with which the Soviet people have greeted these developments.

Little need be said about justice in the Stalin era; the memory of that perversion has not yet faded. At first the Bolsheviks paid scant attention to the principles of justice, since they believed that the Revolution would create a new society which would have no need of laws, that crime would disappear with all the other evils of the past, and that a penal code would therefore be unnecessary. Crime, they imagined, would be confined to the actions of the 'mentally deranged', to gestures of despair on the part of a dying *bourgeoisie*, and to counter-revolutionary outbreaks. Just to deal with these, they would have to retain the punitive sword for a time in the new state.

Only towards the end of the 1920's, when it became clearer every day that the state was not withering away, but was, on the contrary, becoming more and more powerful under Stalin, and that crime, to say the least, had not diminished—only then did they change their attitude. The almost contemptuous disregard of the criminal code had hitherto been lauded as evidence of Marxist orthodoxy. Now it was suddenly denounced as anti-Marxist and nihilistic, and for people who had championed it— the most notable of whom was Professor Pashukanis—the *volte face* had fatal consequences.

Then came the time when everybody sensed crimes everywhere against the security of the state. The notoriously elastic nine-page Paragraph 58 of the Criminal Code, which deals with counter-revolutionary offences, was stretched in many directions —by the official incorporation, for instance, of the principle of guilt by family association; under Paragraph 58 1c, the relatives of a deserter from the armed forces, even if they had no knowledge of his intentions, could be sentenced to five years' exile 'in the remoter regions of Siberia'.

The year of this decree, 1934, saw a further increase in authorized legal repression. The notorious *troyka* (three-man groups) of the equally infamous *Osso* (an abbreviation of *Osóboye Soveshchániye*, the Special Council), sent millions of 'socially dangerous persons' to the concentration camps or death. The murder of Kirov, Leningrad Party secretary, was followed on 1 December 1934 by the introduction of still another special law, the Lex Kirov, which sent further untold numbers to their doom. People charged under this law could not defend themselves. The charge was made known only twenty-four hours before the opening of the case, which was heard in the absence of the accused; appeals against verdict or sentence on the grounds of clemency were not allowed. In his famous 1956 'secret speech' Khrushchev described the Lex Kirov as 'the basis for a general abuse of socialist justice'. In 1937 its powers were extended; procedure was accelerated in the cases of persons accused of acts of terrorism or of counter-revolutionary sabotage. This threw open the door to despotic tyranny in its most virulent form. In the same speech, Khrushchev confirmed what had long been common knowledge —that from 1937 onwards confessions had been extracted by torture. There no longer existed anything even remotely resembling justice, at any rate for people suspected of being political opponents in the widest sense of the term or indeed for those who were branded as political opponents to obtain 'recruits' for the penitentiary labour camps and for work in the exile territories.

From 1934 until the death of Stalin, the course of justice ran along two separate tracks. The vast majority of prisoners were convicted without proper trial, and also most of those convicted under the Labour Legislation Act of 26 June 1940[1] were not given a fair trial. One of the most sinister blots on the Soviet regime is the grotesque discrepancy between this complete lack of justice for the people and the provisions of Articles 125–128 of the constitution, which guaranteed the inviolability of the individual, his home, his private correspondence and also freedom of speech and of the press, and the right to hold meetings and organize demonstrations. Yet, side by side with all this, there existed a more or less normal form of procedure against ordinary criminals and a civil code that functioned with comparative justice.

Stalin's death was followed immediately by several amnesties.[2] The first, three weeks afterwards, expressly excluded political prisoners; the second, on 17 September 1955 (issued in connection with a treaty that had just been concluded with the German Federal Republic) granted amnesty to those convicted of collaboration with the enemy; the third, on 1 November 1957 coincided with the fortieth anniversary of the Bolshevik Revolution and followed the same lines as the amnesty of 1953, once again excluding political prisoners.[3] These amnesties came as a blessing to millions of people, though the movements of a great number of those released remained restricted to specific and often very remote territories. At the same time, rehabilitation proceedings were begun, by which many of the surviving victims of the Stalin purges were freed and their names cleared; in Khrushchev's secret speech people were even rehabilitated posthumously. The same thing happened in the East European countries.

In September 1953 *Osso* and its *troykas* were abolished. This vital measure was not made public until the beginning of 1956, and then not officially, but through the medium of a legal journal.[4] After that, so-called counter-revolutionary crimes were tried by legally constituted courts in accordance with the general criminal law. The supervision of the penitentiary camps was transferred from the MVD (the Ministry of the Interior, formerly called the NKVD) to the Ministry of Justice, although the State Security Service remained an independent unit directly under the Council of Ministers. In November 1957 special commissions were set up in the local soviets for the supervision of prisons and camps, and these commissions were granted permission to initiate appeals for amnesties. On 19 April 1956 the Lex Kirov was abolished, and a week later the worst aspects of the Labour Legislation Act of 1940 were annulled.

Why this change in favour of the Soviet citizen? There are, I believe, three reasons. First, Stalin's death; second, the readiness of his successors to make up in popularity what they lacked in authority by paying some attention to the wishes of the people —which Stalin had never considered; and third, the efforts of the 'new class' (including the lawyers) to put an end to the arbitrary despotism under which they had suffered for so long. In a land that for many years had been under a reign of terror, where the brutal hand of the secret police left its mark on every family, where no one, high or low, had ever been sure that he would not be dragged from his bed by the State Security Service—in such a land riddled by an unparalleled system of espionage and denunciation where millions were hounded to their doom without trial, all must have longed from the depths of their hearts to put an end to this constant and overwhelming horror.

Thus the new elite, and particularly the legal profession, seized the first opportunity—the death of Stalin—to seek improvements in the judicial system. Since 1956 legal experts and professors of law—M. S. Strogovich, P. Nedbaylo, R. Rakhunov, P. Romashkin, to mention a few—have published many articles demanding an extension of the legal safeguards for the individual in his relations with the state, strict observance of the principle that every man is deemed innocent until proved guilty, absolute independence of the courts, the right of the defence to be present at preliminary investigations, and the abolition of collective punishment for the members of a defector's family. They have attacked the principle of guilt by analogy, insisting that only crimes specifically named in the criminal code should be liable to punishment.[5]

The Supreme Soviet issued a decree on 25 December 1958 laying down the fundamental principles of criminal law.[6] (This referred to principles and not to the code itself, because in the Soviet Union justice is the concern of the individual republics. The law states the principles on which the separate republics have to base their respective criminal codes.)

The new criminal code incorporates some of the proposed reforms mentioned earlier in this chapter. In future only crimes specifically laid down in the code can be the subject of proceedings and punishment. The code specifies what is liable to punishment and what is not. The principle of guilt by analogy has been abolished, and retroactive application of the code is forbidden. Punishment, which for decades has been regarded as 'a measure for the protection of society'—in other words, as a deterrent—has now been made to fit the crime; the maximum deprivation of liberty has been reduced from twenty-five years to ten (fifteen in exceptional cases), and the absolute authority of the courts in criminal matters, which had been violated by the *Osso* of the MVD, has been reaffirmed and incorporated in the code. The defence will in future be allowed to be present at the preliminary investigation of a case; and—a point of particular interest—in the very first paragraph of the principles, in contrast to the law previously in force, 'protection of the person' is named as the object of the legislation.

In many ways, even this new code does not correspond to Western ideas. A person becomes liable to criminal proceedings at fourteen or sixteen years of age. A new article declares that it is an offence for a Soviet citizen to refuse to return to the Soviet Union from abroad. Most important of all, the principle that the burden of proof lies on the prosecution has not been incorporated in the code, although it was in the draft. Another proof of a persisting totalitarian element is the fact that legal measures do not necessarily have to be made public before they come into force; among the measures that have not been made public is the 'Ordinance regarding Labour Reformatory Colonies and Prisons of the MVD of the U.S.S.R.'[7]

Finally, the new regulations regarding crimes against the state and military crimes—the crux of the criminal code in the political field—have not been materially altered and still contain the essentials of the old Paragraph 58: high treason, espionage, subversive activities, anti-Soviet agitation—these are the headings under which, as before, proceedings can be taken for the suppression of any opposition, real or presumed.

Worse still, paralleling the symptoms of a movement toward the rule of law apparent in the new criminal code, opposite tendencies are to be observed—for example, the Anti-Parasite Law[8] which, since 1957, has been adopted in the majority of the Soviet republics, including (on 4 May 1961) the most important of them, the R.S.F.S.R.[9] Under the provisions of this law (as in general under the new criminal legislation), groups of persons not trained to act as judges and practically appointed by

Party organs have been given the power to condemn a citizen who may be innocent of any indictable offence to years of forced labour by a simple majority vote, the sentence being subject only to confirmation by the local executive committee. The raising of a workers' militia—in addition to the regular militia, the police—is another step in the same direction. At the Twenty-first Party Congress Khrushchev proposed that criminal proceedings be conducted outside the jurisdiction of the courts, in line with the gradual withering away of the state.[10]

It is also alarming that in 1961 the application of the death penalty has been widened three times: on 5 May, for theft of state or public property, and forgery; on 18 May, for revolts in prisons; and on 1 July, for violation of foreign currency regulations.[11]

Also ominous, and reminiscent of the days of Stalin, was the Ivinskaya case. After Pasternak's death on 30 May 1960, Olga Ivinskaya—his friend and inspiration, the model for Lara in *Doctor Zhivago*—was arrested and sentenced at a secret trial in December 1960 to eight years' detention, and her daughter Irina was sentenced to three years, both on rather unconvincing charges of violation of the currency laws. The world has taken this action as nothing but a petty revenge by the Soviet Government against the dead genius.

Events such as these are reminders to Soviet citizens not to overestimate the value of the written law. Reintroduction of the Stalinist system of rule by terror would undoubtedly cause a revulsion of feeling among the people against the leaders, and particularly among the more demanding elite. But it would presumably be no more than a very cautious opposition, seeking expression in theoretical legal dissertations. There is such an overwhelming weight of power in the hands of the rulers that reformers in the Soviet Union stand a chance of success only if the state is predisposed to accept the reforms they advocate.

The centuries-old acceptance of the individual's subordination has led the people not to expect any improvement in the painfully neglected question of their personal security, except through legal measures within the framework of the existing system. Few have given serious consideration to the possibility of a new political order that would make the system more humane, and would more effectively guarantee the fundamental rights of citizenship. The old habit of subordination and the new spirit of bureaucracy together constitute a formidable barrier to independent political and legal thinking.

But I don't want to sound pessimistic. Even a quarter-century of Stalinist terror has not been able to stifle the people's desire for personal security. Scarcely was the dictator dead than they began to curb despotism and injustice—in other words, to turn their attention to their civic rights. These are the same throughout the world, and can be summarized as the right to preserve inviolate a measure of personal freedom from state despotism. In the West the freedom of the community as a whole was won in the fight for the freedom of the individual; in the Soviet Union, behind the struggle for the freedom of the individual citizen there rises, even if only in outline, the image of freedom itself.

CHAPTER 18

CRISES — AND REPERCUSSIONS

AN INCLINATION to withdraw into a private life away from politics and attempts to set up legal safeguards against the arbitrary intrusion of the state—these tendencies among the people of a totalitarian state are of real political significance. They do not, however, amount to a direct threat to the state itself; the apolitical citizen, it is true, has never been the ideal subject from the point of view of a totalitarian regime, but at the same time he has never been regarded as a troublemaker. Are there, then, any forces or movements that go further, that, deliberately or otherwise, refuse to recognize state authority, and that in the long run might undermine it? Are there at least the germs of a resistance movement?

An unequivocal 'No' to this question would represent a truly formidable triumph for Bolshevism. For in Tsarist Russia— and not merely among the subject peoples, whose nationalistic opposition we need not consider here—various forms of resistance existed. Russians have anarchy in their blood; some people attribute this to a fundamental element in the composition of the race, to the restlessness of the Cossacks, the Russian frontiersmen.

The nineteenth-century European anarchist movement had, in the Russians Bakúnin, Nechàyev, and Kropótkin, men who not only were formidable revolutionary theorists, but were also determined to translate their theories into action. The extent to which these men prepared the way for Lenin and company is well illustrated by a sentence from *The Revolutionary's Catechism*, drawn up by Bakunin and Nechayev:

> To the revolutionary, all things are moral that help the revolution, and all things that stand in its way are immoral and criminal.

Kropotkin, in his thesis *Anarchist Morality*, conceded to the terrorists who murdered the Tsar Alexander II 'the right to kill'.

The same fundamental streak of anarchy is to be found in

many of the sects, like the Dukhobors, that are so typical of Russia. These sects reject any form of state authority; but it is also worth remembering that this has never prevented them from imposing completely dictatorial rule over their own members.

Many Russians joined in the Revolutions of 1905 and 1917, not because they had a clear picture of a new form of government, but simply because they wanted to overthrow the existing one and were lured by the revolutionaries' proclamation that once victory had been won, the state would wither away and cease to exist.

They were inevitably disillusioned, as were all who fought to bring the Bolsheviks to power; gradually they were all either brutally subjugated or liquidated by the Bolshevik leaders. The sole surviving Party was itself organized along a most rigid chain-of-command system—and that is the essential meaning of the formula 'democratic centralism'.

The Tsarist regime was hard and exacting, often downright brutal; but now this severity has been systematized. Despite their obvious differences, Ivan the Terrible, Peter the Great, Nicholas I, Lenin, and Stalin can all be grouped together, although, of course, the bloodshed under Lenin and Stalin was incomparably greater than that under the Tsars. All of them exacted unconditional obedience to the will of the state, of which they claimed to be the sole representatives; they all paid scant attention to the aspirations and feelings of the people under their dominion—the Tsars because they regarded themselves as infallible by divine right, Lenin and Stalin because they were convinced that the Bolshevik leaders alone understood the immutable laws of social evolution. Even Tsar Alexander II, 'the liberator', described his reforms of the 1860's as 'a revolution from above', while Lenin both advocated and implemented the claims to power of a conspiratorial political elite. Stalin later elaborated a complete doctrine of 'revolution from above', designed to give ideological sanction to the arbitrary will of the rulers. The dictatorship of the proletariat means the dictatorship of the Party as 'the vanguard of the proletariat'—which, in turn, means the Party leadership.

Lenin and his disciples, and Stalin even more so, admittedly attached considerable importance to obtaining the consent of the people. One of the most effective methods they employed was the so-called 'election'. The conduct of these elections shows, however, that the underlying intention has never been to ask the people for their opinion, but to demand from them an unequivocal declaration of faith in the absolute authority of their leaders, that would reject all criticism and discourage all opposition.

The Bolshevik leaders demand obedience and discipline. But for them it is not enough that the people should merely obey; they demand constantly reiterated, enthusiastic assurance from the people that they are convinced of the infinite wisdom of their leaders. The people dislike the endless gatherings held day after day throughout the country, not only because these are boring and rob them of the leisure time they richly deserve, but also because they are constantly called upon to reaffirm their faith in the state, its ideology, and its leaders.

Some time ago I heard of a Soviet professor who, before he fled to the West during the war, used to smoke a pipe because he found it was the only way he could control his facial expression; he had observed that a man's mouth could give him away even more effectively than his eyes. In the Soviet Union one is always running into people who lead double lives. Externally they are enthusiastic supporters of Bolshevism; in reality they stand aloof from it, often viewing it with abhorrence. Others, admittedly, may be influenced by outside pressures. When millions of people are compelled day after day to show smiling faces to the world, those in power can be reasonably certain that this make-believe will eventually affect their characters and personalities. The authorities believe that they can accomplish with human beings what the great physiologist Ivan Pavlov achieved with his dogs.

Has this attempt at the mass conditioning of 200 million by no means unintelligent people succeeded, has it killed the tendency towards anarchy that seems inherent in the Russian character? Is the Western conception of a standardized 'Soviet robot' accurate? If the answer is 'Yes', it amounts to admitting that in the brief space of forty years the Bolsheviks have, as they claim, changed human nature. We should not shrink from this admission—if it corresponds with the facts. But to think that it does is to confuse appearance and reality.

Things that are unfamiliar often give the impression of being

uniform. At first sight all Chinese look alike to Western eyes;
later, however, one realizes that they are no more alike than the
people of any other nation. To be sure there is greater external
uniformity among Russians than among the nationals of the
Western world. It begins with their clothing, which shows little
variety in quality or style. More important is the compulsory
conformism in external behaviour, that habit of doing what the
other fellow does. The old soldier's maxim 'Stick to the middle
of the rear rank' has even more meaning in a totalitarian state,
where the best chance of survival lies in being as inconspicuous
as possible, since any clearly defined and strong personality is
suspect. Hundreds of thousands of such individuals were swept
aside by Stalin, and the survivors have reduced themselves to a
colourless conformity. People feel most secure when they keep
close to the conventional lines approved by the men at the top.
Hardly anybody wants to take an exceptional risk—and for very
good reasons. Dudintsev's celebrated novel, referred to earlier,
gives a drastic and convincing description of the fate that awaits
the individualist, however necessary to the state he may be:
ridicule, want, hunger, suspicion, and finally a Siberian prison.

Experiences like this, repeated year after year, cannot fail to
make their mark on a nation, and definite patterns of behaviour
emerge. Camouflage becomes a habit. Discussions that might
have political repercussions are deliberately avoided, or are confined to small groups generally inaccessible to foreigners. This,
as we have seen, applies particularly to the humanities; Soviet
periodicals are full of articles complaining that the vast majority
of savants expend their energies along paths either long since
fully explored or leading back to ancient history.

All this is incontestable. It is hard to say how far this external
adaptation leads to a genuine inner change and the emergence of
mass-produced robots. I have never felt that it does. Since 1929
I have spent approximately the same number of years in the
Soviet Union and the United States, and I don't believe that
Soviet citizens are much more uniform in their thoughts and
responses than Americans. No sooner had the death of Stalin
slightly eased the pressure than the old Russian began to re-
emerge.

Two small and very ordinary incidents will show what I mean.
One evening after I had been to the Puppet Theatre, I got on

a bus in Mayakovsky Square to go back to my hotel. Passengers board Moscow buses at the back and get off at the front; the conductress stands at the rear entrance to collect the fares. At the third stop an inspectress got on the bus. Two seats in front of me was a blonde girl about seventeen years old. As soon as the inspectress appeared, the girl got up and walked towards the back of the bus.

'Where are you going, citizen?' the inspectress asked sharply.

'To get my ticket.'

'Where did you get on?'

The girl murmured something I didn't catch, but I knew that she had already been inside the bus when I got on. The conductress folded her arms—she had no intention of issuing a ticket to the 'hare' (as people who try to travel without a ticket are called in Russia). The rest of the passengers watched with interest.

At the next stop a few more people got on, among them three young students who, quickly sizing up the situation, bought four tickets. The conductress did not notice the discrepancy; she issued the four tickets mechanically without counting the students. A moment later the inspectress reached the blonde girl.

'You'll have to pay a fine of five roubles,' she said with a hard stare.

At that, the girl handed over a ticket, which one of the students had slipped into her hand. The inspectress was furious.

'You can't get away with it like that!' she shouted. 'When I got on you had no ticket. Five roubles!'

The girl was embarrassed and also obviously reluctant—or perhaps unable—to pay the fine. Hesitantly, she still held out the ticket while the inspectress berated the students for having tried to shield the 'delinquent' from the punishment she deserved.

Meanwhile the other passengers had begun to murmur, at first softly and then more and more insistently. 'Such nerve!' seemed to be the general comment. Well, I thought, the passengers who paid for their tickets obviously are against the 'hare'. But then I realized, with some surprise, that they were grumbling not against the girl but against the inspectress.

'The girl's got a ticket, so why all the fuss?'

'What's it got to do with the inspectress, anyway, where she got it from?'

'That's right. She's got a ticket, and that's all that matters.
'Why should we put up with these petty bureaucrats?'

The inspectress, now thoroughly roused, turned on the passengers and began to defend herself. But it was no use; the general feeling was against her. The bus stopped, and the girl jumped off, followed by the three laughing students.

'There's a nice thing for you!' the inspectress shouted furiously, 'a young girl accepting money from three strange men! What will happen next?'

The second incident occurred a few years later, in the spring of 1959—also, as it happened, in Mayakovsky Square. One sunny morning I was photographing the newly erected statue of the poet when I heard a voice behind me. 'I find that shocking...'

I turned around and saw two young men.

'What's shocking about it?' I asked.

'The inscription, of course.'

I admitted that I hadn't looked at it. This is what I read:

TO VLADIMIR MAYAKOVSKY
POET OF THE REVOLUTION AND OF THE PROLETARIAT
FROM THE SOVIET GOVERNMENT

I still didn't see what had aroused the indignation of the young men, and I looked at them inquiringly.

'Why, "by the Soviet Government"!' one of them said. 'The statue was paid for by taxes. If they'd put "by the Soviet people", well and good. But "by the Soviet Government" is nonsense—and offensive nonsense at that.'

A remark of this kind, made to a complete stranger, would never have been heard in Stalin's time. It is a sign of the greater self-assurance of Soviet citizens and particularly of the younger generation. This is evident, too, in their dealings with the police. As I have pointed out elsewhere, the police have not succeeded in making Soviet citizens respect the sanctity of state property. Many citizens have evolved an amorality of their own to set against the amorality of the state; the unscrupulousness with which millions abuse state property is on a par with the unscrupulousness of the state towards its citizens. In general the people are fully capable of differentiating between amorality in public affairs and the ethics of private life. There are, of course, some who have learned to reason 'dialectically' about their private lives as well. In my experience, however, there are just as many (or as few) in Russia as in the West who take a proper ethical standard in their relations with their fellow men for granted. I would go so far as to say that revulsion from Stalin's openly amoral philosophy greatly contributed to anti-Stalinist feeling. For the Russian people as a whole retain their healthy outlook and have a moral code that does not vary with circumstances or with the decisions taken by their leaders. Their natural ethical standard finds strongest expression in their conception of *pravda* (justice and truth), which is in irreconcilable contrast to the concept and to the theory and practice of Bolshevism—particularly Stalin's brand of Bolshevism.

In his day loyal supporters of the regime, and even true sons of the Party, knew that at any time they might be pounced upon and liquidated as dangerous saboteurs. In Stalin's eyes everyone was a potential traitor. His attitude did not change after the war, although the people had risked their lives to defend his regime. Many felt that this offended their human dignity, just as his repeated demands for an enthusiastic affirmation of support for the regime insulted their intelligence.

At the outset Stalin's successors appear to have followed the same insulting policy. How can one otherwise explain, for example, the fact that after the shooting of Beria, the man who for so many years had been the omnipotent chief of the State Security Police, subscribers to the *Great Soviet Encyclopaedia* received a letter asking them to cut out pages 21-24 of Volume V (containing Beria's biography) and to substitute a detailed thesis on the Bering Straits? And how can one account for the fact that the publication of Volume XL (SOK-STI), which should have appeared in 1956, was postponed for two years (though Volumes XLI to L appeared in regular sequence), while the authorities were trying to decide how to deal with the biography of Stalin?

The outstanding example, however, was the de-Stalinization itself. I happened to be in Moscow at the time. Officially, the Twentieth Party Congress ended on a Friday. Word had gone around that a great demonstration was to take place in Red Square, where the people of Moscow would be expected to indulge in one of their 'spontaneous demonstrations of allegiance'. The rumour was confirmed when on Thursday and Friday groups

of men began to paint the lines used in marshalling the hundreds
of thousands who join in these monster rallies. But no demonstration took place. Instead, an unusually large number of cars
was observed outside the Kremlin on Saturday. Obviously a
very important conference was in progress, but nobody knew
what it was about.

Nevertheless, the few hints dropped during the Congress had
set people thinking. The Russian is no fool; even the villagers
possess a peasant cunning that enables them to weigh a political
situation with astonishing speed and accuracy. The people have
acquired the knack of reading between the lines and working
things out for themselves. I was given a fresh example of this
when, five days after Khrushchev's public speech, I accepted an
invitation from the American Ambassador, Charles Bohlen, to
a skiing-party at his country house. While passing through a
village I got into conversation with a peasant who was chopping
wood outside his cottage. For want of anything better to say,
I asked him the name of his *kolkhoz*.

The peasant, a man in his fifties with an artful, wrinkled face,
looked at me quizzically for a moment before replying. Then—
quietly, but with a twinkle in his eyes—he said: '*Poká yeshchó
Stálinsky*' ('For the moment, it's still the Stalin *kolkhoz*').

He evidently had a very keen nose, for it was not until a fortnight later that the bombshell exploded. At a French Embassy
reception in honour of President Auriol I talked to a Western
Ambassador regarded as one of the best-informed men in Moscow. He told me about rumours that Khrushchev had wound up
the Congress with a speech *in camera*, in which he had violently
attacked Stalin. Others had heard the same story, and the news
spread rapidly in whispers among the guests. Little groups
began to form in the corners, their heads close together. I spoke
to a few of the Russians who were there, but they all stared
blankly at me and changed the subject.

As the censors refused for several days to release anything
about Khrushchev's secret speech, the foreign journalists, normally tight-lipped in the presence of their rivals, pooled their
findings, and very soon they had got hold of the bare bones of
the speech. In the meantime it had been read at a number of
closed Party meetings in Moscow and other important cities.
(The text was published only some months later by the U.S.

State Department, which had obtained it through a 'leak' from one of the East European countries.[1])

I was less concerned with such details of the speech as had become known than with the people's reaction to it. During the following weeks I raised the subject with everyone I met, not only with those famous 'voices of the people', the taxi drivers, but with people sitting next to me in buses and restaurants, with cloakroom attendants at the theatre, streetcar conductors, and the people beside me in lines or at the cinema. The answers I got were far more varied than one would have expected from a nation of 'robots'.

First of all, there were the bitter enemies of the dead tyrant, to whom the destruction of the myth had given immense satisfaction. They expressed themselves in no uncertain terms: 'Serves him right, the blood-sucker! Just think of the number of people whose lives he ruined! It won't help those he murdered, of course, but it will at least be some consolation to their relatives. . . . It's a pity they didn't tell the truth about him a long time ago. . . . Well, let's hope they pull his corpse out of the mausoleum. . . . He murdered all the best of our people—men like Bukharin and Rykov—and don't tell me *they* were enemies of the people! They disagreed with him, that's all, so he got them out of the way because he was determined to be the sole boss.'

At the other extreme were Stalin's diehard admirers, mostly younger people: 'It's a dirty, low-down trick to throw a great man into the mud like that, three years after his death. Who won the war for us? Who raised Russia from a backward country that was a laughing-stock to the most powerful state in the world? Stalin! He was the true disciple of Lenin, and he carried on Lenin's work. He was a great man, like Ivan or Peter. Of course some bad things happened under his rule . . . but there were a hell of a lot more good things!'

Then there were the people who expressed misgivings about Stalin's successors: 'For years, these people worked closely with him and ate out of his hand. Three years ago they were falling flat on their faces before him. After his death they still trembled at the thought of him, and it's only now they've summoned up the courage to attack him. Where were they, anyway, while all these atrocities were being committed? They were at his side, supporting him, and they must take their share of the blame.

And are things all that much better now? Last week my sister-in-law was sentenced to three years and her property confiscated, simply because she made a bit extra by selling a few fish she'd bought. Speculation, they called it. It's always the same—the little man gets the kicks, and the bosses have so much money they don't know what to do with it. How can we manage, anyway, if we don't make a bit on the side?'

On the other hand, there were people who defended Stalin's colleagues: 'They were against him, but there was nothing they could do about it. Stalin had all the power in his own hands—and the GPU as well. Voroshilov even shot at him once, and wounded him in the right hand; but the Lord God evidently wasn't ready yet to put an end to our miseries.'

Finally, there were many who displayed complete indifference. One day soon after the Party Congress I visited the Tretyakov Art Gallery and noticed that all the portraits of Stalin were gone. When I mentioned this to a middle-aged man nearby, he merely shrugged. 'It's always the same,' he said, 'the new tenant moves the furniture around so as not to be reminded of his predecessor.'

A great many people showed by their replies that they were influenced far less by pro-Stalin or anti-Stalin feelings than by great confusion. A workman I talked to on a building site, a man in his middle thirties, said: 'For years, since my earliest childhood, Stalin had been held up to me as Stalin the Great, the Benevolent, and the Wise, and I believed it implicitly. Now the whole picture has suddenly changed, and I simply don't know what to believe. Not that it matters very much . . . ' He made a disparaging gesture. 'What does worry me is how I'm going to explain it all to my kids. Never mind about me; I'm a grown man and can take it. But to have to tell the kids, who've been singing nothing but hymns of praise to Stalin in kindergarten and school, that their good, kind Stalin was a tyrant and an oppressor—that's tough. I don't think I can do it.'

The intelligentsia had little or nothing to say against de-Stalinization as such; it was among their ranks that Stalin had caused the most damage. As the brutal autocrat who set himself up as high priest of the arts, he had been the object of their bitter hatred. It was bad enough that his successors should within a few days have indulged in so complete a *volte face*, from worship to the most vicious condemnation; but that they should also expect the nation to follow suit was something many of the more clear-minded regarded as an insult to their intelligence. On the other hand, those who had degraded themselves by becoming tools of Stalin's tyranny were completely disconcerted; an extreme example, Alexander Fadeyev, who was general secretary of the Writers' Association from 1936 to 1954, shot himself a few weeks after Khrushchev's denunciatory speech.

The weeks following the Twentieth Party Congress are among the most astonishing I have ever experienced in the course of a very varied life spent among a multitude of people. It is only when one looks back on these events that one fully realizes how completely the Party leadership disregarded the intelligence of the nation. Here, too, a few personal impressions may be illuminating.

The Moscow theatres have solved the problem of people jostling for their hats and coats by admitting only a specified number into the cloakroom at a time. The ornate theatre in the Soviet Army Centre follows this practice. When I was there one evening in the middle of February 1956, just as I got to the top of the stairs the attendant happened to stop the flow of people into the cloakroom on the floor below. For five minutes or so, therefore, I patiently gazed down the great neo-baroque staircase at a vast canvas, a copy of the well-known painting by A. M. Gerásimov, showing Stalin and Voroshilov striding through the Kremlin together—a striking study of the two Marshals in their long, flowing greatcoats, and an appropriate ornament for the imposing staircase of the Army Centre. Then the attendant opened the barrier, and we moved on.

Three weeks later I visited the same theatre again. As chance would have it, the attendant again stopped us as I reached the top of the stairs. I suddenly realized that the picture was missing. I glanced round hurriedly. Everything was as before—except for the painting. In its place stood a huge bust of Lenin against a dark red velvet curtain. The white bust against the dark red was most effective. But where was the picture? To make quite sure, I asked the attendant. 'Behind the curtain,' she answered drily and then opened the barrier.

In Gorki, some twenty miles from Moscow, the house where Lenin lived during his last illness and where he died in January 1924 has been preserved for many years as a museum. Visitors who are shown Lenin's room were also, until recently, shown the room in which Stalin spent the night whenever he visited Lenin. The guide never failed to point out the two chairs in the garden in which, as a well-known photograph documents, Lenin and Stalin used to sit and talk. When I visited Gorki not long after the Twentieth Party Congress, Stalin's chair had disappeared, and his room was tersely described as a 'guest room'.

The third anniversary of Stalin's death, which occurred a few days after the Twentieth Party Congress, was officially ignored. But Stalin had not been entirely forgotten. On that day I stood for a while in Red Square in front of the tomb in which the embalmed bodies of Lenin and Stalin lie side by side. That day the mausoleum, through which for many years long lines of people had filed, was closed. The anniversary happened to fall on a Monday that year, and on Mondays the mausoleum is not open to the public. Nor was there the usual big crowd flowing through Red Square on its way to the great GUM store, for that, too, is closed on Mondays. So on that particular Monday the whole of the vast square was almost deserted.

And yet it was a Monday with a difference. All day long little knots of people stood by the entrance to the tomb. Some of them had probably not realized the significance of that particular day. Why should they? Even *Pravda*, the only newspaper published on Mondays, had not written a line about the anniversary. But some people obviously had remembered. One man, who had been standing motionless for a long time with tears streaming down his face, approached the policeman on duty and asked whether he could go into the mausoleum, as he had come a long way. 'No,' the policeman replied, 'today's Monday.'

About midday, above the noise of the traffic—which is also much reduced on Mondays—I heard a woman's voice. Between the Spassky Gate in the Kremlin wall and the white stone bastion on the site of the mediaeval execution place there stood a woman of about fifty, simply dressed, reciting a hymn of praise to Stalin. It was not a poem I knew; but like thousands of similar tributes, it called him the father of his people and the wise disciple of Lenin. The woman was reciting from memory; her face was pale and tense, and her eyes were fixed unwaveringly on the tomb. No one interfered with her, but no one took much notice of her either, except for three or four men who stood near by, listened, showed no emotion, made no comment, and went away in silence after the woman had finished and made her way across the square.

This tribute from a solitary woman, the tears of a man from the provinces, and a few modest bunches of flowers placed on the red balustrade of the mausoleum—to me they seemed to symbolize a protest against the manner in which the de-Stalinization had been carried out, a protest from people who were not prepared to let themselves be manipulated like puppets on a string.

Since then, of course, rehabilitation has begun. Events in Poland and Hungary showed Khrushchev how dangerous it was to arouse doubts and misgivings in the minds of the people. Very soon after the Hungarian uprising, he began to speak of Stalin with greater respect. As early as January 1957 the new line became clear. At a reception at the Chinese Embassy in honour of Chou En-lai, Khrushchev spoke of the 'Stalin tragedy'. Stalin's mistakes, he said, had been made in the conviction that he was serving the cause of the Revolution and socialism, and as far as the decisive questions were concerned—protection of the workers' interests, socialism, the fight against the enemies of Marxism-Leninism—'may God grant that every Communist will be prepared to fight as Stalin fought'. The newspapers reported that there was 'enthusiastic applause' after this sentence. Roused by this response, Khrushchev continued:

> For all of us who have dedicated our lives to the revolutionary struggle in the interests of the workers and their militant vanguard, Lenin's Party, the name of Stalin is indissolubly linked with the doctrine of Marx and Lenin. It is therefore the desire of each one of us as members of the Communist Party of the Soviet Union to be as true to the Marxist doctrine and as staunch in our fight in the interest of the workers as Stalin was.[2]

In the bare space of twelve months, then, the verdict passed by his successors on Stalin had come full circle—worship, condemnation, and back to renewed veneration—with, admittedly, certain reservations. Since then the curve has been unsteady, but criticism on the whole has prevailed. It was quite strong in Alexander Tvardovsky's poem *That's how it was*,[3] in the 1961 film *Clear Sky* (the sky clearing when the word spread that Stalin had died), and again in connection with the twentieth anniversary of Hitler's invasion of the U.S.S.R. when Stalin was declared responsible for the dreadful reverses during the first phase of the war.

As one would expect, the more intelligent people, who do not merely repeat set phrases, can only view these mental acrobatics with cynicism. Khrushchev himself is fully aware that a too sudden change of policy might cast doubt on his own sincerity; witness his speech to the writers in spring 1957—'We were sincere in our veneration of Stalin when we wept over his coffin.'[4]

Khrushchev eventually summed up his assessment of Stalin in one simple formula. Stalin, he said, had made just one mistake —he had succumbed to the cult of individual leadership; and from that one error all the other mistakes had followed. The new Party leader was probably trying to find a simple explanation so as not to confuse the public unduly. However, since it was considered essential to have an infallible prophet, even if only a dead one, the condemnation of Stalin was linked with a renewed glorification of Lenin. Indeed, it might well be said that the leadership cult was not diminished by the denigration of Stalin, only that the balance of authority between the two prophets was shifted. During the last years of his life Stalin enjoyed perhaps 80 per cent of leadership authority and Lenin 20 per cent; after de-Stalinization the entire 100 per cent was transferred to Lenin; at present one might estimate it as 60 per cent to Lenin, 35 per cent to Khrushchev, 5 per cent to Stalin.

Since then internal opponents of the regime have been in the habit of disguising their opposition as Leninism. Khrushchev, of course, counter-attacks them not as Leninists—to do so would be to disavow himself—but as 'revisionists'. Everything which doesn't suit the Party leadership is brushed aside as 'revisionism', to which a very loose definition has been given. The ideological principles more or less precisely defined under Stalin are now, therefore, in a state of flux.

Above all, the inevitable rewriting of Soviet history has completely confused the historians. This has been reflected in the central journal of Soviet historians, *Voprósy Istórii*. The official history of the Revolution, of the civil war, and of the 1920's and 1930's now looks like a heap of rubble. The distortions forced on historians are almost indescribable. For example, there was an article in which E. N. Burdzhálov, then editor of the historians' journal, criticized Stalin's attitude in 1917, before Lenin had arrived from abroad.[5] Burdzhalov was attacked by Professor Bondarévskaya, and she in turn was attacked by the historian Nosov.[6] Finally *Pravda* launched an attack on the whole of the journal's editorial staff,[7] which was thereupon reorganized.

Stalin's role during the civil war provided another quarrel. Is it true, for instance, that Stalin was the leading figure in the defence of Tsaritsyn against the Whites in 1918 and 1919? And if not, is it right that the town should bear its present name of Stalingrad? It is difficult enough for the historian to record events that occurred in times of universal chaos, but when at the same time he has to follow the constantly changing line of those in power his task becomes impossible.

We are concerned, however, not with the occupational hazards of Soviet historians, but with the people who, as the result of events since Stalin's death, gaze more sceptically and with more bewilderment than ever at the Kremlin stage and its swiftly changing scenery. Their bewilderment was increased in 1956, when world events clearly demonstrated the gaping discrepancy between slogans and reality. For the Soviet press gave more detailed, albeit prejudiced, information about these events than is generally realized in the West.

During the Hungarian uprising, for example, the Soviet citizen suddenly read in the Moscow newspapers that a veteran Hungarian Communist (to whom even as late as the end of October the press had referred to as Comrade Nagy) had joined the ranks of the enemy; that a large portion of the workers, particularly the younger elements, had followed his example, motivated by honourable and patriotic convictions; that Soviet troops had been forced to intervene; and finally that bitter fighting had brought the economic life of the country to a complete standstill and had led to enormous destruction and a state of chaos. They even learned from a message sent by Eisenhower to Bulganin (published in Moscow, it is true, after a delay of five days) that:

... the fresh use of force by the Soviet Union against the government and the people of Hungary had occurred at a moment when negotiations between the representatives of the Soviet and Hungarian governments were actually in progress.[8]

The Soviet soldier is trained for every kind of warfare except the business he was called on to carry out in Hungary—the suppression of a genuine popular uprising which followed precisely the revolutionary rules laid down by Lenin, but was directed against Lenin's successors. Aware of the danger of 'infection', the government kept pulling troops out and sending new troops in; as a result, there must have been several hundred thousand Soviet soldiers who served tours of duty in Poland and Hungary during the autumn of 1956. Did they become 'carriers of infection', like the Tsarist troops who followed Napoleon into France in 1814 and saw for themselves the Western way of life? The more naïve readers of *Pravda* were perhaps prepared to swallow the stories about the 'fascist hordes' whom the Soviet troops were supposedly fighting in Hungary; but the Soviet officers and men on the spot knew better.

Hungary's fight for freedom could be presented to the Soviet reader as the work of foreign agents; but since Moscow had reached an agreement with Gomulka, it was not possible to keep a great deal of authentic information about Poland's 'Spring in October' from reaching the Soviet Union. Soviet readers learned, for example, that respected Polish Communist writers had turned passionately against the tyranny of 'socialist realism' to which Soviet literature was subjected; that they held socialist realism responsible for 'the complete standstill in Soviet literature since the 1920's' and described it as a scourge that the 'boot lickers and toadies' of the regime had fashioned for their own purposes.[9]

What were the demands made by Poland and Hungary? To name some of them: more liberty, greater personal security, slightly improved wages, a little more intellectual freedom, trade unions that safeguard the interests of their members instead of enforcing the state's will, and the right to share in the direction of affairs through genuine workers' councils. Things like these are desired equally by the people of the Soviet Union, though their wishes have so far not been expressed with the same directness as in Poland and Hungary.

What must have been the effect when hundreds of thousands of the Soviet intelligentsia read the full text of a protest against Soviet action in Hungary, drawn up by leading writers of the French left, including Jean-Paul Sartre and others well known as 'friends of the Soviet Union'? This protest contained the sentence 'Socialism can no more be enforced by bayonets than can freedom'.[10]

The reports of criticism and opposition emanating from countries in their own camp—the states of the eastern bloc who, with the sole exception of the arch-heretic, Tito, had always been described as trustworthy friends—must have had a strong and confusing effect. Even Tito had been welcomed back into the fold with honour by Khrushchev on his 1955 visit to Belgrade, when he repudiated the 1948 curse of the Cominform against Tito, representing it as the work of that sinister conspirator Beria. What, then, can one make of Khrushchev's speech made three years later in Sofia, in which he once more imposed the curse that he himself, in 1955, had lifted?[11]

Even the new big brother in Asia, to whom it was no longer possible to deny political and ideological equality of rights, contributed to the shattering of the belief in the infallibility of dogma. In the autumn of 1957 I stayed in Moscow on my way back from China. Russian friends often questioned me about Mao's celebrated 'contradiction speech' of 27 February 1957, which was published in *Pravda* some months later. Mao had declared that even under socialism contradictions between the government and the governed could arise—and, as in Hungary, could lead to open hostility. The Soviet ideologists had always maintained that all contradictions in a socialist state could be resolved by discussion and reform.

Mao's thesis caused considerable speculation among the Soviet intelligentsia. The Soviet ideologists busied themselves as never before with the problem of contradiction. *Kommunist*, the principal journal of the Party, with a circulation of 560,000, reported a great number of readers' queries on the subject; there were some people, the journal said, who believed that genuine progress could emerge only as the result of a struggle between opposites[12]—implying that an absolute dictatorship, without the will of the people to counterbalance it, must eventually stagnate, at least intellectually.

Mao's speech aroused many Russians. A fellow-passenger on the trans-Siberian train said to me quite bluntly: 'It is a very long time since we have heard from Russian lips any ideological pronouncement as interesting as Mao's. It was a *krupny trud* [a great work].'

There are, then, other things besides 'capitalist propaganda' that cause uneasiness among the Soviet people.

CHAPTER 19

CRITICISM—METHODS AND TARGETS

WHAT CHANCE, apart from confidential talks with friends, has the Soviet citizen of giving expression to the criticisms that the shattering experiences of recent years must have evoked in the mind of every intelligent man?

Organized facilities for free, democratic discussion simply do not exist. In the Western world there are tens of thousands of clubs, associations, unions of every description in which the state takes not the slightest interest provided they respect the law. In the Soviet Union everything is directed and supervised from above. Except the organizations directly controlled by the Party and the state, there is an absolute ban on 'associations' of every kind. Trade unions, factory groups, football clubs, chess circles —the Party keeps tabs on every one of them. It is the Party that organizes everything, and if anyone attempts to arrange independent discussions, the Party will do its utmost to listen in.

Anything resembling the emergence of a group is investigated with grave suspicion and at once labelled a 'splinter movement'. Personal loyalty to one's immediate superior is considered undesirable; what is demanded is loyalty to the heads of the state and of the Party pyramid, to the Party as a whole, and to the country, but certainly not to any individual who may stand between the citizen and the men at the top. Not the least important reason for frequent transfers of political and economic officials is to avoid the formation of cliques.

The Soviet citizen is always aware of the threat that hangs over him. Fear is his constant companion; of all the forces that prevent him—even in thought—from trying to change the regime, fear is the strongest. For the older generation the bloody 1930's remain a sinister, vivid memory. Nor do they forget the postwar years, when Zhdanov sounded the call for an attack on any kind of independent thinking. Recently the state has taken pains to show a slightly more civilized face to the world, but the people know that it is still powerful and ruthless enough to strike without mercy. Who can feel safe, after all, when Khrushchev denounces as enemies of the Party six of the ten men who sat with him a short while ago in the Presidium of the Central Committee?

Opposition precluded in its open form can emerge only in disguise. One variety of criticism that has existed for many years in the Soviet Union and is accepted as legitimate is the so-called 'self-criticism'. This, in its narrower sense, first appeared when individuals—or collectives such as the employees of a factory or a *kolkhoz*—beat their breasts and publicly confessed that they had fallen down on the job, had lied, or had harboured erroneous ideas. The twofold political objective of this device is obvious: first, to conceal the absence of personal freedom and give the impression that misdeeds are not covered up, but rather discussed freely by all concerned; and second, to convey the idea that, if anything in the Soviet Union is not quite as it should be, it is not the state that is responsible, but the laziness, stupidity, and even sometimes the wickedness of the individual.

Self-criticism is at the same time a weapon wielded with great skill by the Party against the citizen. It places him in the position of having to expiate his sins either by more zealous endeavour or fervent protestations of loyalty to the regime—sometimes even by acting as a spy for the political police.

This type of self-criticism, of course, can hardly be expected to contribute to any modification of Bolshevism. But there is another type, in the same general category, in which the individual criticizes not himself but things in general with which neither he nor his collective have any direct connection. This, too, has been practised for many years and has become a standard form of criticism in the press. The officially inspired satirical humour of *Krokodil* is on the whole intolerably boring, and is therefore in no great demand among Soviet people; but it is nevertheless worth reading by the foreign observer because it does, in fact, often contain critical articles, poems, and caricatures. The major newspapers, too, sometimes contain such articles, not entirely without humour.

The Brothers Tur, like many of their colleagues, have specialized in the fight against bureaucracy, and many of their satires are based on actual events. Here is an example dating back to the 1920's:

Some time ago (they wrote), a little bookkeeper came to

them with a tale of woe. He had recently buried an uncle in one of the Moscow cemeteries. In accordance with the regulations, he had handed in his personal papers for scrutiny by the cemetery officials. When the funeral was over, he had collected his papers and gone home. Shortly afterwards he arranged to get married. The guests were all assembled, and the happy couple hurried off to the registry office for the brief formality that would put the seal of state approval on their bliss. Imagine the bookkeeper's horror when the registrar returned his papers to him with a curt 'I don't marry the dead'. And, indeed, on the bridegroom's identity certificate was an entry stating that he had been buried on 20 May in grave No 4945. The guests went home sadly. The bride burst into bitter tears. The bookkeeper's life was in ruins. Without valid identity papers he might as well not exist; he could not draw any money, he could not travel. Everyone he approached steadfastly refused to have anything to do with a man officially recorded as dead. The cemetery authorities, whom he pestered, said quite bluntly that he had been given a decent burial according to the regulations and that he would be well-advised to hold his peace. The only recourse left to the poor man was to turn to the Brothers Tur, who published his story. A week later *Izvestia* announced that the charge against the cemetery authorities of making a mistake in their records had been proved, and those responsible had been dismissed.

Through the years thousands of similar stories have appeared in the Soviet press, and they serve a useful purpose in a country where direct criticism by the individual is hardly possible. I personally have seen more than once how useful this outlet can be. While I was on a flight to Central Asia in 1955, for example, my plane landed early one morning at Uralsk for a twenty-five minute stopover. I was just going to hurry over to the canteen for breakfast when the man next to me in the plane, a friendly young officer, persuaded me not to.

'Wait till we get to Aktyubinsk,' he suggested.

'Why?' I asked.

'The Aktyubinsk airport restaurant,' he replied, 'has recently been sharply criticized in the press. You can bet your life everything will be ship-shape now. . . . They've probably even got paper in the lavatories.'

At Aktyubinsk the restaurant manager, eager and smiling, was waiting to greet us as we stepped out of the plane. The whole place was spotless. There were clean white cloths on all the tables, and the waitresses were wearing freshly laundered aprons. The washed leaves of the rubber plants shone like mirrors.

Criticism is not confined to the satirical magazines, but is also frequently to be found in more serious media. I remember a film called *Shadows on the Path*. The 'negative hero', a Party official, is anxious to acquire a decoration. He decides to do this by becoming a 'hero of land reclamation' and gives orders that a large tract of pasture in his district is to be ploughed up. The shepherds whose flocks graze there try in vain to get the order rescinded. The climax of the film comes when the flocks return from their summer grazing grounds. When they reach the pasture that has been ploughed, they find no fodder, and the film gives a vivid picture of their starvation and death.

The film exposed the perverse and stupid behaviour of one Party official, who in the end was made to pay for his misdeeds; but it was also a protest against bureaucratic despotism in general. It aroused great interest, and the audiences clearly showed their condemnation of the wrongs it exposed.

This officially licensed self-criticism is, of course, strictly controlled by the regime. Only the small fry may be attacked; criticism must remain as shy of the leaders as it does of the official dogmas. Anyone seeking to aim higher—to take a shot at one of the despots themselves or to bring about a change in the system as a whole—must therefore resort to more subtle methods. The new Party leader showed how this could be done —and astonished the whole world—when, referring to certain undeniable aspects of the past from which he wished to disassociate himself, he said they were attributable to personal mistakes and errors of judgment, by the wicked Beria and (he added after 1956) by Stalin.

The seeds of the greater glorification of Lenin fell on fertile ground. For some time antipathy to the Stalin regime had in many minds assumed the form of an exaggerated veneration of Lenin. Anti-Stalinism became synonymous with pro-Leninism. For those who rejected not only Stalinism but the whole system, and yet were unwilling to plunge into the hazardous venture of independent thought, the slogan 'Back to Lenin' gave an opportunity to criticize the regime without risking expulsion from the ranks of the faithful. Others went a step further—they said 'Lenin', but what they really meant was liberty. For all of them an avowal of devotion to Lenin was the only way they could give their opposition the appearance of legality. Leninism, in fact, had become an alibi for opponents of the system.

A second method of making veiled criticisms is to pass on opinions, for which one does not care to admit personal responsibility, in the form in which they were expressed by a foreign journalist or broadcaster. This is done, of course, in a tone of lofty indignation at such capitalist infamy, and the wicked wolf thus led into the Soviet arena on the end of his journalistic chain is afterwards cut to pieces with all the resources of dialectical criticism. But these polemics sometimes fall strangely flat, while the publicity given to the 'exposed' Western comments shows clearly where the real interest, and perhaps the real sympathies, of the critic lay. From the 'negative' of the critical analysis put before him the reader can obtain a most illuminating 'positive'.

Consideration for some of my Russian colleagues prevents me from giving more precise details, for to involve them in political embarrassment would be a poor return for their perspicacity and courage; but that this method of airing sharp criticism is so widespread seems to indicate that the newspapermen who use it must enjoy the tacit consent of many of their superiors—and of their readers.

The feeling 'Enough of this despotism of party and state' is widespread among the Soviet people, and their criticism, both overt and concealed, is centred on it. But does this mean that they would revert, if they could, to the old, pre-Bolshevik conditions or change over to the Western way of life? Any illusions about this would only be damaging to ourselves; the concrete desires of the Soviet people are concerned not with a distant past or a distant future, but with the realities and experience of the present.

It is, of course, quite possible to make an intelligent Soviet citizen recognize that private enterprise is a better and more efficient system of economics; that—to use his own jargon—the 'surplus value' the Western businessman withholds from the workers and puts into his own pocket is, in fact, incomparably less than that which the Soviet state claims as its own. So small a minority realizes this, however, that it is insignificant. The vast majority of the people have never known anything but a state-owned economy, and for the shortcomings that they know exist, most of them blame not the system but the failure of individuals. It is true, people grumble about the bad service in the state-owned shops and the shoddy repairs made by collectively run workshops. 'If this were your own business, you wouldn't dare treat your customers like this' is a complaint frequently heard; but this doesn't mean that the speaker really wants to see a return to private enterprise in trade—to say nothing of industry—or even regards such a return as possible. The people honestly believe, as some of the conversations I have mentioned show, that a state economy is the better system. The fact that a free market can operate as an incentive and a regulator is something only very few can appreciate.

Also, Soviet newspapers always emphasize Western unemployment figures with malicious satisfaction, implying that free enterprise and large-scale unemployment are two sides of the same coin. In short, the disadvantages of a state-planned economy and the lack of personal freedom inherent in it are less keenly felt than people in the Western world imagine, because the Soviet citizens have no idea what the working of a free economy is like. What they all yearn for is a relaxation of the pressure imposed on them by the plan, the norm, and the quota. Their 'welfare state', however, must on no account be tampered with in the process.

Payment for labour performed, which is at present the guiding principle of economic life in the Soviet Union, has the approval of all those who gain by it—at least in industry and related activities. They feel it is just that the man who works harder than others, or has higher qualifications, should earn more. But among the ordinary labourers there is undeniably a desire to see the abuses in the piecework system eradicated and the basic wage raised within the framework of the total earnings. Today the basic wage is so low that to subsist at all a man must supplement it with an inordinate amount of piecework. Most of the workers, I think, would like to have their basic wage increased, but still scaled according to age and qualifications.

Higher basic wages, less exacting quotas, lower prices, more consumer goods, a greater variety in the shops, more space to live in, better business methods so that they do not have to stand in line for hours—these, by and large, are the things the Soviet people want.

In the villages things are somewhat different. Most of the rural population no longer have any clear recollection of an independent peasantry. I have talked to many peasants, and I have no doubt whatever that what they long for is less compulsion in the *kolkhozes*, more land of their own, higher prices for their produce, and an easing of the pressure of plans and quotas. But whether they would really like to see the whole of the agricultural land divided again into smallholdings among the individual *kolkhozniki* seems doubtful. There are, of course, some peasants with initiative who dream of land and a farm of their own. But the younger ones, who have acquired technical knowledge as tractor drivers, threshers, zoologists, and mechanics are not moved by any such urge. If they were given land of their own, they would probably want to cultivate it with collectively owned machines. In the villages there is no solidarity of ideas and purpose which, if Bolshevism collapsed, could put forward a clear-cut alternative.

We in the West may well say that the shortcomings of the Soviet economic system are indissolubly linked with the political system, which is concerned only with its ultimate aim of world domination and not with the people's needs. But this argument will not convince the Soviet elite (and they are the people who count) because in recent years, without any change in the political system, their standard of living has undeniably risen, and they hope to see this improvement continue. They do not recognize that the state still regards the satisfaction—or otherwise—of the needs of its subjects as dependent on the answer to a purely tactical question: How much must we give the people to keep them going? Nor do they quite realize that the increase or decrease in consumer goods will continue to be determined by an arbitrary policy.

The elite still appear to believe that an even higher standard of living can be achieved without any drastic change in the economic system. The masses, on the other hand, feel that they have been thoroughly exploited under the present economic system and sense that this exploitation will continue as long as the political system is unchanged. The fact that they see no chance of a change only adds to their sense of grievance; however, they have nothing to say about anything.

Inevitably, the predominant influence of the elite will make itself felt in politics; for the new and essential factor in the Soviet social structure is not the 'dictatorship of the proletariat' (which is pure fiction—the Party, not the proletariat, is the real dictator) but this 'new class', already numbering millions, to which the most hated word in the Bolshevik vocabulary, *bourgeoisie*, can be aptly applied in many respects. The absence of this stratum and thus of a solid social foundation led to the failure of the attempt to create a democratic state in the spring of 1917—an attempt that the Bolsheviks had at that time no difficulty in frustrating. But now, for the first time in Russian history, there exists a large, markedly bourgeois class. In the West it has been the free citizens who have carried the torch of democracy. Will the 'new class' be willing and able to play the same role in the Soviet Union?

This question goes far beyond the individual's desire for a higher standard of living and a legal guarantee of personal security; it leads straight into politics. It is a difficult question to answer, if only because in the Soviet Union there is not that freedom of discussion which is essential for the clear and convincing formulation of political ideas. Nor, of course, do people reveal their political aspirations or convictions in reply to a casual question; many long and earnest conversations are needed to discover what they really think and feel.

From my own observation I would say that the breeding ground of political thinking among the critically minded is found in the very institutions that gave the Soviet state its name—the soviets, or councils. The Soviet state consists, in theory, of a pyramid of councils, with the village soviets as the base and the Supreme Soviet of the U.S.S.R. as the apex. If the Soviet state were in reality and not merely in name a state of councils, it would still differ sharply from the Western democracies; but the designation of a democratic state—that is, a state conforming to the will of the people—could then not necessarily be denied it. Ever since Lenin assumed power with the help of these councils, however, they have been nothing more than a façade behind which the Party has wielded its monopoly of power; for the Party has the right—granted in Articles 126 and 141 of the Constitution—to select the candidates, even those called 'independents'. It is obvious, therefore, that the forces in the country who want democracy are not at the moment asking for a constitution along French or American lines, but want first to liberate the existing councils from the unworthy status of 'yes men', thus endowing them with a genuine political character and influence.

An initial, though modest, success is reflected in the new and far-reaching statute which increases the powers of the village councils. This was promulgated in the summer of 1957 by the Supreme Council of the R.S.F.S.R. (Russian Socialist Federal Soviet Republic), by far the most important of the republics that form the Union. It gave village councils the right to ask for reports from local economic authorities and to comment on them.[1] It is interesting that the preamble to the statute specifically states that the provisions are drawn up on the basis of a large number of proposals and suggestions. For some time, too, there has been talk of the need to make rules that will enable the electorate to dismiss a council member whose work has proved unsatisfactory[2]; the right to dismiss elected members who disregard the wishes and interests of their constituents, could not fail to strengthen the electors' self-esteem and interest in politics.

During one of my recent visits to Moscow I asked if there were any interesting new novels about intellectuals and technicians. Among others, a novel by Daniil Granin, *The Seekers*, was recommended to me.[3] In it there is a description of a Party meeting at a scientific institute where officials are to be elected for the coming term. The 'negative hero' of the story, an engineer named Viktor Potapenko, is determined to win a place on the Party committee. With Dolgin, the local Party secretary and chairman of the meeting, he maps beforehand the exact course the procedure is to follow—who will catch the chairman's eye and be called upon to speak, who will propose whom for what office. Nevertheless, things do not go quite according to plan. Potapenko is nominated (out of turn), but when Dolgin blandly ignores all the raised hands and continues to call on speaker after speaker according to his prearranged list, the members of the meeting become very indignant.

Eventually Borisov, one of Potapenko's opponents, acts. Ignoring the rulings of the chair, he strides up to the rostrum, seizes the list from the chairman's hand, and begins to ridicule it. 'Comrade Dolgin seems to have arranged everything very nicely!' he says scornfully.

By this time the meeting has got completely out of hand. People who at first were nervous or apathetic are now aroused and determined to exercise their right to choose their own candidates. Discussion becomes fast and furious. Gradually the list of candidates grows. Eventually the new Party committee is complete, and the first task entrusted to it is to inquire into the conduct of Dolgin, Potapenko, and their followers. The people have shown that they will no longer tolerate intrigues and the complete disregard of the wishes of ordinary Party members.

This Party meeting might well be described as the birth of a democracy in microcosm. A previously docile and acquiescent community had suddenly taken matters into its own hands and exercised its rights. It is significant that a widely read Soviet novel should espouse the fundamental principle of democracy, the participation of everyone in the affairs of the community. Every reader must have realized that the methods condemned by the author were exactly those employed by the Party leaders in the national elections. The only difference between the 'elections' to the Supreme Council of the U.S.S.R. and the intrigues described by Granin is that the former affect the whole country, while the latter are confined to a small institute.

It will probably be some time before the readers of Granin's book (and, indeed, the whole population of the Soviet Union) can understand that democracy on this miniature scale will be of no use to them while the vital decisions continue to be made by a handful of men in the Kremlin, independent of the people. But by openly refusing to remain supine under the dictates of local Party bosses, the people have taken the first, and perhaps the most difficult, step.

Intrigues such as those Granin described occur constantly in real life. In many cases—probably the majority—the official wire-pullers win, but quite often they are defeated. The important thing is that they are challenged at all. We also hear of cases where criticism from Moscow is not taken seriously at the local level.[4]

Something I have rarely encountered in the Soviet Union is

the demand for more than one political party. The highly exaggerated descriptions of Western inter-party rivalries that the Soviet papers publish with such glee naturally do not encourage the Russians to emulate them. Moreover they prefer a dynamic form of government that never ceases to set targets for the future. They have become accustomed to seeing the development of the country in terms of continuous progress. They don't want the exploitation of the country's vast resources to falter in any way, and they fear that a multi-party system, with all the delays caused by conflicting views and changing majorities, might well be a serious hindrance to development; at the same time they are incapable of envisaging the many advantages a multi-party system has to offer.

History has shown—the Germans and the Japanese are cases in point—that people who feel they have arrived belatedly on the scene and must hurry to catch up with those ahead are usually prepared to support a strong, even rigorous, form of government, provided it promises to win them a place in the sun.

If you ask a Russian whether he would like to see a government really responsible to the Supreme Soviet, a government that the Supreme Soviet appoints and can dismiss at will, you will see from his expression that he has never thought of such a possibility. If you mention the Communist Party, reactions are more definite. 'We're not particularly fond of it, but—could we get along without it?' seems to sum up the attitude of most people.

But on one point they all agree—the Party's hitherto unlimited despotism must be checked. The idea of a division of power, of a government held in check by a parliament, is one I have never come across in the Soviet Union. The Russians have hardly any idea how a Western democracy works. Perhaps one could put it this way: we in the West love the freedom our form of government and economy give us, but we feel—and this applies particularly to the younger generation—that not enough is demanded of us, that we are not sufficiently 'involved'—in short that we live alone in a world where everybody can do, or not do, as he likes. The Soviet people, on the other hand, live in a condition of super-integration. They thoroughly approve of the fundamental principle—the integration of the individual into the state—but feel that an exaggerated application of it imposes too great a demand on the individual. What we need, then, is a good strong dose of the communal spirit, and what the Russians need is an even stronger dose of personal liberty. The ultimate aims of both are not too far apart, although the basic differences, of course, remain.

On this point American interrogations of former Soviet citizens have elicited a number of facts that largely corroborate the opinions expressed in this book. Here, for example, is an extract from the summary of an American report:

> So far as the formal declaration of belief in civil liberties, such as freedom of the press, assembly, and religion, is concerned, former Soviet citizens show a marked and uniform propensity to declare themselves in favour of them. When specific limiting conditions or concrete situations are mentioned, however, a good deal of the support for civil liberties melts away in favour of varying degrees of governmental control and intervention.[5]

To sum up, it can be said that the Soviet man in the street wants a 'good' state, but does not quite see how he can compel the state to be good—in other words, how it would be possible to create institutions that could prevent the state from becoming 'evil'. But I think it is undeniable that the yearning for a better state is becoming both stronger and more apparent, and this seems a good sign.

Here I would like to quote Dudintsev's novel again. In its remarkable concluding pages, Lopatkin recalls something a friend once said to him: 'You mark my words—one of these days you'll go into politics.' Then follow these memorable sentences:

> This was probably the first time that he had really understood this man, whom he had regarded for some time as an elder brother. Although his machine had been built and was serving the people, he once more saw the endless road stretching into the distance before him; it was waiting for him, and it fascinated him with its mysterious twists and grave responsibilities.

His path had so far brought success to Lopatkin the inventor. Where would it now lead Lopatkin the man of politics? We do not know. But that the author should take leave of the inventor of yesterday by greeting him as the man of politics of tomorrow has a logic that is not to be denied.

At present, it doesn't matter much that no clear-cut ideas for the future are discernible; the vital point is that men have begun to seek new solutions and, above all, that most of the seekers belong to the rising generation. None of the younger writers has epitomized this trend more convincingly than Yevgeny Yevtushenko in 'Station Zimá', published in 1956.[6] This auto-biographical poem describes his return home to the Siberian hamlet of Zima, which he decided to visit because he realized that in his early life he had 'said things he should not have said, and left unsaid things he ought to have said'.

Until then, he explains, he had lived almost without a care, but that carefree life had seemed so simple only because every-thing that was difficult in it was settled for him by other people. Then suddenly things changed, and he knew that from now on he must seek the answers for himself.

The visit to Zima takes place after the execution of Beria, at a time when people were still concerned about the alleged 'doc-tors' plot' against Stalin. One of the poet's relatives says to him 'The people have begun to wonder . . . is it true that the doctors were not guilty after all? Why, then, were they so viciously attacked? Was it all the fault of the wicked Beria?'

Shortly before he leaves the village he meets Vovka, a child-hood friend, who senses that the poet is preoccupied, seeking answers and not finding them:

'Today, we all are thinking, brother, in this land . . .
'You want a quick solution of all problems.
'The time will come—don't worry—for the answers.
'Long thinking is required.
                    Hurry not.'

The crucial words are 'all are thinking'. The appeal to think independently is powerful and unmistakable. It is the most en-couraging call that has come from the Soviet Union in recent years, and all the more so because it comes from the pen of a young poet.

Finally, I am prepared to venture a cautiously optimistic prognosis. The evolution of democracy, beginning in the days of Cromwell, was by no means rapid or continuous during the succeeding centuries. In eighteenth-century Europe, the unchecked absolutism of Louis XIV was followed by the enlightened absolutism of Frederick the Great, Joseph II, and Catherine II. Later, in Russia, the autocrat Nicholas I was succeeded by Alexander II, 'the liberator'. By the same sort of evolutionary process it is possible that the Bolshevik totalitarianism of the first and second generations may be followed by a species of 'enlightened totalitarianism', though not, as yet, in my opinion, by a democracy as we understand it. I have met no Soviet citizen whose thoughts about the future ran along Western democratic lines; but I know a great many who envisage and hope for the evolution of the Soviet state into a modern autocracy that will respect the needs of its people.

CHAPTER 20

THE WORLD OUTSIDE

THE SWING of the pendulum between admiration and contempt for everything foreign has been characteristic of the Russians since before the days of Peter the Great, and it is still evident today.

In the 1930's everything foreign was wonderful. A good suit, a camera, a car, a fountain pen that worked, and an electric torch —all these were, as a matter of course, *zagranichny* (from abroad). At that time there was little evidence of the traditional Russian diversity of opinion about the West. The Russian admired and envied the West. In his eyes the United States was the remote, unattainable utopia; visitors from the West were mortals dazzlingly favoured by fate, to be admired as if they were demi-gods.

I noticed this particularly in 1934, when my wife accompanied me to Russia for the first time. On the long drive from Berlin through Poland and the Baltic states to Moscow I spent some time each day trying to teach her a little Russian. To encourage her I said how helpful it would be for her, when she went shopping, to be able to speak the language of the country. The day we arrived I took her to the big food store known before the Revolution as Yeliséyev's, but now renamed Gastronom No. 1. As I speak Russian without a foreign accent, I was always treated like a Russian and made to stand in line for a long time before being served. But my wife was at once recognized as a foreigner by one of the saleswomen and whisked out of the bread line. 'What can I get for you, madam?' the saleswoman asked in German. 'White bread? Certainly!' She walked briskly past the line to her colleague behind the counter and brought back the bread. The whole thing took, perhaps, half a minute. After that, whenever I ventured to reproach my wife gently for her lack of eagerness to learn Russian, I was firmly slapped down with 'Remember Gastronom No. 1!' Thereafter I made a practice of talking 'foreigner's Russian' whenever I wanted something that was scarce, as nearly everything was, including even theatre and railroad tickets.

In those days all the best domestic products were reserved for export, and the Russians accepted this as a matter of course. During a journey through the endless forests of northern Russia in 1935 I came across a primitive sawmill in what had once been a cemetery on the banks of the Dvina. As far as I could see, only women worked there—poor, miserable souls in rags and worn shoes. But when they heard that a foreigner had arrived, they began to work with redoubled zeal.

'Come on, girls!' called one of these women. 'Let's show the foreigner how we work for the export drive!' As she took me round the mill, she kept on repeating proudly: 'All for export! Everything we turn out here goes abroad!' The tone in which she said 'export' and 'abroad' was eloquent testimony to the awe in which she held the great world beyond Russia's frontiers.

Since that time the attitude towards foreign countries has changed. One of the causes was the treatment accorded to the occupied or imprisoned Russians on Hitler's and Himmler's orders. But a stronger and more lasting reason has been the Russian's pride in their own achievements and their vast industrial expansion. The improvements in their standard of living and the constant assertion that nearly a billion people are now 'in the socialist camp' have not been without effect.

Great interest in foreign countries is no longer associated with a despairing inferiority complex. Indeed, many Soviet citizens have reverted to a feeling of superiority and look upon the rest of the world much as the Orthodox Russians of old used to look down on the 'foreign heretics' of the West. On the other hand, the Russians' self-confidence has been severely shaken by the glimpses of the outside world many Russians have had since 1944—first during the conquest and occupation of other European countries, and more recently since Russians have been allowed to attend international conferences, and the volume of tourist traffic in both directions has increased.

When I reached Moscow a few days after the Youth Festival, organized so lavishly in the summer of 1957, I asked every Russian I met for his impressions of the great event. Their answers naturally varied according to their background. When I asked a bootblack who was cleaning my shoes what he thought of the visitors from abroad, he replied: 'I'll tell you one thing. . . . They have the most marvellous shoes!'

A taxi driver to whom I put the same question at first screwed up his face and was silent for a few moments. Then he said, 'They're a damned sight better off than we are'.

A student told me of a conversation he had had with a young Norwegian visitor. Asked how he paid for his studies, the Norwegian replied that his father was quite well off and naturally paid the bills. Of course, he added, there were also government allowances—and he beckoned to a compatriot, the son of a working man, who was studying on a government grant and drawing a monthly allowance equivalent to the price of two new suits. 'Just think of it!' the young Russian said to me. 'Why, that would mean more than 1,000 roubles a month!'

Hundreds of thousands of Russians made their first acquaintance with the quality of Western products during World War II, when the Allies poured in goods of every description, from medical stores to trucks, accompanied by a host of Americans in uniform and in mufti as maintenance men and instructors. Stalin's suspiciousness, however, more or less successfully prevented any fraternization, and in the years that followed he carefully controlled the trickle of friendship visits, until the dwindling stream was at last completely frozen by the cold war.

The extent to which the West has succeeded during the cold war in reaching the Soviet citizen with Russian-language broadcasts is, in view of the extreme caution the listener has to exercise, hard to determine. The number of radio sets in the Soviet Union is, of course, enormous (production rose from 1,070,000 sets in 1950 to 3,772,000 in 1956 and 4,035,000 sets in 1959[1]; most of them, however, are merely relay loudspeakers. Anyone who has travelled in a Russian train knows that there is a loudspeaker in every compartment that broadcasts only what the train's radio operator decides to pass on from the programme he picks up on the master receiver. The same system is followed all over the country. The receivers offered for sale are mainly limited to medium- and long-wave reception; there are few that can pick up foreign broadcasts, and the great array of jamming stations constantly operating helps to make such reception even more difficult. Nevertheless, a fair amount does seem to seep through. At all events the Soviet press is always fulminating, not only against the broadcasts by *émigrés* over Radio Liberation which the Soviets particularly detest, but also against the Voice of America and the B.B.C.

Anyone interested in the way Western democracy works can obtain absolutely no factual information from the Soviet press or radio. An unbiased account of the evolution of British democracy would make fascinating and thought-provoking reading for young Russians—and for that reason, the authorities make sure that nothing of the kind is available. A Scandinavian Ambassador, when he was given a few minutes on Soviet television, had the excellent idea of setting forth an exact and factual account of the constitution and institutions of his country, and it was shrewd of Mr Macmillan to use his television time in Moscow for a description of British achievements.

Soviet readers are given a mass of disjointed information in their own newspapers. It is all heavily biased and the questions that interest readers are only discussed sporadically. The Soviet press publishes only the news that currently suits the Party and the government. In the Soviet Union 'objectivity' is a dirty word; what is demanded instead is *partíynost'* (Party loyalty), 'engagement', the presentation of only one side of the question. The Soviet citizen knows very well that he is kept insufficiently informed by his press; hence his mistrust of the newspapers, but also his reluctance to judge for himself and his shoulder-shrugging attitude of *Im vidnéye* (they, the bosses, know best).

Here, however, we are concerned more with the Soviet people's hunger for news than with their limited opportunities to get hold of it. Where the urge for contact with others exists, it will always seek satisfaction, whatever the obstacles. When men are cut off from all sources of foreign information, the greater the value they will place on the foreign news they do hear and the more cunning will be their efforts to obtain it.

Towards the end of the Stalin era, not even the savants of the Soviet Union were allowed to keep abreast of developments in the West. Anyone who persistently asked for foreign publications, or quoted foreign colleagues too frequently, exposed himself to the charge of 'toadying to degenerate capitalism'. The great scholars of the West were dismissed as reactionaries or fools, and all the major inventions of recent times were attributed to Russians.

This has by now changed, partly because the Soviet scientists' demand for information about developments in the West has become increasingly insistent, and partly because Stalin's successors have been intelligent enough to recognize that by barring access to up-to-date information they were only injuring themselves. Einstein, who for years had been cited in the Soviet Union as the prototype of the scientist who succumbs to idealism and mysticism, was rehabilitated posthumously. A gigantic organization, the Institute of Scientific Information of the Academy of Sciences of the U.S.S.R., was set up in 1952 for the express purpose of studying thousands of foreign technical journals and informing Soviet scientists as quickly as possible of everything valuable they contained. It has a permanent staff of about 2,500, as well as about 11,000 to 13,000 scientific correspondents. It publishes thirteen journals containing abstracts and reports that are more comprehensive and better co-ordinated than anything comparable in the West, and it also issues thirty-six mimeographed reports every week.

These new and direct contacts with Western thought are having considerable influence on political thought in Russia, particularly when the fruits of these contacts become available to a wider public through the press. In this way, for example, it became known that Western sociologists regarded the social structure of the Soviet Union as that of a class state. Many Soviet citizens had reached a similar conclusion, but had not been allowed to say so. Soviet intellectuals were tremendously interested to find in their own newspapers and magazines reports from Soviet representatives at international Congresses of Sociology; from the attacks launched by the Soviet delegates on opinions expressed by Western sociologists, the Russians were able to get some idea of Western opinions. This is the sort of thing they read:

> Some bourgeois sociologists, seeking to praise capitalism and denigrate socialism, assert that the abolition of private ownership and its replacement by socialist state-ownership has not put an end to the exploitation of the individual. . . . In their vain efforts to find at least some small tear in the social fabric of the Soviet Union, the bourgeois ideologists have done their best to portray in a false light that small

measure of inequality that still exists in our standard of living. They maintain that socialism, far from preventing the emergence of class distinctions and differences in the living standards of various members of society, has merely enhanced them. These misrepresentations are frequently presented in a scientific manner, making full use of the class-formation theory held by Western sociologists. In this theory, a word borrowed from geology—'stratum'— is substituted for the normal term 'class'; instead of class distinctions it refers to social strata, which differ according to income and position in the social framework. The bourgeois sociologists use this theory to prove that under capitalism class distinctions are vanishing, while under the socialist system, on the contrary, new privileged strata— 'the new elite'—are emerging.[2]

This is exactly what countless Russians have been telling themselves for a long time, as I know from many conversations. Similarly, by using the 'negative' of Soviet denials to produce a 'positive' of what has been said in the West, the Soviet reader was also able to glean the views of the anti-Tito Yugoslav Djilas, author of *The New Class*.

Another thing the Soviet citizen has learned through the newspapers is that in the West, particularly the U.S.A. and Germany, there is considerable support for a kind of 'people's capitalism', involving the ever-widening spread of ownership, to be achieved primarily by encouraging employees to acquire more shareholdings, often in the firms they work for—a development that is expected to reduce the traditional hostility between capital and labour. This theory is, of course, anathema to the Bolsheviks, for its success would cut the ground from under their feet. The whole of their argument is based on the opposite premise— that the conflict between capital and labour cannot be settled by peaceful negotiation, but only by force and revolution.

None the less, the idea of a 'people's capitalism' has aroused lively interest in the Soviet Union; a special conference of Russian experts on Western economic affairs was held in Moscow to discuss it.[3] From the ever-increasing number of reviews of foreign books in Soviet periodicals, the Russian reader has been able to learn far more than in Stalin's day about

Western trends of thought, and even to read critical dissertations by foreign students of Soviet affairs.

The Soviet citizen who has any conception of the Western world knows that there is more freedom in it, but he is inclined to believe that this freedom leads—indeed, must lead—to chaos. He feels that this is confirmed by the reports and critical comments in Western newspapers on rising prices, over-production, and unemployment. These are faithfully served up to him every day in the Soviet press, which is usually scrupulously careful to quote the exact source of the information. The smooth working of a free market is something he cannot grasp at all. The Russian does not doubt that the standard of living in the West is higher than in the Soviet Union, but only, of course—it cannot be otherwise if one believes Marx—among the exploiting, predatory class, while the masses are starving; he is all the more ready to believe this because it is, in fact, what he is familiar with in his own country. Soviet tourists abroad are therefore less impressed with the magnificence of the main shopping streets in our cities than they are with the housing for workers. This shows them that in the West the *entire* population has a higher standard of living.

The Russians know that life in the West is in many ways easier and more pleasant than life in their own country, but propaganda has taught them that these gains have been made at the cost of a general degeneration and that the West is filled with a decadent lust for profits and material comfort. Many Russians look upon the West as Cato, the Roman, once looked upon Hellenic civilization, and as the Russian Slavophiles of yesterday used to regard the rest of Europe. The Western nations, with their gangster films, sadistic comic strips, and sex-filled entertainment, make things altogether too easy for Soviet propaganda, which takes full advantage of its opportunities. Yuri Trifonov's novel *The Students* contains the following fragment of dialogue (probably taken from life) between two young men comparing wartime experiences:

'I ran into the Americans,' said Lagodenko, 'in Austria. Technically they are strong, but they're not soldiers—they're just tourists, people on motor bikes.'

'And that's just how they behaved all through the war. Guest artists, playing in Europe!'[4]

Even more characteristic were replies given to Americans by Soviet *émigrés* in the United States. One of those questioned was highly critical of the way young people in America were allowed to see films that tended to encourage sexual precocity. Another said quite bluntly, 'Thank God *we* have never had the demoralizing comics and the filthy publications that every child can get hold of in this country.'[5]

Whenever I talk to a Russian about life in the free West as compared with life in the Soviet Union, with its brutal laws, forced-labour camps, and frightful privations, I remember a boy I used to know at school. Two or three times every month his very strict father gave him a severe thrashing. The boy didn't enjoy these thrashings, of course, but nevertheless they gave him a feeling of superiority over the rest of us; he looked down on us as mother's pets. There is no other people in the world in whose proverbs chastisement and love go hand in hand so often as in those of the Russians.

Something else that frequently crops up in conversations with Russians and makes them feel superior to their chief rivals, the Americans, is the trouble the Americans have with their domestic racial problems. Little Rock seemed to the Russians further proof of persistent racial discrimination. They point out that it couldn't happen in the Soviet Union, and that in their factories, schools, and colleges, all races work amicably side by side. Indeed, even in Tsarist Russia there was always less consciousness of race—except, of course, for the pogroms against the Jews—than in other colonial powers. The conquests of Siberia and Central Asia under the Tsars was as ruthless as anything that has ever happened anywhere. But once conquest was achieved, racial and social integration proceeded fairly quickly. Leading families of the subject peoples were raised to the nobility of the Russian Empire and were received at the Imperial Court.

It is true that there has been a certain amount of racial tension, heightened to some extent by increased industrialization. Nevertheless, and in spite of the brutal treatment of whole races by the Kremlin, most of the people of the Soviet Union think that there is more racial tolerance in their country than anywhere else in the world.

The Russians are engagingly friendly to non-European visitors, particularly Asians. Friendliness towards other people is inherent in most human beings, but in the Russians it seems to be an exceptionally pronounced trait; besides, the state constantly encourages it for political reasons. Anyone who has seen the enthusiasm with which the Russians embrace their Asian or African guests cannot help feeling that this welcome probably makes a more lasting impression on these guests than does the reception given to them by any other white nation.

In recent years interest in France has also increased. I have frequently been asked about current French intellectual trends and especially about existentialism. It is from Paris that the younger generation primarily expects intellectual stimuli that seem to them to be lacking in other Western countries. I imagine that books about India, which for political reasons have recently depicted that country in a very favourable light, have turned the thoughts of the younger generation towards ideas regarded as undesirable by the Kremlin. I remember, for example, how a young Russian engineer questioned me very closely on the subject of yoga and the Indian practice of meditation.

This traditional admiration of foreign countries that has been revived recently is offset by the newly-awakened pride in Russia's war-time achievements, in the Sputniks, and in the world records broken by Russian athletes—all of which seem for the first time to have brought within reach the fulfilment of the slogan 'We must catch up—and overtake them', a slogan the Bolsheviks have been proclaiming for so many years. I felt something of this spirit in the tremendous jubilation when the Russian long-distance runner Kuts, at one of the first big international sports events in Moscow, beat his most serious rival, Gordon Pirie, by a whole lap.

For a long time the Russian seems to have been saying to himself: The West treated us as barbarians, not to be taken quite seriously; now at last we can enjoy the feeling that technically and in the economic sphere we have beaten them—or will certainly be able to beat them in the not-too-distant future.

CHAPTER 21

SOVIET MAN AND THE WEST

LET US NOW turn back to a question that is crucial for Russia and the rest of the world. Have the Soviets succeeded in transforming the Russian into a new man, a collectivized robot, who in thought, deed, and desire reacts exactly as they want him to react, a being unapproachable by and incomprehensible to us—in short, Soviet man as the Bolsheviks see him?

Whatever the reason, whether it is the influence of industrialization and mass civilization or the result of an indoctrination carried out over forty years with all the resources of a totalitarian state, the indisputable fact remains—Soviet man is not the Russian our fathers knew and often saw in a romantic light. Many 'typically Russian' characteristics have disappeared, and —particularly among the upper class—have often been replaced by diametrically opposite traits. The wild, primaeval forces have been tamed, unpredictable spontaneity and impulsiveness have given way to the steady discipline of modern, workaday life; a firm determination to succeed and a strong faith in technological progress have been superimposed on the old, irrational Russian temperament; religious beliefs have been thrust back inside the church walls. But at the same time I have found little or no trace in the vast majority of the Russian people of the trait that has been described as 'typically Bolshevik' and is, in fact, typical of the Party officials and their kind—the cold-blooded, calculating determination of the fanatic, for whom the end justifies any and every means. It is true that most Russians have accepted without much protest the state's omnipotence and its monopoly of the means of production, and have recognized its claim to be the executor of the 'law of progress' from capitalism via socialism to Communism; but this has not yet made them Bolsheviks at heart. On the contrary, from all I have seen and heard over a period of thirty years I am convinced that the answer to the question I posed at the beginning of this book— Is Soviet man more Soviet or more man?—is emphatically 'More man'. And his salient characteristics, which we can regard as constant, certainly for the next ten or fifteen years—his growing demand for personal security, for a private life of his own in the family circle, free from state interference, for freedom of thought and intellectual evolution—are themselves the surest indication that within another ten or fifteen years he will still be no Bolshevik.

The Bolsheviks wanted industrialization, and they achieved it, but in the process they created something else that they didn't want at all—a stratified society, with an increasingly self-assured upper class that has taken the first opportunity to strengthen the legal guarantees of its own personal security.

The Bolsheviks wanted a higher standard of general education as a prerequisite of industrialization. In this, too, they largely succeeded, with the help of a broadly-conceived and intensive educational system which has taught the people to think —but also to think for themselves.

The Bolsheviks wanted law and order firmly established throughout the country, and they found that they had to foster the family life they had previously scorned, with the result that millions of families in the Soviet Union today are leading their own lives, in small groups which the power of the state can scarcely penetrate.

Earlier in the book I examined in detail the findings I have summarized in these last few pages. The reader therefore knows that—like all human questions—the problems of Soviet man are really much more complicated. And I must warn him once more against jumping to conclusions. That only a small proportion of the Soviet people has become Bolshevik and that most of the country doesn't much care for politics does not imply a serious defeat of the Party. On the contrary, it may be to their advantage in some ways, particularly in relation to Soviet penetration of Africa and Asia, which has been achieved under the label of 'economic assistance', and which is not without its dangers for the West. Thousands of Soviet citizens are being employed in these ventures, and it is highly important for the Kremlin's purpose that these people should be efficient technicians, engineers, instructors and officers; that their work should be reliable; that they should behave in a disciplined manner; and that they should make themselves as pleasant as possible, so that the people they work with in their new surroundings should say, 'What nice people these Soviet Russians are!'

We come now to the decisive question: Of what significance for the peace and future of the world is Soviet man as we have met him in this book? Is there any likelihood that he would rise and turn against his government if, either deliberately or by miscalculation in the years ahead, it led him into war? One can only say that it is not likely. In spite of the people's obvious desire for peace, their obedience to their leaders, and their readiness to accept the government's decisions are as yet stronger than their hatred of war.

When I talked to people about their worries I found that they were now aware of the frightful possibility of a third world war. Earlier Soviet propaganda, according to which only the corrupt West needed to fear an atomic war, had had no effect. 'If there is a third world war,' a Soviet officer said to me, 'our planet will be left as barren as the moon: completely without life.'

The Soviet people's desire for peace has not diminished; a call to 'die for Berlin' would have about as much appeal to them as 'die for Danzig' once had to the French. This will to peace could be our best ally, but unfortunately the Soviet citizen knows very little of what takes place in the world, and even less of the role his leaders play in endangering its peace.

One evening I was sitting with two young Soviet lieutenants in a Moscow restaurant. One was from the air force, the other the navy. We had a most agreeable conversation, with many friendly toasts. We talked about everything, including our differences of opinion. One of them, as we were about to take leave of each other, said to me that he particularly enjoyed the clash of conflicting ideas. 'Man has been given understanding, to distinguish him from the beasts,' he said. Then he added, 'And he must use every opportunity of forming his own opinion —that's the most important thing of all.'

This sounded good to all of us, so I said: 'It was a great pleasure for me to sit and chat with you like this. I'd rather see you with me around a table than above me in a bomber.' A shadow fell across the friendly face of the Soviet airman, and his expression hardened a little as he said, 'That's something over which we have no control. We have to obey orders.'

His reply reflected not only his own outlook, but the outlook of the great majority of Soviet citizens. Their behaviour towards us and towards the West in general depends not on their own desires or views, but on the orders of their leaders. Thus it will remain for quite some time, and we must know this.

Things might become different if, as time goes on, the people of the Soviet Union should be able to influence the shaping of policy and thereby assert more actively their great desire for peace. The people are far less interested in world revolution than are their leaders. The Kremlin, I think, might accept the risk of war to wean some key country of Asia or the Near East away from its Western ties or if it saw a chance of turning such a country into a Communist state. Not so the people: to them world revolution isn't nearly important enough to justify such a risk. Any increase in the people's share in policy-making, therefore, would reduce the danger of a war undertaken with the purpose of Sovietizing another nation.

Reduce—but not eliminate. A sense of obligation to fulfil a specific mission in the history of mankind is in the Russians' blood. It is always possible that the Soviet leaders might still be able to strike a responsive chord in the hearts of the people —even if they had obtained wider democratic rights—with a rallying-cry like 'The triumph of peace in the world depends on us. One last battle, and then—paradise on earth is guaranteed!' I deliberately rate this as possible, not probable, because the Kremlin would not find it easy to kindle enthusiasm for such a cause; after years of sacrifice and disillusionment, the public's yearning to be left in peace has become very strong.

Up to now there has been no chance of a democratic foreign policy, nor will there be in the foreseeable future. But the growing political influence of the 'new class' has become apparent. There is no doubt that they feel the need for peace very strongly, for in any disaster resulting from a gamble in foreign politics, they stand to lose more than any other section of the population. But wars are—and have been for thousands of years—fought not only on ideological grounds, but also for reasons of national policy, in defence of so-called vital national interests; and a German does not have to delve very deeply to find proof that even a thoroughly bourgeois and prosperous upper class is capable of indulging in power politics and even chauvinism— more so, indeed, than the workers.

In this connection we must remember that the Bolshevik

leaders, with their doctrine of two types of war, have for many years deliberately prepared the grounds on which to attack any moral reservation with regard to the use of military force. According to this doctrine, which was enunciated by Stalin (though Lenin held similar views), there are two kinds of conflict—a just war and an unjust war:

> A *just* war is a war that aims not at conquest, but at liberation, a war that is fought either to defend the people against a sudden onslaught and an attempt to subjugate them, or to free a people from the slavery of capitalism, or, finally, a war whose object is to liberate colonies and dependencies from the yoke of imperialism.
>
> An *unjust* war is a war of conquest, waged with the object of conquering and enslaving foreign countries.[1]

Note that these definitions are worded loosely enough to cover all contingencies, including a war of aggression. Khrushchev, in a speech on 6 January 1961, has spoken of three kinds of wars —world wars, local wars, and wars of liberation—and what he said about the wars of liberation was practically identical with Stalin's thesis about 'just wars'.[2]

Pacifism is strictly forbidden in the Soviet Union; in the Soviet interpretation pacifist is all but synonymous with traitor—but only, of course, if he is a Soviet citizen. Military training of the youth—apart from national service—is carried on openly. In the universities students are drilled in the handling of arms, and in the para-military organizations millions are trained in partisan warfare.

Patriotism and familiarity with the handling of arms, both of which are much greater than in the West, could therefore create a situation in which a Soviet population, endowed with democratic rights, supported or even demanded a policy dictated purely by power politics and nationalism, even though such a policy threatened world peace. But this, again, is unlikely. The section of the population content with its lot will not lightly hazard the advantages it has so laboriously won, and the other sections who are still dissatisfied would say to themselves that war would make things even worse.

I wish I could assert with confidence that the Soviet people, or at least the elite, will do their utmost to restrain the government from rash adventures. But if I speak of hopes, and not assertions—although the hopes, I think, are justifiable—it is because I have had talks with Soviet citizens that make me feel it would be irresponsible to give such a facile and simplified answer to a question of such importance to the world.

Not too long ago, when I talked with a Russian about the world situation, we discussed whether a third world war was conceivable. I had complete faith in the desire of the Soviet people for peace, I said, but none in that of their government; the government's aim, I said, was not world peace but world domination, and one of these days this might bring about a situation fraught with the gravest danger of war. My companion contested this, claiming that the Soviet Government had never started a war or tried to gain an advantage by threatening war.

'You must have a very short memory,' I countered. 'What about the attack on Japan in 1945, or on the Baltic states and Poland, with all of whom the Soviet Union had signed non-aggression pacts? And, above all, what about Finland in 1939?'

'Finland,' he replied heatedly, 'was a special case. At that time the Finnish border was barely twenty miles from the second most important city in our country. Finnish guns were emplaced all along the border, and the Western powers were pressing Finland to open fire on Leningrad. It was a situation we couldn't tolerate indefinitely. Surely you must see that. For months we negotiated with the Finns. We offered them territory in exchange for a withdrawal from the Leningrad area. But they were obdurate. So there was nothing left to do but . . . '

At this point he stopped short, realizing that he had gone too far.

'Now think over what you have just told me,' I said. 'In your opinion a preventive war against Finland was justified, because Finnish guns were within twenty miles of Leningrad and constituted a threat to that city. By now practically every city in the world will be within range of potentially hostile rocket bases. Now put yourself in our place—or in the place of any other nation you like. Suddenly something we do upsets you. Suppose you call this a potential threat and demand that we bow to your wishes on the issue. We must either accede to these and any subsequent demands you may make, or assume that you will attack us. The fact that you should think this perfectly reasonable shakes my whole faith in the Russians' desire for peace. If there are people in the U.S.S.R., decent people like yourself, who are prepared to argue that a preventive war against weaker nations is justifiable in certain circumstances—which you yourself specify!—then you mustn't be surprised if I prefer to entrust my own future and that of my country to a strong alliance and its powerful deterrents, rather than to the goodwill of the Soviet Union.'

To sum up: so long as the decision rests solely with the Kremlin, war on ideological grounds and as the outcome of national power politics is possible; if the voice of the people should ever begin to carry more weight, the danger from ideological pressures would be reduced, while the danger from power politics would not automatically disappear. At the same time it would be easier for the rest of the world to deal with a Soviet Government that no longer imposed a dictatorship on its people, but allowed them to share in making decisions.

The most important need today is to be ready for that situation when it arises, and in the meantime to take advantage of whatever meagre opportunities are available now. This brings us to the final question, implicit in all we have discussed so far: What can we do, as nations or as individuals; what should be our attitude towards the Soviet people—towards the people, not the Soviet Government or the Communist Party—in order to strengthen the possibility of peaceful co-existence in this nuclear age, without sacrificing positions that are vital to us?

The first imperative is self-evident. By our behaviour we must make Soviet man understand that we have no unfriendly feelings towards him or towards the Soviet people as a whole, that, on the contrary, we feel the highest admiration for their cultural and economic achievements and regard them as one of the great peoples of our time, people whose friendship we seek.

If others treat me as an outcast, then they are responsible if I behave like one. Everybody would rather be loved and respected than hated and despised. This is true of the Russians— and of the Americans—perhaps even more than of any other people. We must help the Russian to get rid of the idea that the rest of the world regards him as a mad dog and fears him accordingly.

Some people in the West build their hopes on the human

frailties of the Russians and gloat when they read in the Soviet press reports of drunkenness or juvenile crime. 'Ah!' they say, 'the Soviet state will soon crumble.' This kind of reasoning is unworthy of free men. Besides, if the Soviet state were to collapse, it would be for reasons other than these; after all, these same phenomena can also be found in the West.

The hope of the world is that the finest qualities of the Russian people will grow stronger with the years, stronger than the evil forces of Bolshevism, that they will modify Bolshevism and in the end triumph over it.

If we wish to appeal to the positive qualities of Soviet man, we must show that we sympathize with him. But at the same time we must make it clear that there are limits to the concessions we are prepared to make for the sake of friendship, and that under no circumstances will we tolerate our or our friends' forcible conversion to Communism. But there again we must stress the positive aspect. We must make far greater efforts to convince Soviet man that the desire for peace in Western Europe and in the United States is certainly no less sincere than it is among the Russians or the Uzbeks. We must continue to try to give him a true picture of Western conditions, for thus far all he has been told has been radically distorted. We must try to point out to him the advantages of our way of life rather than hammer away at the defects of his own.

Why not undertake together some enterprise that could really bring about a dramatic change in the relationship between our peoples and the Soviet Union? Of course, it would have to be of a magnitude to fire the imagination—for example, a joint expedition to the moon. A flight to the moon will certainly be attempted fairly soon by both Russians and Americans separately. Why not join forces and achieve this epoch-making breakthrough together?

Such co-operation, of course, would in no way change the outlook of the present Kremlin leaders. But the sharing of a great enterprise would do more than anything else to dissipate mutual suspicion. For its progress would be followed not with gloating triumph on the one hand and consternation on the other—as in the case of the Sputniks—but with tremendous enthusiasm and excitement on both sides. The fact that the Russians seem to have a slight lead in this field at the moment would make them readier to agree to a joint effort. It would be immensely flattering to their pride and to their sense of magnanimity to be the donors rather than the recipients.

To make any prophecies is impossible, but this much can be said: If, contrary to the opinions put forward in this book, the Soviet people become, from year to year, more and more Bolshevized, more and more intent on world domination, then the chances that mankind will enter the third millennium of our era both alive *and* free are meagre indeed. Ever-increasing pressure by Communism on the rest of the world would then be inevitable. The rest of the world would either have to fight back in self-defence—and go down in flames with the Communist state —or capitulate and give up its freedom. Humanity's chances of survival would be immeasurably greater if, during the next ten or twenty years, peace, based at present precariously and unavoidably on mutual fear, finds a more secure foundation in mutual trust. And mutual trust would surely emerge if Soviet man were to achieve a gradual modification of Communism.

NOTES

Chapter 1: WHAT CAN AND CANNOT BE SEEN

1   *Izvestia*, 10 June 1947

Chapter 2: THE SOCIAL FRAMEWORK

1   These and the following figures are taken from the official Soviet handbook *Narodnoye Khozyaystvo SSSR v 1959 godu* (Moscow 1960), especially pp. 307, 589, 604, 682
2   *Pravda*, 30 January 1959
3   This figure has been calculated on the basis of the decree of Council of Ministers, Central Committee, and Trade Unions' Central Council of 8 September 1956, *Izvestia*, 9 September 1956

Chapter 3: THE RUSSIAN CHARACTER

1   *Literaturnaya Gazeta*, 8 April 1958
2   Arvid Brodersen, 'Der russische Volkscharakter', *Kölner Zeitschrift für Soziologie und Sozialpsychologie*, No. 8 (1956), pp. 477-506, and Nathan Leites, *A Study of Bolshevism* (Glencoe, Illinois 1953), p. 232
3   M. Ilyin, *Kotory chas?* (Moscow 1933)
4   K. Merkuleva, *Fabrika tochnosti* (Moscow 1933)
5   An example for the survival of what the world considered as 'a typical Russian' can be found in Yu. Kazakov's novel 'Otchepenets', *Oktyabr'*, No. 7 (July 1959)
6   A. Sofronov, *Oktyabr'*, No. 2 (February 1949)
7   See his speeches to XIII Komsomol Congress (*see Pravda*, 19 April 1958) and to the villagers of Kalinovka (*see Pravda*, 21 October 1958)
8   *Komsomolskaya Pravda*, 19 November 1953
9   *Izvestia*, 22 January 1956
10 The sale of indecent postcards was referred to in the article 'Bez skidki na zhalost', *Pravda*, 11 June 1958
11 L. Solovyov, *Oktyabr'*, No. 8 (August 1957), p. 107
12 I. Sabelin, *Oktyabr'*, No. 7 (July 1954), p. 77
13 N. Davydova, 'Lyubov' inzhenera Tzotova', *Novy mir*, 1960, Nos. 1, 2 and 3 (especially No. 3, p. 73 *et seq*).
14 For a summary of this investigation, see: Raymond A. Bauer and others, *How the Soviet System Works* (Cambridge, Mass. 1957) and Alex Inkeles and Raymond A. Bauer, *The Soviet Citizen* (Cambridge, Mass. 1959)
15 Yulia Dubrovkina, *Yunost'*, No. 6 (June 1957), p. 45

Chapter 4: FAMILY AND HOME

1 Decrees of 19 December 1917, and 19 November 1926. For texts, see *The Family in the USSR: Documents and Readings* Ed. by Rudolf Schlesinger (London 1949)

2 Klaus Mehnert, *Youth in Soviet Russia* (New York and London 1933)

3 Law of 27 June 1936. For text, see *The Family in the USSR, op. cit.*

4 Law of 8 July 1944. For text, see *The Family in the USSR, op. cit.*

5 Vladimir Lidin, *Oktyabr'*, No. 1 (January 1956), p. 82

6 These rules are dated 2 August 1953. For the text, see George S. Counts, *The Challenge of Soviet Education* (New York 1957), p. 74

7 John N. Hazard, *Law and Social Change in the USSR* (London 1953) p. 265

8 *Literaturnaya Gazeta*, 24 December 1955

9 *Narodnoye khozyaystvo SSSR v 1959 godu* (Moscow 1960), p. 594

10 S. Shatrov, *Ogonyok*, No. 35 (1956) p. 30

11 G. Kalinovsky, *Oktyabr'*, No. 6 (June 1956), pp. 98-111

12 See Vera S. Dunham, 'The Strong Woman Motive in Soviet Literature', in *The Transformation of Russian Society: Aspects of Social Change since 1900* (Cambridge, Mass. 1900), pp. 459-483

13 Malte Bischoff, *Die sowjetische Familie* (unpublished monograph)

14 Warren W. Eason, 'Population Changes', in *The Transformation of Russian Society, op. cit.* pp. 72-90

15 *Dostizheniya sovetskoy vlasti za sorok let v tsifrakh* (Moscow 1957) p. 346

16 *Narodnoye khozyaystvo SSSR v 1956 godu* (Moscow 1957), p. 247

17 *Dostizheniya sovetskoy vlasti za sorok let v tsifrakh* (Moscow 1957) p. 34

18 *Narodnoye khozyaystvo SSSR v 1959 godu* (Moscow 1960), p. 36

19 *Narodnoye khozyaystvo SSSR v 1956 godu* (Moscow 1957), p. 269, and *Narodnoye khozyaystvo SSSR v 1959 godu* (Moscow 1960), p. 45

20 *Izvestia*, 4 April 1954

21 Kent Geiger, 'Deprivation and Solidarity in the Soviet Urban Family', in *The American Sociological Review*, Vol. 20, No. 1 (January 1955), pp. 57-68

22 Malte Bischoff, *op. cit.*

23 See Natalie Tarassowa, *Osteuropa*, Nos. 7/8 (July-August 1961)

24 *Pravda*, 13 October 1952

25 *Bol'shaya Sovetskaya Entsiklopediya*, 2nd Ed., Vol. 38 (1956) p. 491

Chapter 5: PROSPERITY

1 Law of 27 November 1942. For details see John Hazard, *Law and Social Change in the USSR* (London 1953), pp. 204-207

2 For detailed description of the bonus system see Joseph S. Berliner, *Factory and Manager in the USSR* (Cambridge, Mass. 1957), pp. 25-56

3 *Pravda*, 18 December 1957

4 L. Malyugin, *Moskva*, No. 5 (May 1957), p. 155

Chapter 6: *PROPERTY*

1 *Izvestia*, 6 January 1954
2 Decree of 9 January 1943 in *Vedomosti Verkhovnogo Soveta SSSR*, No. 3 (1943)
3 James Burnham, *The Managerial Revolution* (New York 1941)
4 Milovan Djilas, *The New Class* (New York 1957)
5 *Krokodil*, 30 July 1954
6 See speech in Minsk (*Pravda*, 25 January 1958) and on Twenty-first Party Congress (*Pravda*, 28 January 1959)
7 Moscow Radio broadcast, 25 February 1956
8 Law of 7 August 1932

Chapter 7: *SUCCESS*

1 *Izvestia*, 15 June 1954
2 *Pravda*, 18 January 1958
3 *Izvestia*, 4 September 1960
4 The severity of these punishments was increased by a decree of the Presidium of the Supreme Soviet of the U.S.S.R., promulgated on 24 April 1958. See *Pravda*, 19 May 1958
5 A. Smirnov-Cherkesov, *Ogonyok*, No. 4 (1956), p. 30 *et. seq.*
6 *Pravda*, 14 January 1961
7 Joseph S. Berliner, *Factory and Manager in the USSR* (Cambridge, Mass. 1957), p. 155
8 *Izvestia*, 21 December 1956
9 *Pravda*, 12 April 1957
10 Alf Edeen, 'The Civil Service. Its Composition and Status', in *The Transformation of Russian Society. Aspects of Social Change* (Cambridge, Mass. 1960), pp. 274–292
11 Decree of 16 September 1943, in *Sbornik zakonov SSSR i ukazov Presidiuma Verkhovnogo Soveta SSSR* (Moscow 1956), p. 241

Chapter 8: *AND EQUALITY?*

1 *Kommunist*, No. 2 (1958), p. 24
2 Decree of 8 September 1958 (see *Izvestia*, 9 September 1956)
3 *Pravda*, 3 January 1958
4 *Pravda*, 15 February 1956
5 *Pravda*, 19 April 1958
6 *Oktyabr'*, No. 2 (February 1955)
7 *Komsomolskaya pravda*, 17 May 1954
8 *Trud*, 25 October 1950
9 Robert Feldmesser, 'The Persistence of Status Advantages in Soviet Russia', *American Journal of Sociology*, July 1953, pp. 19–27
10 *Izvestia*, 28 March 1954
11 *Pravda*, 27 May 1954
12 *Kommunist*, No. 12 (1957), p. 25
13 *Osteuropa*, No. 6 (1954), pp. 431–435

Chapter 9: *THE PURSUIT OF KNOWLEDGE*

1 See chapter 'The Kollektiv'
2 *Cf.* Alexander Steininger in *Osteuropa*, Nos. 7/8 (July and August 1958)
3 *Izvestia*, 1 June 1958
4 B. Gorbatov, *Obyknovennaya Arktika* (Moscow 1946), p. 4
5 *Narodnoye khozyaystvo SSSR v 1959 godu* (Moscow 1960), p. 727
6 *Ibid.*, p. 731
7 Decree of 2 October 1940 (*Bol'shaya Sovetskaya Entsiklopediya*, 2nd ed., vol. 12, 1952, p. 308)
8 *Uchitel'skaya gazeta*, 6 August 1955
9 *Narodnoye khozyaystvo SSSR v 1956 godu* (Moscow 1957), pp. 251 and 246
10 *Pravda*, 16 January 1959
11 Speech to XIII Komsomol Congress (see *Pravda*, 19 April 1958)
12 *Izvestia*, 7 June 1958
13 *Narodnoye khozyaystvo SSSR v 1956 godu* (Moscow 1957), p. 250
14 *Narodnoye khozyaystvo SSSR v 1959 godu* (Moscow 1960), p. 740
15 *Ibid.*, p. 750
16 *Pravda*, 16 April 1956
17 *Pravda*, 15 February 1956
18 *Sovietskaya pedagogika*, No. 4 (1957), p. 16 *et seq.*
19 *Pravda*, 19 April 1958
20 *Komsomolskaya pravda*, 6 June 1958, and *Pravda*, 16 January 1959
21 *Komsomolskaya pravda*, 6 June 1958
22 *Pravda*, 21 September and 16 November 1958
23 *Pravda*, 25 December 1958
24 *Trud*, 10 December 1958
25 For example Professor N. N. Semyonov, winner of the Nobel Prize for chemistry, in *Pravda*, 17 October 1958
26 *Uchitel'skaya gazeta*, 10 July 1960
27 For a summary of what happened to the school reform see Oskar Anweiler, 'Zwischenbilanz der sowjetischen Schulreform', *Osteuropa*, No. 4/5 (April/May 1961), pp. 285-301
28 *Pravda*, 16 December 1956
29 Ordinance of the Minister of Education of the R.S.F.S.R., 29 August 1959, in *Sbornik prikazov i instruktsii Ministerstva Prosvechcheniya R.S.F.S.R. 1959*, No. 40, pp. 3-13. The figures for the pre-reform period are taken from *Narodnoye obrazovaniye v SSSR*, Moscow, 1957, p. 91

Chapter 10: *A WORLD TO DISCOVER*

1 *Literaturnaya gazeta*, 8 April 1958
2 *Ibid.*
3 Boris Isakov in *Literaturnaya gazeta*, 3 January 1957
4 *Pravda*, 6 February 1956

5 Vladimir Seduro, *Dostoyevski in Russian Literary Criticism 1846-1956* (New York 1957), p. 96 *et seq.*
6 *Istoriya russkoy literatury*, ed. N. L. Brodsky, vol. 2 (Moscow 1950)
7 *Pravda*, 6 February 1956
8 *Komsomolskaya pravda*, 16 March 1961
9 *Literaturnaya gazeta*, 25 May 1957
10 *Komsomolskaya pravda*, 28 November 1957

Chapter 11: FREEDOM OF THOUGHT

1 *Literaturnaya gazeta*, 16 April 1953
2 *Znamya*, No. 10 (1953)
3 *Novy mir*, No. 12 (1958)
4 Ilya Ehrenburg, 'Ottepel', *Znamya*, No. 5 *et seq.* (1954)
5 *Novy mir*, No. 8 (August 1956)
6 *Literaturnaya gazeta*, 22 May 1957
7 *Kommunist*, No. 12 (1957), p. 24
8 *Literaturnaya Moskva*, Vol. 2 (Moscow 1956)
9 *Den' poezii* (Moscow 1956)
10 Ten poems appeared in *Znamya*, No. 4 (1954)
11 A. Wal'tseva, 'Kvartira Nr. 13', *Moskva*, No. 1 (1957)
12 *Pravda*, 26 December 1956
13 *Literaturnaya gazeta*, 15 January 1957
14 *Ibid.*, 10 January 1957
15 *Ibid.*, 22 January 1957
16 *Ibid.*, 19 March 1957
17 *Ibid.*, 22 May 1957
18 *Kommunist*, No. 12 (1957), pp. 11-29
19 *Vechernyaya Moskva*, 6 December 1957
20 *Novy mir*, Nos. 10 & 11 (1958)
21 *Oktyabr'*, Nos. 7, 8, 9 (1958)
22 *Neva*, Nos. 6 & 7 (1958)
23 *Literaturnaya gazeta*, 25 October 1958
24 *Pravda*, 29 October 1958
25 *Komsomolskaya pravda*, 30 October 1958
26 *Pravda*, 2 November 1958
27 *Novy mir*, No. 1 (1960), pp. 78-96; published in an English translation in 1960 by E. P. Dutton, New York
28 Among others: Anatolij Gladilin, 'Dym v glaza', *Junost'*, No. 12 (December 1959), and Anatoly Kuznetsov, 'Zhenshchina', *Junost'*, No. 5 (May 1961)
29 *Novy mir*, No. 4 (April 1957), pp. 75-78
30 *Komsomolskaya pravda*, 28 April 1957
31 *Literaturnaya gazeta*, 25 June 1957
32 *Komsomolskaya pravda*, 13 January 1959
33 Yunna Morits, 'Stichi o solntse', *Junost'*, No. 8 (August 1960)
34 Viktor Nekrasov, 'Vtoraya noch'', *Novy mir*, No. 5 (May 1960), p. 46
35 Nina Ivanter, 'Snova avgust', *Novy mir*, No. 9 (September 1958), p. 39

36 A. Kalinin, *Surovoye pole* (Moscow 1959), and Sergey Voronin, 'V rodnych mestach', *Neva*, No. 9 (1959)
37 Vladimir Tendryakov, 'Za begushchim dnyom', *Molodaya gvardiya*, No. 12 (1959), p. 106
38 Vladimir Dudintsev, 'Novogodnyaya skazka', *Novy mir*, No. 1 (January 1960), p. 80
39 Nikolay Dubov, 'Zhostkaya proba', *Novy mir*, No. 9 (September 1960), p. 69. See also for the preceding paragraphs Barbara Bode's reviews of Soviet literature in *Osteuropa*, No. 12 (December 1959), No. 9 (September 1960), No. 1 (January 1961) and the April-June 1961 issue of *Survey*, No. 36 (April-June 1961), London.
40 Too numerous to be quoted; particularly interesting are *Izvestia*, 15 January 1959, and *Pravda*, 26 August 1960

Chapter 12: THE KOLLEKTÍV

1 Raymond A. Bauer and others, *How the Soviet System Works* (Cambridge, Mass. 1957), p. 224
2 Semyal shkola, June 1948 (quoted)
3 Klaus Mehnert, 'Moskauer Theatersaison 1959', *Osteuropa*, Nos. 7, 8 & 9 (July, August and September 1959)
4 *Novy mir*, No. 6 (June 1956), pp. 121-132
5 *Novy mir*, No. 10 (October 1956), pp. 181-196

Chapter 13: DO 'THEY' KNOW BEST?

1 *Pravda*, 16 January 1950
2 For a detailed discussion of 'Transition to Communism', see the series of articles in *Osteuropa*, Nos. 4/5 (April/May 1961) and in the following issues, and also *Pravda*, 30 July 1961
3 For example S. Strumilin, 'Rabochy byt i kommunizm', *Novy mir*, No. 7 (July 1960)
4 Daniil Granin, 'Posle svad'by', *Oktyabr'*, No. 7 (July 1958), p. 14

Chapter 14: THE FATHERLAND

1 Klaus Mehnert, *Stalin versus Marx* (London and New York 1953)
2 *Pravda*, 12 June 1958
3 Klaus Mehnert, *Asien, Moskau und wir* (10th ed. Stuttgart 1960), pp. 187 *et seq.*

Chapter 15: THE CONTENTED AND THE DISCONTENTED

1 Raymond A. Bauer and others, *How the Soviet system works* (Cambridge, Mass. 1957), p. 106
2 *Ibid.*, p. 122
3 *Ibid.*, p. 105
4 *Pravda*, 9 May 1958
5 Louis Fischer, *Russia Revisited* (New York 1957), p. 45
6 *Pravda*, 23 February 1958

7 *Pravda*, 3 November 1957
8 Raymond Bauer and others, *op. cit.*, p. 204
9 *Komsomolskaya pravda*, 14 April 1960

Chapter 16: *RETREAT FROM POLITICS*

1 *Komsomolskaya pravda*, 28 April 1957
2 Patricia Blake in *Reporter*, 14 November 1957
3 *Pravda*, 25 November 1956
4 *Yunost'*, No. 4 (1957), p. 73
5 *Pravda*, 16 April 1958
6 At the XII Plenary Session of the Komsomol Central Committee, 30 April 1944
7 *Komsomolskaya pravda*, 28 December 1956
8 *Literaturnaya gazeta*, 25 May 1957
9 B. Pasternak, *Doctor Zhivago* (London and New York 1958), p. 502
10 *Christ und Welt* (Stuttgart), 27 November 1958
11 Yu. Trifonov, 'Sluchayny sosed', *Ogonyok*, No. 32 (1956)
12 *Izvestia*, 7 August 1959 and 16 October 1960; *Pravda*, 16 June, 13 July and 31 August 1960; *Kommunist*, No. 17 (September 1960), pp. 13-21

Chapter 17: *DESIRE FOR PERSONAL SAFETY*

1 *Vedomosti Verkhovnogo Soveta*, Nos. 20 and 28 (1940)
2 *Cf.* Dietrich A. Loeber, ' "Sozialistische Gesetzlichkeit" im Zeichen des XX. Parteitages der KPdSU', *Osteuropa-Recht*, No. 2 (1956), pp. 243-255
3 For text of these three amnesties see *Pravda*, 23 March 1953, *Izvestia*, 18 September 1955, *Pravda*, 2 November 1957
4 *Sovetskoye gosudarstvo i pravo*, No. 1 (1956), p. 3.
5 *Sovetskoye gosudarstvo i pravo*, No. 4 (1956), pp. 24 *et seq.*, and No. 6 (1957), pp. 20-29; *Izvestiya*, 27 March 1957, and 27 July 1957
6 *Izvestiya*, 26 December 1958
7 Speech of Presecutor General Rudenko, *Pravda*, 27 December 1958
8 See *Osteuropa*, No. 1 (January 1958), pp. 10-16, and No. 5/6 (May/ June 1959), p. 285
9 *Vedomosti Verkhovnogo Soveta RSFSR*, No. 18 (1961)
10 *Pravda*, 28 January 1959
11 *Vedomosti Verkovnogo Soveta SSSR*, Nos. 19, 21, and 22 (1961)

Chapter 18: *CRISES — AND REPERCUSSIONS*

1 For full text with commentary see Bertram D. Wolfe, *Khrushchev and Stalin's Ghost*, (New York 1957), pp. 99-253
2 *Pravda*, 19 January 1957
3 A. Tvardovsky, 'Tak eto bylo' in *Novy mir*, No. 5 (May 1960)
4 *Kommunist*, No. 12 (1957), p. 20
5 *Voprosy istorii*, No. 4 (April 1956), pp. 38-56
6 *Ibid.*, No. 7 (July 1956), pp. 186-189

7   *Pravda*, 20 November 1956
8   *Pravda*, 9 November 1956
9   See *Literaturnaya gazeta*, 20 September 1956
10 *Literaturnaya gazeta*, 22 November 1956
11 *Pravda*, 4 June 1958
12 A. Sobolev in *Kommunist*, No. 2 (1958), p. 16

Chapter *19*: *CRITICISM—METHODS AND TARGETS*

1   *Pravda*, 16 August 1957, and *Vedomosti Verkhovnogo Soveta RSFSR* No. 1 (1957)
2   *Literaturnaya gazeta*, 7 February 1957
3   Daniil Granin, *Iskateli* (Leningrad 1956)
4   For example in Astrakhan, see *Pravda*, 29 March 1961
5   Raymond Bauer and others, *How the Soviet system works* (Cambridge, Mass. 1957), p. 122
6   *Oktyabr'*, No. 10 (October 1956), pp. 26–47

Chapter *20*: *THE WORLD OUTSIDE*

1   *Narodnoye khozyaystvo SSSR v 1959 godu* (Moscow 1960), p. 265
2   Kommunist, No. 15 (1956), p. 39
3   *Mezhdunarodnaya zhizn'*, No. 7 (1957), pp. 60–109
4   Yury Trifonov, *Studenty* (Moscow 1956), p. 205
5   Raymond A. Bauer and others, *How the Soviet system works* (Cambridge, Mass. 1957), p. 132

Chapter *21*: *SOVIET MAN AND THE WEST*

1   *Geschichte der Kommunistischen Partei der Sowjetunion (Bolschewiki). Kurzer Lehrgang* (Berlin 1946), S. 202
2   *Kommunist*, No. 1 (January 1961), pp. 17–20

INDEX